AN AMERICA CHALLENGED

An America Challenged

*Population Change and the Future
of the United States*

Steve H. Murdock

TEXAS A&M UNIVERSITY

Westview Press

BOULDER • SAN FRANCISCO • OXFORD

Copyright © 1995 by Westview Press, Inc.

Published in 1995 in the United States of America by Westview Press, Inc., 5500 Central Avenue, Boulder, Colorado 80301-2877, and in the United Kingdom by Westview Press, 36 Lonsdale Road, Summertown, Oxford OX2 7EW

Library of Congress Cataloging-in-Publication Data
Murdock, Steven H.
  An America challenged : population change and the future of the
United States / Steve H. Murdock.
      p. cm.
  Includes bibliographical references and index.
  ISBN 0-8133-1808-4. — ISBN 0-8133-1809-2 (pbk.)
  1. Population forecasting—United States.   2. United States—
Population.   I. Title.
HB3505.M868   1995
304.6'0973'01—dc20   94-29676
                                                                         CIP

Printed and bound in the United States of America

  ∞   The paper used in this publication meets the requirements
       of the American National Standard for Permanence of Paper
       for Printed Library Materials Z39.48-1984.

10   9   8   7   6   5   4   3   2   1

To my nieces and nephews,
Karen, Julie, Denise,
Diane, David, and Mark

Contents

PART TWO
*The Implications of Population:
Change for America's Future*

Tables and Figures

REFERENCE TABLES

FIGURES

Preface

For nearly 20 years, I have been involved in applied demographic research. During most of that period, the work completed has been either descriptive of demographic trends or methodologies or has involved conceptually based analysis of academically oriented research topics. Applied users of our data frequently ask questions related to the implications of the descriptive or empirical analyses. What do these values mean? What difference will this trend make? Why is this important? This volume is an attempt to address such questions by identifying how projected demographic trends are likely to be important to the United States in the coming decades. Its intended users are private- and public-sector officials involved in strategic and other forms of planning, students wishing to obtain an overview of major demographic trends impacting the United States, and all persons interested in knowing what the demographic future may mean for the social and economic structure of America.

Such analyses are inherently difficult, risky, and potentially controversial. Any social scientist examining given societal phenomena is aware that the future state and trends related to it will be determined by a multitude of complex factors. Any attempt to examine the implications of one set of factors, such as those related to population change, will likely appear either naively simplistic or overly deterministic. This is especially true when the factors being examined are based on projections of the future, which are always fraught with error. Despite such limitations, and the qualifications that are necessary in such an analysis, I have chosen to proceed because examining what the future may be is essential if we wish to change it.

Specifically, this volume examines the socioeconomic implications of three major patterns evident in recent population projections completed by the U.S. Bureau of the Census. These three patterns include slower population growth and the increased importance of immigration in determining growth, the aging of the population, and the increasing ethnic diversity of the population. These three patterns are examined as they impact the labor force, income and poverty, businesses, public and private services, and fiscal conditions in the United States between now and the middle of the twenty-first century.

The work begins with a brief introductory chapter and then presents seven chapters organized into two parts. Part One, entitled "The Demographic Context of Change in America," contains two chapters. Chapter 2 examines current demographic patterns in the United States, and Chapter 3 describes recent projections of the U.S. population completed by the U.S. Bureau of the Census for periods through 2050. It also provides detailed documentation of the three demographic trends noted above, delineating their nature for each decade from 1990 to 2050.

Part Two, entitled "The Implications of Population: Change for America's Future," contains five chapters. Chapter 4 examines the implications of demographic change for the labor force, and Chapter 5 looks at the impacts on income and poverty levels. Chapter 6 then discusses the implications for American business, and Chapter 7 evaluates some of the potential effects of population change on selected public- and private-sector services and on the fiscal resources that pay for such services. The final chapter presents overall generalizations from the work and delineates their potential implications for America's future.

In each of the substantive chapters in Part Two, the population projections described in Chapter 3 are used to project implications in the topical area of interest. Population-based rates are used to project specific factors (such as the size of the labor force, using labor-force participation rates), and 1990 rates are assumed to prevail throughout the projection period. Rates for 1990 are clearly unlikely to prevail over such an extended period of time, but the intent is not to provide projections of future numerical values for detailed planning purposes but to identify the direction of future trends. In addition, it is often easier to understand the implications of future change if one can evaluate the future relative to the present. Thus, although it is likely that rates of occurrence as well as demographic patterns will change in the future, comparisons are facilitated by holding rates of occurrence (within given age, sex, and race/ethnicity groups) constant at current levels.

After presenting such projections, the implications of the projected patterns are described for selected aspects of the topical area. Those implications examined must, of course, be selective, but an attempt has been made to examine a sufficiently diverse set of issues to indicate the extent of the effects of population in each topical area.

The substantive chapters in both Part One and Part Two have concise summaries at the end of each chapter that highlight the key findings as well as the implications of these findings. In addition, graphical and tabular presentations of key trends are provided. Thus, by reading the introductory and concluding chapters, reading the summaries for the substantive chapters, and examining the graphs, a reader can obtain a basic overview.

The findings of the volume suggest that the population and other factors that reflect its change will grow more slowly than in the past, that immigration will be increasingly important to such growth, that the population will age, and that it will become substantially more ethnically diverse. These patterns will result in dramatic changes in the United States that will potentially lead, because of the historical linkages between certain demographic characteristics and socioeconomic resources, to numerous changes in American society.

The findings also suggest that such changes may lead to a labor force that is less well educated and perhaps less competitive, to reduced worker compensation, and to substantially increased retirement costs for the society. They may lead as well to an increase in the number of households but to a reduction in the average income available per household and to an increase in the overall rate of poverty. Population growth will result in substantial increases in consumer and discretionary income but not as much as if the characteristics of the population remained stable. Markets for goods and services will likely become more complex and will be sharply divided into upper- and lower-income segments. Public- and private-sector services will be differentially affected depending on the population segments they serve. Thus, educational services are likely to grow more slowly than in the past while health care services will grow rapidly. Public-sector costs and revenues will increase as well, but deficit spending may lead to increased public-sector debt. Overall, the results suggest that inequality may increase and American society may develop increased bases for diversity and division. Future population change may lead to numerous challenges for American society and its leaders in the coming decades.

Throughout the discussion, an attempt is made to clearly point out that the projected implications result from the current relationships between demographic trends and characteristics, and socioeconomic resources. For example, minority population growth leads to reduced aggregate income relative to growth from majority population groups only because minority populations have, due to historical discriminatory and other factors, had less access to resources. A major point of the discussion is that increased opportunities for minority and other disadvantaged population groups could lead to substantial benefits for American society as well as for the members of the groups themselves. Given projected demographic trends, changing the historical relationships between some demographic characteristics and socioeconomic resources is likely to be essential to altering the less-positive implications of future population patterns.

This book's analysis is clearly limited, and the implications of its findings are likely to be altered by future demographic, as well as by socioeconomic, change. It is nevertheless a work that I hope will be useful to its users, both for describing the changes likely to affect them in the coming decades and for providing insights into how the future may be changed. My hope is that this work's most positive projections will prove to be too pessimistic and that its most negative projections will fail to materialize. In sum, this work will be most successful if its projections are made to be inaccurate.

Steve H. Murdock

Acknowledgments

In the completion of this work, the support, assistance, and encouragement of numerous persons and agencies must be acknowledged. The Department of Rural Sociology and the Texas Agricultural Experiment Station in the Texas A&M University System provided financial support for this effort and receive my sincere appreciation. I also extend appreciation to the Texas State Data Center and Texas Population Estimates and Projections Programs, which have brought me into contact with numerous persons who have forced me to examine not only the nature of population change but also the implications of that change.

In the preparation of the book, numerous people have provided assistance in data preparation, in manuscript preparation, and in the provision of critical reviews of the volume. First I wish to thank my editor, Dean Birkenkamp, who has provided encouragement and guidance throughout the work's development and completion. Dean's efforts have clearly made it a better work. I wish to especially thank several reviewers who provided reviews on very short notice. These include Karen White and Clare Dyer from the Texas Legislative Council and Dudley Poston, Rogelio Saenz, and Mary Zey from the Departments of Sociology and Rural Sociology at Texas A&M. Their comments have substantially improved the work. Special appreciation is due to Md. Nazrul Hoque, who tirelessly performed repeated computer runs to produce data for this work, and to Beverly Pecotte, who proofread the entire work, made numerous useful criticisms, and produced the graphic presentations included in the text. Steve White is also due special thanks for thoroughly searching for the data necessary to implement several of the projections, for proofing the entire work, and for making numerous important criticisms that improved the work. I also wish to express appreciation to Darrel Fannin, who assisted in the computer analysis, and Joann Fritz, who provided technical editing assistance. Special appreciation is due Charla Adkins, Michelle Mach, Delma Jones, and Ben Matthews, who typed repeated drafts of the work. Teresa Ray is due special appreciation for preparing numerous computations and for typing key sections of the work. I owe my most sincere thanks to Patricia Bramwell, who was instrumental in the completion of every phase of the work and who ensured the quality of the manuscript's preparation. The work clearly would not have been completed without her extraordinary efforts in organizing and directly participating in nearly all aspects of the work.

Finally, I extend my thanks to my colleagues, staff, and friends, who endured my impatience and neglect of other activities during the completion of the work.

S.H.M.

CHAPTER ONE

The Implications of Future Population Change in America: The Rationale and Scope for an Assessment

Mounting budget deficits, a changing world order, and increasing competitiveness in international markets are among the dramatic changes that Americans recognize as having an impact on their lives both now and in the future. Such issues receive widespread attention in the press and in public debates and are recognized as unlikely to be easily or quickly altered.

Changes in the characteristics of the American population are less often recognized, equally difficult to alter, and slow to evolve but also promise to change the future social, economic, and political structure of the nation. Because population changes are not adequately understood, the implications of demographic change for the social and economic patterns of the United States in the coming century have seldom been thoroughly examined. As a result, many Americans are not aware of the extent to which the United States today is a product of the characteristics of its population or of how changes in these characteristics in the coming decades may alter the American way of life. This book is intended to provide an understanding of some of the demographic bases of America's future.

FOCUS, RATIONALE, AND INTENDED USES FOR THE WORK

This book describes changes in the population of the United States expected in the remainder of this century and first half of the next. Rather than simply describing these patterns, however, it examines the implications of these patterns for numerous areas of American life, attempting to address such questions as:

- How much will the population of the United States grow in the coming years and will that growth be sufficient to maintain markets for key goods and services and the tax base of federal, state, and local governments?

- What will the aging of the population do to the availability of entry-level workers and the overall productivity of the American workforce?
- How will the characteristics of consumers change in the coming decades? How will marketers need to alter the nature of goods and services in U.S. markets to address the increasing cultural and ethnic diversity of consumers?
- How will the changing population alter health care costs and the markets for housing, educational, recreational, and other services?

Although no one work can adequately address all of these issues, and population patterns represent only some of the many dimensions impacting America's future, it is nevertheless important to understand the demographic dimensions of the future. This book attempts to address such areas as they are likely to be affected by the future population of the United States.

Why write such a book? First, as noted above, is the simple fact that the implications of future population change are not well known. This book describes the implications of future demographic events and thereby addresses an important information need. Second, although there are several other works intended for professional demographic audiences, they are based largely on pre-1990 patterns and examine the potential implications of population change in substantial detail (for example, Robey 1985; Fosler et al. 1990; Gill et al. 1992); this work is intended to meet the need for a more succinct overview of demographic trends and their implications for those who are not professional demographers. Finally, this is one of the first works to utilize post-1990 Census information to examine the nation's future population trends and patterns. In sum, this work provides one of the first relatively concise summaries of the social and economic implications of future population change in the United States, utilizing results from the 1990 Census and post-1990 projections of the population.

This book is intended for use by corporate planners and others who wish to understand the bearing of demographic change on social, economic, market, and other patterns in the United States; by public officials who wish to know the effects of population change on public services and fiscal bases; and by students who wish to obtain a brief overview of the demographic patterns likely to impact the United States in the coming decades. Thus its audience includes all those who desire to obtain knowledge of future demographic trends in the United States and of their implications for American Society.

TOPICAL ORGANIZATION OF THE TEXT

Specifically, this book examines the impacts of three major patterns in the future population of the United States. These include:

- the rate of future population growth and the role of immigration in that growth;

- the changing age structure of the population;
- the increasing ethnic diversity of the population.

Historical trends in these factors are described and future patterns projected. Most importantly, the implications of future patterns for many of the issues noted above are examined.

The work is organized into this introductory chapter, six substantive chapters, and a conclusions chapter. In the substantive and conclusions chapters, extensive tabular and textual descriptions are provided. In addition, each chapter ends with a summary of the major findings from the analysis and discusses the implications of such findings. Finally, a set of reference tables is included at the end to provide additional detailed data on factors examined in each chapter.

Chapters 2 and 3 are organized into Part One, entitled "The Demographic Context of Change in America." Chapter 2 provides an overview of past demographic trends and contains a brief history of past patterns along with a description of expected future directions of change in these patterns.

Chapter 3 presents an analysis of projected future population patterns for the United States. Specifically, the impacts of differential levels of population change, and of change in the ethnic and age composition of the population, are examined for the United States, noting areas of uncertainty in such projections and aspects of projected patterns least likely to be altered by future events. The effects of alternative assumptions on the projections are discussed and the projections are thoroughly described. Chapter 3 provides the reader with an understanding of the projected trends in the population, which are the foundation for the analyses in succeeding chapters.

Part Two is entitled, "The Implications of Population: Change for America's Future." It contains five chapters, four of which examine the implications of future demographic change for a key social and economic area. Each of the four chapters presents projections of the impacts in the topical area and an extensive discussion of the implications of the projected trends.

Chapter 4 examines the implications of population change for the future rate of growth in the labor force and for the characteristics of the labor force over the coming years. It examines the implications of such changes for the future competitiveness of the U.S. workforce in world markets.

Chapter 5 examines the effects of the projected demographic trends on the socioeconomic characteristics of the population, concentrating on households as the unit within which socioeconomic changes are manifested. Chapter 5 also examines how the projected changes in population and households may affect the economic well-being of Americans both in terms of aggregate incomes and in terms of income distribution. The effects of demographic and household change are examined both as they relate to income and to the incidence of poverty. Chapter 6 describes the impacts of projected population trends on business products and services. Because no single chapter can examine the impacts of population change for all business and service sectors, general patterns of potential change are described in relation to general consumer expenditures relative to selected areas such as investment services, real estate, and recreation.

Chapter 7 examines the implications of future demographic trends for private- and public-sector services. As for business-related impacts, only general patterns can be presented and examples of these patterns are described for selected service areas. Special attention is given to the impacts of future population patterns on health care services and costs and on the size, composition, and likely needs of students in elementary and secondary and higher education. Chapter 7 also examines the implications of future population change for federal expenditures for services and for the resource base to pay for such services.

Chapter 8 provides a summary and conclusions for the work. In addition to providing a brief summary of the major findings from the analyses presented in the book, Chapter 8 speculates on the potential social, economic, and political changes that may be brought about by the demographic changes projected to impact America in the twenty-first century.

Thus the book is organized to provide a sampling of the diverse range of impacts of future demographic change on life in the United States. It is intended to provide substantive knowledge about the impacts of future demographic change on selected topical areas and stimulate interest in additional examinations of the implications of changing demographics for the private- and public-sector development of the United States in the coming years.

LIMITATIONS OF THE BOOK

In pointing out the implications of future population change, it is important to note that population projections are limited both in their accuracy (Murdock and Ellis 1991) and in their utility (Ascher 1978). As one writer has facetiously noted, "Prediction is very difficult, especially about the future" (Niels Bohr as quoted by Coffey 1983:93). In fact, virtually every assessment of long-term forecasts (be they economic, demographic, financial, clinical, recreational [sports], or related to totally nonhuman-impacted dimensions such as the weather) has found that projections for long periods of time are often inaccurate (Ascher 1978; Armstrong 1985; Camerer and Johnson 1990). It is important, then, to examine any work that uses population or any other type of projection with the understanding that events will not likely occur exactly as assumed in the projections. In fact, projections often become inaccurate because actions are taken on the basis of the analysis of expected patterns that alter the future. Projections are perhaps best seen as means of examining the implications of alternative assumed patterns rather than as point forecasts of what the nation's population **will** be in the future.[1]

With such qualifications, it might appear that one should not bother to examine either projections or their implications. However, many of the projected directions of change are much more certain than the exact magnitude of change. In particular, it is likely that patterns highlighted in this work will move in the directions projected, although the exact extent of that movement may be less certain. It is important to know the implications of these patterns while remaining cognizant of the limitations inherent in projections.

This book is also limited by its examination of only the demographic correlates of selected socioeconomic patterns when, in fact, the causes of such phenomena are often much more complex. The implications of demographic change are examined for labor-force patterns, school enrollments, markets, and other important aspects of American society, all of which are also markedly influenced by social, economic, and many other nondemographic factors. No attempt is made to provide a multivariate analysis or establish the statistical relationships between demographic and other factors because the intent is to be descriptive of potential, rather than to analyze empirical, effects. The intent is not to suggest demographic determinism of the patterns discussed but rather to highlight the importance of demographic factors in these areas. Demography is not destiny, but many social and economic patterns are markedly influenced by demographic change.

It should also be recognized that, due to space limitations, the analysis presented is selective of topics and analytical approaches for examining these topics. It examines only some of the dimensions of only some of the factors affected by, and affecting, demographic change. Others could have been examined. It is equally obvious that although this analysis examines patterns only within the United States, international patterns would have been equally interesting and important to examine.

CONCLUSION

This work attempts to inform its readers about the consequences of demographic changes likely to occur in the United States in the remainder of this century and the first half of the next. It does so by examining projections of the population and the implications of population change for the labor force; income and poverty; businesses; and services in the United States. Although its results are admittedly limited by the inherent limitations of projections, and by the author's interpretation of the implications of demographic change, the work will hopefully provide readers with insights into the implications of demographic change for the United States in the twenty-first century.

PART ONE

The Demographic Context of Change in America

CHAPTER TWO

America's Demographic Past: Setting the Framework for the Future

Much of what will occur in the population of the United States can be seen as a product of past and present patterns. Before examining the major patterns likely to affect the United States in the coming decades, it is, therefore, essential to establish the existing condition of the U.S. population. What is the position of the population of the United States relative to that of other nations? What have been the recent patterns of population growth and change in population characteristics that are likely to provide the bases for future trends? This chapter presents a general description of the demography of the United States to provide the reader with an understanding of the context for future demographic change.

What is demography? Analyzing the demography of an area's population means analyzing the size, geographical distribution, and characteristics of that population and of the major demographic processes of fertility (births), mortality (deaths), and migration (including both the internal movement of persons within a country and international migration between nations) that determine the size, distribution, and characteristics of a population (Murdock and Ellis 1991). An examination is therefore provided of the overall rates of population change and trends in fertility, mortality, and migration; the distribution of the population across different regions and states in the United States; and the age, sex, race/ethnicity, household and family, education, income and poverty, and employment characteristics of the population, with emphasis placed on the most recent trends in these factors. The population of the United States in the context of the world's population is examined first, followed by a description of the various aspects of population change within the United States.

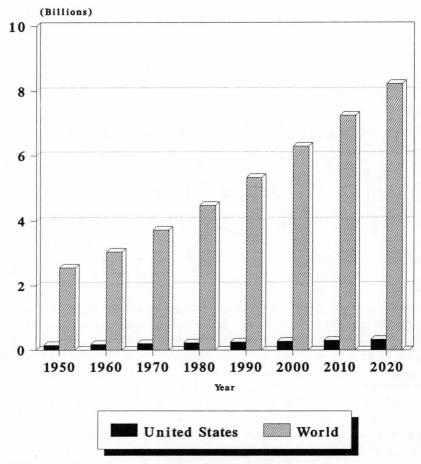

FIGURE 2.1   United States and world population growth, 1950–2020.

THE INTERNATIONAL CONTEXT OF
POPULATION CHANGE IN THE UNITED STATES

With 252 million persons, the United States ranked as the third most populous nation in the world in 1991, after China with nearly 1.2 billion and India with nearly 870 million (Jamison 1991). The former Soviet Union ranked as the third-largest nation before its breakup. By 1992, the 255 million persons in the United States accounted for about 4.6 percent of the world's 5.5 billion persons (United Nations 1992). The United States' number-three rank is expected to continue through the second decade of the next century, but by then will account for only 3.9 percent of the world's more than 8.2 billion persons (see Figure 2.1). As with other developed nations, the U.S. rate of growth (about 1.0 percent per year from 1980 to 1992) is substantially less than that in the developing nations of the world. Thus, the developed nations (defined by the United Nations as all countries in North America and Europe as well as the former Soviet Union, Japan, Australia, and New Zealand) accounted for about 1.2 billion of the world's 5.5 billion persons in 1992 and grew at an average annual rate of 0.5 percent per year. However, developing nations (all remaining nations in the world) accounted for 4.3 billion persons and grew at an average annual rate of 2.0 percent per year. As a result, "of the 88 million persons added to the world population each year during 1985–1990, only 8 million persons were in the more developed regions while 80 million were in the less developed regions" (United Nations 1992:2). Because of such differentials, roughly 94 percent of all population growth in the world between now and the end of the first quarter of the next century is projected to occur in developing nations. The population increase in developed nations from now until 2025 is projected to be only about 179 million persons compared to a 2.8-billion increase in the developing nations. Developed nations' share of the world's population is projected to shrink from 22 percent in 1992 to 17 percent by 2025.

In understanding population patterns in the United States, it is essential to note that the United States is likely to be of decreasing demographic significance in the world. The international context of America's population is one of increasing competition from an ever larger world community.

AN OVERVIEW OF DEMOGRAPHIC CHANGE IN THE UNITED STATES

Population Growth

Table 2.1 shows the population of the United States to have grown rapidly during its more than 200 years of census history. Growth rates exceeding 30 percent per decade were evident in the first decades of the nation's history, followed by rates of 20 percent per decade during the latter part of the nineteenth century. Rates were lowest during the depression of the 1930s, with the nation increasing its population by only 7.2 percent from 1930 to 1940. Growth rebounded during the baby-boom era in the 1950s (with the population increasing by 18.5 percent from 1950 to 1960). Rates then began to decline; during the decade of the 1980s the population of the United States increased by less than 10 percent. Table 2.1 shows that the general trend in population change in the United States is and has been toward reduced growth.

Components of Population Growth in the United States

Population change results from two components: natural increase, which is the difference between the number of births and deaths, and net migration, the difference between the number of persons moving into and the number moving out

Table 2.1: Population and Population Change in the United States by Components of Change, 1790-1992

Year	Total Population	Population Change	Total Immigrants[a]	Total Natural Increase[a]	Percent Population Change	Percent of Population Change Due to Immigration[a]	Percent of Population Change Due to Natural Increase[a]
1790	3,929,214	-	-	-	-	-	-
1800	5,308,483	1,379,269	-	-	35.1	-	-
1810	7,239,881	1,931,398	-	-	36.4	-	-
1820	9,638,453	2,398,572	-	-	33.1	-	-
1830	12,866,020	3,227,567	132,237	3,095,330	33.5	4.1	95.9
1840	17,069,453	4,203,433	553,567	3,649,866	32.7	13.2	86.8
1850	23,191,876	6,122,423	1,498,815	4,623,608	35.9	24.5	75.5
1860	31,443,321	8,251,445	2,760,469	5,490,976	35.6	33.4	66.6
1870	39,818,449	8,375,128	2,139,652	6,235,566	26.6	25.6	74.4
1880	50,155,783	10,337,334	2,759,650	7,577,684	26.0	26.7	73.3
1890	62,947,714	12,791,931	5,248,079	7,543,852	25.5	41.0	59.0
1900	75,994,575	13,046,861	3,692,612	9,354,249	20.7	28.3	71.7
1910	91,972,266	15,977,691	8,350,637	7,627,054	21.0	52.3	47.7
1920	105,710,620	13,738,354	6,194,488	7,543,866	14.9	45.1	54.9
1930	122,775,046	17,064,426	4,248,435	12,815,991	16.1	24.9	75.1
1940	131,669,275	8,894,229	656,639	8,237,590	7.2	7.4	92.6
1950	151,325,790	19,656,515	901,216	18,755,299	14.9	4.6	95.4
1960	179,323,175	27,997,385	2,503,320	25,494,065	18.5	8.9	91.1
1970	203,302,031	23,978,856	3,240,731	20,738,125	13.4	13.5	86.5
1980	226,545,805	23,243,774	4,375,330	18,868,444	11.4	18.8	81.2
1990	248,709,873	22,164,068	6,583,679	15,580,389	9.8	29.7	70.3
1992	255,081,838	6,371,965	2,030,100	4,341,865	2.6	31.9	68.1

[a]Because immigration data were not systematically collected prior to 1820, components of population change could not be computed until the 1820-1830 period.

Source: Population Data from the appropriate decennial censuses as reported by the U.S. Bureau of the Census in Historical Statistics of the United States: Colonial Times to 1970, Washington, DC: U.S. Government Printing Office, 1975. Values for 1980 and 1990 are from the decennial censuses for the respective years. Values for 1992 are estimates from the U.S. Bureau of the Census. Data on immigration from the 1991 and 1992 Statistical Yearbooks of the Immigration and Naturalization Service, Washington, DC: U.S. Immigration and Naturalization Service, 1992 and 1993. Data on natural increase computed by subtracting net immigration from population change.

Decade

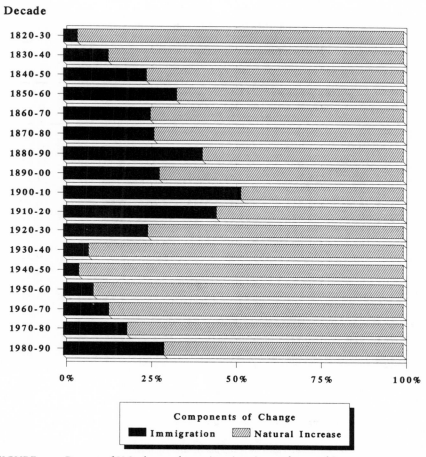

FIGURE 2.2   Percent of U.S. change due to immigration and natural increase.

of an area. Table 2.1 and Figure 2.2 also show population change in the United States resulting from the two components of change for each of the decades since immigration data first began to be collected by the United States in 1820. As the data suggest, the majority of population change throughout nearly all periods of U.S. history has been due to natural increase, with immigration being responsible for a much smaller proportion of population change.

The data also suggest that the proportional contribution of immigration to overall population growth has recently increased. Thus, historically, immigration accounted for more than 50 percent of population growth in only one decade, 1900 to 1910, and accounted for less than 10 percent of all growth for each of the decades of the 1930s, 1940s, and 1950s, nearly 14 percent in the 1960s, and nearly 19

Table 2.2: Immigration into the United States, by Period and Area of Origin of Immigrants, 1820-1990 (numbers in thousands)

Time Period	Number of Immigrants	Percent by Area of Origin					
		Europe	Asia	Canada	Latin America	Africa	All Other
1820-1830	152	70.14	0.02	1.64	6.23	0.01	21.96
1831-1840	599	82.73	0.01	2.27	3.30	0.01	11.68
1841-1850	1,713	93.24	0.01	2.44	2.93	0.00	1.38
1851-1860	2,598	94.40	1.60	2.28	0.60	0.01	1.11
1861-1870	2,315	89.21	2.80	6.65	0.56	0.01	0.77
1871-1880	2,812	80.79	4.42	13.64	0.73	0.01	0.42
1881-1890	5,247	90.26	1.33	7.50	0.65	0.02	0.24
1891-1900	3,688	96.41	2.03	0.09	0.97	0.01	0.49
1901-1910	8,795	91.59	3.68	2.04	2.07	0.08	0.54
1911-1920	5,736	75.35	4.31	12.94	7.00	0.15	0.25
1921-1930	4,107	59.97	2.73	22.51	14.42	0.15	0.22
1931-1940	528	65.77	3.14	20.54	9.74	0.33	0.48
1941-1950	1,035	60.01	3.58	16.59	17.69	0.71	1.42
1951-1960	2,515	52.70	6.09	15.03	24.61	0.56	1.01
1961-1970	3,322	33.82	12.87	12.44	39.23	0.87	0.77
1971-1980	4,493	17.81	35.35	3.78	41.19	1.80	0.07
1981-1990	7,338[a]	10.38	37.31	2.14	47.13	2.41	0.63

[a]Includes persons who were granted permanent residence under the legalization program of the Immigration Reform and Control Act of 1986.

Source: 1991 Statistical Yearbook of the Immigration and Naturalization Service, Washington, DC: U.S. Immigration and Naturalization Service, 1992.

percent in the 1970s. Its contribution to growth has recently increased; nearly 30 percent of total population change in the 1980s was due to net immigration from other nations. Population growth in the United States is increasingly dependent on immigration.

The information in Table 2.2 demonstrates another important aspect of recent immigration to the United States: the changing origin of immigrants that come here. The data in this table are for slightly different periods than those in Table 2.1 but they clearly indicate a changing focus for U.S. immigration. For each of the decades from 1820 to 1920, between 70 and 96 percent of all immigrants to the United States were from Europe. Since 1920, immigration patterns have shifted;

from 1981–1990 only 10 percent of immigrants were from Europe, 37 percent were from Asia, and 47 percent from Latin America. Immigration has not only become more important in recent decades, it also reflects an increasingly diverse range of people from an increasing number of nations.

Sources of growth and origins of immigrants are important because the impacts of alternative sources of population growth, and of persons from alternative origins, are different. On the one hand, growth through natural increase results, of course, in an increase in the number of infants, which has implications for certain types of goods and services and will eventually impact numerous sectors of a society as infants grow into adults. On the other hand, immigration tends to occur most often among young adults and results in the formation of completely new households in an area, households that require housing and other goods and services necessary to establish a household. Because a large proportion of immigrants are of working age, they also have an immediate effect on the workforce and related incomes and expenditures in an area. In sum, population growth through immigration tends to have larger immediate economic impacts than growth through natural increase.

The origin of immigrants has implications as well because it impacts the preferences immigrants have for goods and services and the ease of assimilation into destination areas where immigrants choose to settle. Assimilation is generally easier for those whose language and cultural characteristics are more similar to the residents of the destination area and more difficult for those who have very different characteristics than those persons already living in a destination area (McLemore 1991). At the same time, immigrants bring with them certain acquired tastes and preferences that may impact the nature of the goods and services they seek. Finally, the socioeconomic characteristics of immigrants as reflected in their levels of education and skills, wealth, and other "human capital" affect the impacts they have on the socioeconomic resource base of an area.

The three major demographic processes of fertility, mortality, and migration determine the level of population change. Knowledge of these three basic processes is, therefore, essential for understanding how a population is likely to change in the future because they vary substantially by key demographic characteristics, particularly by age and race/ethnicity. Thus, as an examination of Table 2.3 indicates, rates of fertility, mortality, and migration have varied across time. After rapid increases during the baby-boom period of the 1950s and early 1960s, fertility rates generally declined until 1980, increased from 1980 to 1990, and are declining again in the post-1990 period. Mortality has declined across time and life expectancy has increased: The life expectancy of the average American was 26 years greater in 1990 (when it was 75) than in 1900 (when it was 49). Although immigration from 1940 to 1970 was much decreased compared to that in earlier periods of the century, it increased in both the 1970–1980 and 1980–1990 decades. It is also evident that the rates of these demographic processes vary extensively among persons with different characteristics. Fertility is concentrated in young

Table 2.3: Birth, Death, and Net Migration Measures for the United States, 1940-1991

	Fertility Measures[a]		
Year	Crude Birth Rate	General Fertility Rate	Total Fertility Rate
1940	19.4	79.9	2.3
1950	24.1	106.2	3.1
1960	23.7	118.8	3.7
1970	18.4	87.9	2.5
1980	15.9	68.4	1.8
1990	16.7	71.1	2.1
1991	16.2	69.6	-

	Mortality Measures[b]		
Year	Crude Death Rate	Infant Mortality Rate	Life Expectancy at Birth (yrs.)
1940	10.8	54.9	62.9
1950	9.6	33.0	68.2
1960	9.5	27.0	69.7
1970	9.5	21.4	70.8
1980	8.7	12.9	73.7
1990	8.6	9.2	75.4
1991	8.5	8.9	75.7

	Migration Measures		
Year Ending	Annual Number of Immigrants	Year	Total Percent of Population Involved in Internal Migration
1940	70,756	-	-
1950	249,187	50-51	5.6
1960	265,798	60-61	6.3
1970	438,000	70-71	6.5
1980	530,639	80-81	6.2
1990	656,111[c]	90-91	6.1
1991	704,005 [c]		

[a]The crude birth rate is the number of births divided by the total population and multiplied by 1,000. The general fertility rate is the number of births divided by the number of women 15-44 years of age multiplied by 1,000. The total fertility rate is the sum of age-specific fertility rates for women 15-44 years of age and indicates the number of children that a woman would have in her reproductive lifetime if exposed to the age-specific fertility rates prevailing at a given point in time.

[b]The crude death rate is the total number of deaths divided by the total population multiplied by 1,000. The infant mortality rate is the number of deaths per 1,000 births. Life expectancy at birth refers to the average number of years someone born in the year indicated could expect to live.

[c]Excludes 880,372 admitted due to IRCA Legislation in 1990 and 1,123,162 in 1991.

Source: Birth and Death Data from the National Center for Health Statistics for the respective years. Migration data for 1940-1980 from Boque, D.J. The Population of the United States, New York: Free Press, 1985. Data for 1990 for migration from United States Department of Commerce, Bureau of the Census. Current Population Reports, P-25, No. 1018, P-25, No. 1057, P-20, No. 456 and P-20, No. 463. Immigration for 1990 and 1991 from the 1991 and 1992 Statistical Yearbook of the Immigration and Naturalization Service, Washington, DC: U.S. Immigration and Naturalization Service, 1992 and 1993.

adults, particularly ages 20 to 29, and is substantially higher among minority groups than among Whites. Similarly, mortality is highest at older ages but is substantially different among racial and ethnic groups, with mortality generally being higher at younger ages for Blacks and Hispanics than for Whites (see Reference Tables 2.1 and 2.2).

Table 2.4 shows rates for different forms of geographic mobility and migration for different types of groups. Data are shown for the total population, for all persons who moved any distance during the 1989–1990 period, and for each of three subtypes of persons who moved. These subtypes include those who moved but remained within the same county, referred to as **movers,** those who moved and crossed county boundaries, who are defined by the U.S. Bureau of the Census as **migrants,** and those who moved to the United States from other nations, referred to as **immigrants.** By comparing the percentages for the three different types of persons who moved with the total population, one can determine whether those with a given characteristic are more or less likely to move than others. For example, it is evident that persons between 20–29 years of age are quite mobile. Although they represented only 16.2 percent of the population, they constituted 32.0 percent of all persons who moved, including 31.9 percent of movers, 32.2 percent of migrants, and 31.8 percent of immigrants. Similar comparisons show migrants are more likely to be male than female, single than married, to have established their residence in the South and West rather than the Northeast or Midwest, to be college rather than noncollege educated, and renters rather than owners. Migrants are similar to nonmigrants in other regards.

Immigrants are also more likely than others to be minority- rather than majority-group members. The data for immigrants are particularly interesting, showing immigrants to be largely young adults, but with characteristics that are either relatively advantaged or relatively disadvantaged compared to the population as a whole. Thus, 25.4 percent of immigrants had less than a high school education compared to 22.4 percent of the population as a whole. Still, 31.2 percent had 4 or more years of college compared to 21.2 percent of the total population. Similarly, although immigrants were more likely to be either unemployed or employed as laborers than other persons in the population, they were also more likely to be employed as professionals. Immigrants are diverse and the impacts of immigration on any given area will vary widely depending on the characteristics of the immigrants who move to the area.

The components of population change–fertility, mortality, and migration–vary by a population's characteristics. Just as they affect overall rates of growth in a population, the rates of occurrence of fertility, mortality, and migration are impacted by the characteristics of a population.

The Distribution of the Population of the United States

The population of the United States is redistributing itself from the Northeast and Midwest to the South and West. In 1900, 62.2 percent of the U.S. population re-

Table 2.4: Selected Characteristics of the Total Population of the United States and
of Movers, Migrants, and Immigrants in the United States, 1989-1990
(values in percents, income in dollars, persons in numbers)

Characteristic	Population	Total Movers, Migrants, and Immigrants	Movers	Migrants	Immigrants
Age					
1-14	20.8	22.2	23.6	20.0	18.9
15-19	7.1	6.9	7.0	6.7	12.4
20-24	7.4	15.6	15.7	15.5	17.8
25-29	8.8	16.4	16.2	16.7	14.0
30-44	24.5	25.7	25.3	26.2	24.4
45-64	19.2	9.5	8.8	10.5	9.8
65+	12.2	3.7	3.4	4.4	2.7
Sex					
Male	48.6	49.8	49.4	50.6	54.0
Female	51.4	50.2	50.6	49.4	46.0
Race/Ethnicity					
White	84.1	81.7	79.4	85.3	73.0
Black	12.3	14.1	16.2	10.7	7.8
Hispanic	8.4	11.0	13.3	7.3	31.9
Marital Status					
Single (never married)	41.6	49.3	50.5	47.5	53.3
Married, spouse present	44.0	34.9	33.6	37.3	34.6
Married, spouse absent	2.5	4.5	4.6	4.3	6.9
Widowed	5.7	2.7	2.5	2.8	2.8
Divorced	6.2	8.6	8.8	8.1	2.4
Region (current residence)					
Northeast	20.6	14.2	14.6	13.5	21.0
Midwest	24.1	22.1	21.7	22.7	10.8
South	34.2	37.2	35.8	39.4	32.1
West	21.1	26.5	27.9	24.4	36.1
Years of school completed					
Elementary					
0-8 years	11.2	7.8	9.3	5.6	19.1
High School					
1-3 years	11.2	11.2	12.5	9.2	6.3
4 years	38.4	37.1	38.5	34.9	28.7

Table 2.4 (Continued)

Characteristic	Population	Total Movers, Migrants, and Immigrants	Movers	Migrants	Immigrants
Years of school completed (continued)					
College					
1-3 years	18.0	20.1	19.5	21.2	14.7
4 years	12.4	14.4	12.5	17.3	17.6
5+ years	8.8	9.4	7.7	11.8	13.6
Median years of					
school completed	12.7	12.8	12.7	13.0	12.9
Median Personal Income	$13,856	$13,260	$12,955	$13,740	$8,016
Household Size					
Average persons					
per household	2.6	2.7	2.6	2.7	4.0
Housing Tenure					
Owner occupied	64.1	28.8	27.3	31.1	16.5
Renter occupied	35.9	71.2	72.7	68.9	83.5
Occupation					
Executive administration					
and management	11.9	10.7	9.7	12.2	6.6
Professional specialty	12.9	12.0	10.1	15.0	14.0
Technical and					
related support	3.1	3.4	3.1	4.0	2.5
Sales	11.5	11.6	11.2	12.2	6.5
Administrative support,					
including clerical	15.2	13.9	14.7	12.6	8.3
Private household service	0.6	0.6	0.6	0.6	1.6
Protective service	1.6	1.5	1.4	1.8	1.0
Service, except protective					
and household	10.3	11.2	12.4	9.2	15.3
Farming, forestry,					
and fishing	2.5	1.8	1.9	1.8	1.6
Precision production,					
crafts, and repair	10.9	11.0	11.4	10.4	11.2
Machine operation,					
assembly, and inspectors	6.3	6.3	7.3	4.5	10.0
Transportation and					
material moving	3.8	3.6	3.9	3.1	2.1
Handlers, equipment					
cleaners, and labor	3.9	4.3	4.5	4.0	6.9
Unemployed	5.5	8.1	7.8	8.6	12.4
Armed Forces	0.5	1.2	0.8	1.7	5.9
Not in labor force	34.0	24.3	23.7	34.3	37.1

Table 2.4 (Continued)

Characteristic	Population	Total Movers, Migrants, and Immigrants	Movers	Migrants	Immigrants
Industry					
Agriculture, forestry, and fishing	2.5	1.8	1.8	1.8	1.8
Mining	0.6	0.6	0.6	0.6	-
Construction	6.1	6.7	6.9	6.5	6.8
Manufacturing	16.9	15.7	16.5	14.3	14.8
Transportation, communication, and other public utilities	6.5	5.8	5.8	5.6	3.0
Wholesale trade	3.6	3.6	3.4	4.0	3.1
Retail trade	15.7	17.1	17.7	16.3	20.9
Finance, insurance, and real estate (F.I.R.E.)	6.5	6.3	6.5	6.1	3.3
Business and repair services	6.1	7.1	7.0	7.3	8.1
Personal services	3.8	4.5	4.5	4.5	4.7
Entertainment and recreation services	1.1	1.1	1.0	1.1	1.6
Professional and related services	20.6	17.9	17.0	19.3	16.8
Public administration	4.5	3.7	3.5	4.0	2.7
Unemployed	5.5	8.1	7.8	8.6	12.4
Armed Forces	0.5	1.2	0.8	1.7	5.9
Not in labor force	34.0	24.3	23.7	34.3	37.1

Source: "Geographical Mobility: March 1987 to March 1990," *Current Population Reports* P-20, No. 456, Washington, DC: U.S. Bureau of the Census, 1991.

sided in the Northeast and Midwest, but by 1990 only 44.4 percent of the population resided in these two regions. During the 1980s, the concentration of growth in the South and West was evident. Just three states—California, Florida, and Texas—accounted for 54 percent of all the population growth in the United States between 1980 and 1990. Of the ten states with the fastest percentage growth in population, only one, New Hampshire, was not in either the South or West.

These patterns of population distribution are sufficiently long-term to suggest that population change is likely to be centered in specific regions of the nation.

The patterns of change noted throughout this book will, therefore, be more prevalent in some areas of the nation than in others.

Population Characteristics

The characteristics of a population—whether it is young or old; dominated numerically by majority or minority groups; has an agricultural- or industrial-based economy; is well or poorly educated; and whether its members are generally wealthy or impoverished—are as important as its growth and its distribution. The composition—that is, the characteristics—of a population determines much of what will happen to it in the future. The characteristics of the population of the United States are briefly examined below.

Age and Sex. The age and sex composition of a population are important because certain biological characteristics, legal rights and responsibilities, and socioeconomic characteristics are a function of one's age and sex. Table 2.5 presents information on the age and sex composition of the U.S. population for selected periods.

Table 2.5 indicates that the population is growing older. Although the change in median age from 22.9 to 32.9 in the 90 years from 1900 to 1990 may not seem large in absolute terms, it is large in demographic terms. Especially important is the relatively rapid aging of the population. For example, the median age of the population was 30.1 years in 1950 and was 30.0 years in 1980—virtually no change in 30 years. From 1980 to 1990, however, the population aged from 30.0 to 32.9 years, an increase of 2.9 years in just a decade. Why the large increase? It is because of the aging of a key group in the population popularly referred to as the baby-boom generation, which is composed of persons born between 1946 and 1964. They comprise one-third of the population and are entering middle age (the first becoming 40 years of age in 1986). Their aging will largely determine the overall aging of the population in the coming decades. For example, because most of the baby-boomers were 25–44 years old by 1990, it was this age group that showed the largest percentage increase from 1980 to 1990 (see Reference Table 2.3). Because baby-boomers will be middle-aged between now and the year 2011, when the first become elderly (65 years of age or older), the population generally will turn middle-aged between now and 2011 and begin to age rapidly thereafter. By 2029, all of the baby-boomers will be 65 years old and older. Thus the general population of the United States will be relatively old, with 20 percent of all persons being 65 years of age or older in 2030 compared to 12.5 percent in 1990.

These data also point to another important aspect of America's age and sex composition. Because females live roughly 7 years longer than males, with a life expectancy of 78.8 years compared to 71.8 for males in 1990 (National Center for Health Statistics 1993), older populations have increasingly higher proportions of females. The U.S. population has shown a decreased number of males relative to females over time, with the number of males per 100 females (the sex ratio) falling

Table 2.5: Median Age and Sex Ratio in
the United States, 1900-1990

Year	Median Age	Sex Ratio
1900	22.9	104.4
1910	24.1	106.0
1920	25.3	104.0
1930	26.5	102.5
1940	29.0	100.7
1950	30.1	98.6
1960	29.5	97.1
1970	28.1	94.8
1980	30.0	94.5
1990	32.9	95.1

Source: U.S. Department of Commerce, Bureau of
the Census. "Characteristics of the Population,"
U.S. Census of Population 1980, Chapter 3,
General Population Characteristics PC80-1-B1
(United States) Washington, D.C.: U.S.
Government Printing Office, 1983. Values for
1990 from the 1990 Census Summary Tape File
1A for the United States.

below 100 by 1950. In addition, although males outnumbered females through age 29 in 1990, the higher rate of male mortality leads to a steady, disproportionate decline. Among those 85 years old and older there were only 38.6 males for every 100 females in 1990. Older populations are generally numerically dominated by women.

Race and Ethnicity. Race and ethnicity are commonly used to refer to differences among population groups based on cultural, historical, and national-origin characteristics. Although race was once thought to denote biological differences, it is now clear that racial differences are largely socioeconomic and cultural. Ethnicity generally refers to the national, cultural, or ancestral origins of a people.

Measuring race and ethnicity is difficult. The U.S. Bureau of the Census has generally measured the concepts of race and ethnicity by asking respondents to identify themselves on questionnaires on two separate items. For example, in the 1990 Decennial Census, persons were asked one question in which they were to identify themselves in terms of the racial categories of White; Black; American Indian, Eskimo or Aleut; Asian and Pacific Islander; or whether they were members of some Other racial group. In a separate question, they were asked whether they were of Spanish/Hispanic origin and, if they indicated that they were of Hispanic origin, they were asked to indicate which Hispanic group they were a member of. As a result of the use of two separate questions, many census reports show data divided by racial groups and also a separate tabulation of data by Hispanic origin. Even when racial/ethnic data are reported together, Hispanic is often shown with a note that "Hispanics may be of any race." Many data users want to add values for Hispanics to the racial categories, but if that were done Hispanics would be counted twice since they are already included in the counts by racial group. In a few tabulations, such as those shown in the projections presented in this volume, Hispanics by race are subtracted from the total population by race to obtain mutually exclusive categories of non-Hispanic Whites or Anglos, non-Hispanic Blacks, non-Hispanic persons of Other racial/ethnic groups, and Hispanics of all races.[2] In still other items asked by the Census Bureau and by other groups, information is collected on the country of birth and on the ethnic identity of persons such that ethnicity comes to have multiple meanings. Users of data on race and ethnicity can only be sure of what is meant by such terms by carefully consulting the sources from which the data are derived.

Race and ethnicity (referring to groups categorized by White, Black, etc., and Hispanic origin) have substantial impacts on the life opportunities of persons because population and socioeconomic patterns for different racial and ethnic groups have historically been very different. Table 2.6 provides data on racial and ethnic groups in the United States.

In general, minority groups (defined here as all non-White or non-Anglo groups) have shown more rapid population growth and have increased their share of the population compared to Whites or Anglos. Thus, during the 1980 to 1990 period, the White population increased by only 5.6 percent; however, the Black population increased by 13.2 percent, the Other population (composed of Asian and Pacific Islanders; American Indians, Eskimos, and Aleuts; and persons from all other racial groups except Whites and Blacks) increased by 72.6 percent, and the Hispanic population by 53.1 percent (see Table 2.6 and Figure 2.3). Of the total net increase in the population from 1980 to 1990, 66 percent was due to minority population growth (see Figure 2.4). As a result, the proportion of Whites

Table 2.6: U.S. Population 1970, 1980, and 1990, Percent Change in Population 1970 to 1980 and 1980 to 1990, and Proportion of Population 1970, 1980, and 1990 by Race and Hispanic Origin, and Ethnicity

Racial/ Ethnic Category	Number			Percent Change		Proportion of Population		
	1970	1980	1990	1970-1980	1980-1990	1970	1980	1990
Race and Hispanic Origin								
White	178,107,190	189,035,012	199,686,070	6.1	5.6	87.6	83.4	80.3
Black	22,549,815	26,482,349	29,986,060	17.4	13.2	11.1	11.7	12.1
Other	2,555,872	11,028,444	19,037,743	331.5	72.6	1.3	4.9	7.6
Hispanic[a]	9,294,509	14,603,683	22,354,059	57.1	53.1	4.6	6.5	9.0
Total	203,212,877	226,545,805	248,709,873	11.5	9.8	---	---	---
Ethnicity								
Anglo	168,812,682	180,602,838	188,128,296	7.0	4.2	83.1	79.7	75.7
Black[b]	22,549,815	26,091,857	29,216,293	15.7	12.0	11.1	11.5	11.7
Hispanic	9,294,509	14,603,683	22,354,059	57.1	53.1	4.6	6.5	9.0
Other[b]	2,555,872	5,247,427	9,011,225	105.3	71.7	1.2	2.3	3.6
Total	203,212,877	226,545,805	248,709,873	11.5	9.8	100.0	100.0	100.0

[a]Hispanics may be of any race. As a result, White, Black, and Other sum to the total population and Hispanics are included among those in these three racial categories as well as being shown as a separate ethnic group.

[b]For 1970, Spanish-surnamed persons were assumed to be Hispanic and all Hispanics were subtracted from the White total to obtain Anglos. The values shown for the Black and other populations for 1980 and 1990 in this table do not include Blacks or persons of Other races who are of Hispanic origin, who are included in the Hispanic total.

Source: U.S. Bureau of the Census, U.S. Census of Population, fourth count census tapes for 1970 and the PL94-171 tape files for 1980 and 1990.

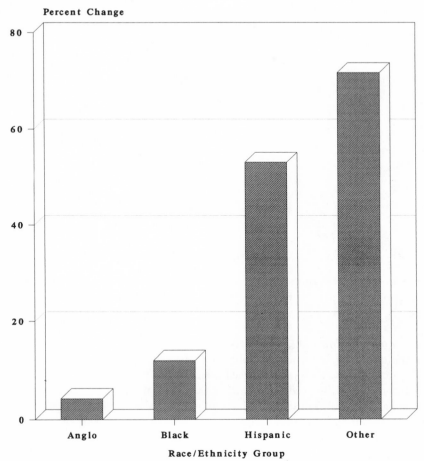

FIGURE 2.3   Percent change by race/ethnicity, 1980–1990.

declined by 3 percent from 1980 to 1990 as the proportion of all other groups increased.

Racial and ethnic patterns differ widely by region and state, however. Minority groups are heavily concentrated in the South and West. Whereas these two regions have 55.6 percent of the total U.S. population, only 53 percent of the White population lives there. However, more than 62 percent of the Black population; 76 percent of the American Indian, Eskimo, and Aleut population; 71 percent of the Asian and Pacific Islander population; 75 percent of the Other population; and 75 percent of the Hispanic population call the South and West regions home. Although the Black population is more widely dispersed among states, the three largest states of California, New York, and Texas had 26 percent of the total popu-

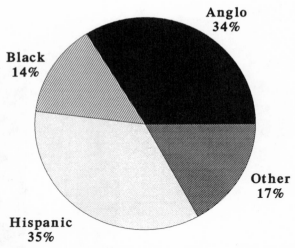

FIGURE 2.4   Percent of net U.S. population change by each ethnic group, 1980–1990.

lation but 53 percent of the Asian and Pacific Islander population, 69 percent of the population of persons from Other races, and 64 percent of the Hispanic population in 1990.

Household and Marital Characteristics. How we group ourselves into households is of critical importance for our social and economic well-being. The characteristics of households have changed dramatically over time. On the one hand, the proportion of divorced persons was 2.5 times greater in 1990 than in 1970; the proportion of family households (those households with two or more persons related by kinship, marriage, or adoption living in a single housing unit) and the proportion of families that are traditional married-couple families have decreased (see Reference Table 2.4). On the other hand, nonfamily households (those households consisting of a single person or two or more unrelated persons living in a single housing unit) and households involving cohabiting adults (adults of the opposite sex who are not married but living together) have increased substantially. (In fact, Bumpass and Sweet [1989] reported 33 percent of men and 37 percent of women 25–29 years of age had cohabited before age 25 and 8 percent of men and 3 percent of women who were 45–49 years old had cohabited before age 25.)

As a result of reduced rates of marriage, higher divorce rates, lower fertility, more diverse living arrangements, and other factors, the average size of households has declined (Table 2.7). The average household has declined from 3.67 persons in 1940 to 2.63 persons in 1990, and although the proportion of households with five or more persons has declined from 27.6 percent of all households in 1950 to only 11.0 percent in 1990, the proportion of one- and two-person households has increased from 31.9 percent in 1940 to 56.5 percent in 1990.

Table 2.7: Number and Percent of Households by Persons in the Household and Average Household Size for the United States, 1940-1990 (numbers in thousands)

Households by Persons Per Household	1940 Number	%	1950 Number	%	1960 Number	%	1970 Number	%	1980 Number	%	1990 Number	%
One person	2,481	7.1	4,737	10.9	6,871	13.0	10,692	17.1	18,300	22.6	22,580	24.5
Two persons	8,667	24.8	12,529	28.8	14,616	27.8	18,129	28.8	25,300	31.3	29,454	32.0
Three persons	7,829	22.4	9,808	22.6	9,941	19.0	10,903	17.3	14,100	17.5	15,970	17.4
Four persons	6,326	18.1	7,729	17.8	9,277	17.6	9,935	15.8	12,700	15.7	13,860	15.1
Five or more	9,646	27.6	8,666	19.9	11,905	22.6	13,215	21.0	10,400	12.9	10,083	11.0
All households	34,949	100.0	43,469	100.0	52,610	100.0	62,874	100.0	80,800	100.0	91,947	100.0
Average persons per household	3.67	-	3.37	-	3.35	-	3.17	-	2.75	-	2.63	-

Source: Data for 1940-1970 from Bogue, D.J. *The Population of the United States: Historical Trends and Future Projections,* New York: The Free Press, 1985 and the United States Department of Commerce, Bureau of the Census. *Historical Statistics of the United States Colonial Times to 1970,* Washington, DC: U.S. Government Printing Office, 1975. United States Department of Commerce, Bureau of Census. Data for 1980 from "Household and Family Characteristics: March 1990 and 1989," *Current Population Reports* P-20, No. 447, Washington, DC: U.S. Government Printing Office, 1990. Data for 1990 from the Summary Tape File 1A from the 1990 Census.

What these changes suggest is that households consist of ever more diverse living and consuming units. Households contain increasing numbers of persons who are living in nontraditional arrangements and in households with smaller numbers than ever before. This suggests that the need to develop new goods and services for these increasingly diverse units is likely to continue in the coming years.

Socioeconomic Characteristics. Social scientists often refer to the education, income, and employment characteristics of a population as its socioeconomic characteristics because these factors are highly interrelated and together largely determine the resources a population's members have to meet their needs. Summaries of key socioeconomic characteristics of the U.S. population (see Reference Table 2.5) show a pattern of progression in educational attainment, a growing labor force in which male participation rates are decreasing and female participation rates increasing, declining manufacturing and extractive- and construction-industry employment, growing service employment, and relatively little real income or other economic growth in the past two decades. Overall, these data suggest that in terms of the educational resources necessary for economic advancement progress is being made, but that stagnation in employment in basic sectors has led to relatively little real income growth for Americans in recent decades.

SUMMARY AND IMPLICATIONS OF CURRENT U.S. POPULATION PATTERNS

The above discussion suggests that population patterns in the United States are characterized by several major trends. These trends can be summarized as follows:

1. The United States is the third-largest nation in the world and will likely continue to be so through the year 2020, but its share of the world's population will decline and so its demographic significance in the world is likely to decrease.

2. The rate of population growth in the United States has slowed over time; by 1992 it was roughly 1 percent per year, and continued slow growth is anticipated.

3. Although natural increase historically has been the major source of population growth in the United States, particularly during the middle part of this century, net immigration has come to be of increasing importance to the recent growth of the nation.

4. Immigration to the United States is characterized by increasing diversity. Although Europeans dominated immigration to the United States for much of the nation's history, immigration is now dominated by persons from Latin America and Asia.

5. The demographic processes of fertility, mortality, and migration, which determine the level of population change experienced in an area, are highly variable

among persons with different characteristics, with age and race/ethnicity being particularly important in the determination of differentials in these processes.

6. The distribution of the population shows an increasing concentration in the southern and western parts of the United States. Three states—California, Florida, and Texas—accounted for more than 54 percent of all population growth from 1980 to 1990.

7. The age and sex composition of the U.S. population shows a population that ages as the baby-boom generation ages. Because women live longer than men, the population is developing an increasing numerical dominance of women.

8. Patterns of change in the racial and ethnic characteristics of the population of the United States show minority populations to be growing more rapidly than White or Anglo populations and increasing as a proportion of the total population.

9. The household and marital composition of the United States population shows a trend toward smaller households with more persons either remaining single or becoming single again after once marrying. Nontraditional household forms (for example, female and male householder families without a spouse present and cohabitating couples) are increasingly prevalent, suggesting the need for a diverse set of goods and services to meet the needs of a wider range of household types.

10. The socioeconomic characteristics of the U.S. population suggest a population that has substantially increased its level of education, is shifting its economy from extractive and manufacturing industries to service industries, and in which income levels are relatively stagnant.

What are the most significant of these trends relative to the public and private sectors in American society and why are they likely to be significant if continued into the future? Nearly all analyses of future trends (Spencer 1989; Day 1992; Fosler et al. 1990; Gill et al. 1992) and the data presented in this chapter suggest that the most significant trends are those related to: (1) the overall level of population growth and the increasing proportion of that growth due to immigration; (2) the aging of the population toward an increasingly middle-aged population in the immediate future and an older population in the long term; and (3) the increase in the minority population, with minorities coming to both dominate growth and to account for an increasing share of the population of the United States.

The magnitude of future change in these three factors and their implications are the topics of the remainder of this book. However, some indication of the potential importance of such trends can be seen by examining Table 2.8, which shows median household incomes of persons of different ages, migration statuses, and race/Hispanic origins. These data show that incomes tend to be higher among those in their middle ages and lower among immigrants and minority populations. Since the trends noted above suggest an increasing number of immigrants, larger minority populations, and an older population, it is evident that a population with an increasing proportion in such groups will likely show

**Table 2.8: Median Household Income in the United States by Age, Migration
Status, and Race/Ethnicity of Householder, 1990**

Characteristic	Median Household Income, 1990
Age of Householder	
15-24	$16,219
25-34	31,497
35-44	41,061
45-54	47,165
55-64	39,035
65+	25,049
Migration Status (1989-1990)	
Nonmigrant	$30,195
Mover	23,152
Migrant	26,369
Immigrant	19,797
Race/Hispanic Origin	
White	$31,231
Black	18,676
Other	33,860
Hispanic	22,330

Source: Data on income by age and race/Hispanic origin, from
"Money, Income of Households, Families, and Persons in the United States:
1990," *Current Population Reports* P-60, No. 174, Washington, DC: U.S.
Bureau of the Census, 1991. Data on income by migration Status from
"Geographical Mobility: March 1987 to March 1990," *Current Population
Reports* P-20, No. 456, Washington, DC: U.S. Bureau of the Census, 1991.

changes in its overall resource base for both private and public uses. Demographic change is likely to impact change in the socioeconomic resource base of
the population with ramifications throughout the public and private sectors.

In sum, the prevailing patterns and trends delineated here seem likely to continue. If these patterns relate to socioeconomic change in the future the same way
they have in the past, they are likely to be of substantial significance. Delineating
the nature of these future trends and their implications is the task addressed in
the remainder of this book.

CHAPTER THREE

America's Future Population: Analyzing Alternative Demographic Futures

The starting point for any analysis of the implications of future demographic change for the labor force, business, and other factors is a thorough examination of the demographic patterns projected for the future. In this chapter, we examine projections of the population of the United States, concentrating on recent projections by the U.S. Bureau of the Census because they provide the basis for much of the analysis provided in subsequent chapters. The intent is to provide a description of the projected size and key characteristics of the future population of the United States.

In beginning the discussion of population projections and what they suggest about the demographic future of the United States, it is critical to note that projections are subject to substantial error (Ascher 1978; Armstrong 1985). The literature (Ascher 1978; Armstrong 1985; Pant and Starbuck 1990) also suggests that projections are most accurate for short periods of time into the future, for areas where future trends depart less from past trends, and for larger population areas where small changes have smaller relative effects.[3] Most analysts argue that projections are unlikely to be accurate for periods that exceed 10 to 20 years beyond the base date from which the projections are made (Keyfitz 1981). Thus caution in using projections, and using them as indications of the direction of change rather than as point estimates, is highly recommended (Murdock et al. 1991a). At the same time, however, it is evident that projections may be useful to indicate what is likely to happen in the future if current trends continue. They indicate what the past may mean for the future and what will happen if the forces of the past are not altered. Thus, projections are important because they provide a means of knowing what the future may be and, therefore, provide a basis for actions that may change the future.

31

THE METHODS AND ASSUMPTIONS UNDERLYING POPULATION PROJECTIONS

Population projections can be made using a variety of methods, including: simple extrapolations of past patterns; methods based on economic models, which use employment patterns to predict population change; multidimensional demographic models; and numerous other methods (Shryock and Siegel 1976; Ahlburg and Land 1992; Murdock et al. 1984). Most population projections, however, rely on a method called the Cohort-Component Projection Method. It is so named because it projects future populations by taking cohorts of a population–that is, groups of people with one or more common characteristics–and projecting the demographic components of mortality and migration for each of the cohorts and fertility for cohorts of women of childbearing age. Summing the projections for individual cohorts produces a projection of the total population. For each of these cohorts, assumptions about mortality, migration, and, for cohorts of women, assumptions about fertility, determine the size and characteristics of the populations projected.[4]

The Projections Used in This Work

Given the uncertainty of projections, it is common to use alternative sets of projections that utilize different sets of assumptions about the three demographic processes of fertility, mortality, and migration. The U.S. Bureau of the Census completes projections that contain alternative assumptions about each of the three processes. The potential combinations for each of the three processes are examined and nine alternative projection series or scenarios of future populations are reported. In addition, to identify the impacts of immigration, a tenth projection series is often provided by the Bureau in which net immigration is assumed to be zero and fertility and mortality are held at the level of the middle scenario. The basic assumptions for the high, middle, low, and zero immigration scenarios for the U.S. Bureau of the Census projection scenarios used in this work are shown in Table 3.1 (see also Day 1992). The resulting total populations projected under each of these assumptions for 1990 through 2050 are shown in Table 3.2 and Figure 3.1.[5] The race/ethnicity groups used in this and subsequent work reported here are the mutually exclusive groups of non-Hispanic whites (referred to as Anglos), non-Hispanic Blacks (referred to as Blacks), all other non-Hispanic social groups combined (referred to as Others), and Hispanics (which includes Hispanics of all races).

PROJECTIONS OF THE FUTURE POPULATION OF THE UNITED STATES

The values in Tables 3.1 and 3.2 point to the uncertainty that may occur in projections of future population patterns. The total populations projected for 2050 vary

Table 3.1: Principal Fertility, Life Expectancy, and Net Immigration Assumptions of U.S. Bureau of the Census' Projections of the Population in the United States from 1992-2050 Under Alternative Scenarios

Projection Assumptions	1992	2050 Level			
		Low Scenario	Middle Scenario	High Scenario	Zero Immigration
Total Fertility Level Per 1,000 Women	2,052	1,833	2,119	2,522	2,119
Life Expectancy at Birth	75.8	75.3	82.1	87.6	82.1
Yearly Net Immigration (thousands)	880	350	880	1,370	0

Source: "Population Projections of the United States by Age, Sex, Race, and Spanish Origin, 1992-2050" by Jennifer Cheeseman Day, *Current Population Reports*, P-25, No. 1092, Pg XI, Washington, DC: U.S. Bureau of the Census, 1992.

from only 275 million, about 27 million more people than were counted in the 1990 Census, to 507 million, 259 million more than in 1990. The differences are much less in the short term, with the differences between the various scenarios being 16 million by 2000, 40 million by 2010, and 75 million by 2020. Nevertheless, substantial differences are evident in these alternative scenarios.

In fact, at first glance it appears there is little that is similar about the alternative scenarios. However, the scenarios show similarities in each of the major trends that have been identified as playing key roles in the future of the United States. They generally show reduced rates of population growth relative to historical time periods, an aging population, and increased ethnic diversity.

Slower Population Growth but Large Numerical Increases

Table 3.3 shows the percentage change in population size for selected time periods for each of the scenarios. If the decade-to-decade changes are examined and compared to those of preceding decades, the slower growth projected in most scenarios is evident. From 1980 to 1990, the population of the nation increased by 9.8 percent; from 1970 to 1980 it increased by 11.4 percent. Under the low, middle, and zero immigration scenarios, there is only one decade for one scenario—the

Table 3.2: U.S. Bureau of the Census' Projections of the Population in the United States by Race/Ethnicity[a] from 1990-2050 Under Alternative Scenarios

Year	Race/Ethnicity				Total Population
	Anglo	Black	Hispanic	Other	
Low Scenario					
1990	188,128,296	29,216,293	22,354,059	9,011,225	248,709,873
2000	193,877,343	33,094,398	28,692,581	12,443,453	268,107,775
2010	193,015,640	35,596,370	33,827,982	15,638,510	278,078,502
2020	189,931,046	37,560,108	38,866,493	18,842,024	285,199,671
2030	182,603,708	38,666,601	43,464,839	21,975,172	286,710,320
2040	170,986,916	39,047,263	47,390,943	24,860,638	282,285,760
2050	158,340,427	38,980,851	50,790;117	27,535,149	275,646,544
Middle Scenario					
1990	188,128,296	29,216,293	22,354,059	9,011,225	248,709,873
2000	196,700,935	33,834,463	30,602,142	13,677,925	274,815,465
2010	201,668,449	38,200,689	39,311,562	18,928,373	298,109,073
2020	206,161,770	42,910,788	48,951,768	24,577,377	322,601,703
2030	207,674,257	47,551,578	59,197,188	30,528,356	344,951,379
2040	205,586,784	52,284,693	69,827,229	36,650,334	364,349,040
2050	201,840,533	57,315,588	80,675,012	42,842,947	382,674,080
High Scenario					
1990	188,128,296	29,216,293	22,354,059	9,011,225	248,709,873
2000	199,638,719	34,485,466	32,342,744	14,839,110	281,306,039
2010	211,185,161	40,346,047	44,328,371	22,035,208	317,894,787
2020	224,370,664	47,187,279	58,445,123	30,119,472	360,122,538
2030	236,654,055	54,682,389	74,717,255	39,076,094	405,129,793
2040	248,211,126	63,013,832	93,465,608	48,996,204	453,686,770
2050	259,720,826	72,277,469	114,903,956	59,837,914	506,740,165
Zero Immigration Scenario					
1990	188,128,296	29,216,293	22,354,059	9,011,225	248,709,873
2000	194,965,334	33,231,157	27,309,887	10,477,149	265,983,527
2010	197,663,449	36,770,882	31,524,275	11,538,507	277,497,113
2020	199,648,747	40,533,600	35,966,836	12,602,334	288,751,517
2030	198,445,572	44,094,173	40,199,015	13,574,332	296,313,092
2040	193,514,146	47,629,160	44,096,785	14,365,552	299,605,643
2050	186,906,199	51,360,897	47,644,286	15,098,474	301,009,856

[a] The racial/ethnic groupings used in this and all subsequent tables are four mutually exclusive categories. Anglo consists of White Non-Hispanics, Black of Black Non-Hispanics, Other of persons in all other (except White and Black) racial groups who are not Hispanic, and Hispanic refers to Hispanics of all races (see footnote 2 for more information on this form of categorization).

Source: Data derived from "Population of the United States by Age, Sex, Race, and Spanish Origin, 1992-2050" by Jennifer Cheeseman Day, *Current Population Reports*, P-25, No. 1092, Washington, DC: U.S. Bureau of the Census, 1992.

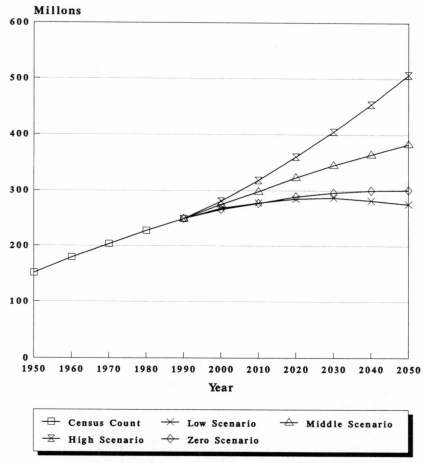

Millons

FIGURE 3.1   U.S. population 1950-1990 and projections to 2050, all scenarios.

1990-to-2000 period under the middle scenario—in which the rate of growth is not lower than during the 1980s. Only in the high-growth scenario are levels of growth similar to those in the 1970s. Similarly, growth would be substantially slower for the total 60-year projection period (1990 through 2050) in most scenarios than during the preceding 60-year period (1930 through 1990). The population of the United States increased by 102.6 percent from 1930 through 1990, but only under the highest growth scenario would the population increase by as much from 1990 to 2050 (103.7 percent). In general, these projections point to a slower-growing population in America in the coming century.

Although growth is expected to increase at a slower **rate** than in the past, the **numerical** increase in population will nevertheless be substantial. The increase of

Table 3.3: Percent Change in the U.S. Bureau of the Census' Projections
of the Population in the United States by Race/Ethnicity from
1990-2050 Under Alternative Scenarios

Time	Anglo	Black	Hispanic	Other	Total
Low Scenario					
1990-2000	3.1	13.3	28.4	38.1	7.8
2000-2010	-0.4	7.6	17.9	25.7	3.7
2010-2020	-1.6	5.5	14.9	20.5	2.6
2020-2030	-3.9	2.9	11.8	16.6	0.5
2030-2040	-6.4	1.0	9.0	13.1	-1.5
2040-2050	-7.4	-0.2	7.2	10.8	-2.4
1990-2050	-15.8	33.4	127.2	205.6	10.8
Middle Scenario					
1990-2000	4.6	15.8	36.9	51.8	10.5
2000-2010	2.5	12.9	28.5	38.4	8.5
2010-2020	2.2	12.3	24.5	29.8	8.2
2020-2030	0.7	10.8	20.9	24.2	6.9
2030-2040	-1.0	10.0	18.0	20.1	5.6
2040-2050	-1.8	9.6	15.5	16.9	5.0
1990-2050	7.3	96.2	260.9	375.4	53.9
High Scenario					
1990-2000	6.1	18.0	44.7	64.7	13.1
2000-2010	5.8	17.0	37.1	48.5	13.0
2010-2020	6.2	17.0	31.8	36.7	13.3
2020-2030	5.5	15.9	27.8	29.7	12.5
2030-2040	4.9	15.2	25.1	25.4	12.0
2040-2050	4.6	14.7	22.9	22.1	11.7
1990-2050	38.1	147.4	414.0	564.0	103.7
Zero Immigration Scenario					
1990-2000	3.6	13.7	22.2	16.3	6.9
2000-2010	1.4	10.7	15.4	10.1	4.3
2010-2020	1.0	10.2	14.1	9.2	4.1
2020-2030	-0.6	8.8	11.8	7.7	2.6
2030-2040	-2.5	8.0	9.7	5.8	1.1
2040-2050	-3.4	7.8	8.0	5.1	0.5
1990-2050	-0.6	75.8	113.1	67.6	21.0

Source: See Table 3.2

nearly 134 million persons from 1990 through 2050 projected under the middle scenario would exceed the number of persons added to the population of the United States from 1930 through 1992. Under the high-growth scenario, the numerical increase in the population of the United States in the coming 60 years would exceed the total population increase since the founding of the nation.

It is also important to note the important role that immigration plays in the projected future growth of the United States. Compare the middle scenario to the zero immigration scenario: The zero immigration scenario is identical in its assumptions about future fertility and mortality to the middle scenario, but assumes no net immigration or emigration (or assumes that the number of immigrants to the United States and emigrants from the United States are equal), so that the addition of immigrants and their descendants are not included. Thus immigration would account for 81.7 million additional persons by 2050 (subtracting from the 382.7 million in the middle scenario in 2050 the 301.0 million in the zero scenario for 2050) compared to what would have been in the population if only natural increase had occurred. Since the total population growth projected under the middle scenario is roughly 134 million, this means that 61 percent of the total net increase in the U.S. population from 1990 through 2050 is projected to be due to immigrants and their descendants. Since the middle scenario assumes annual immigration of 880,000 persons over the 60-year period, this suggests that direct immigration from 1990 to 2050 would be 52.8 million. This increase in immigration would be unparalleled for any period in U.S. history, except the late 1800s and early 1900s. In sum, immigration is projected to play as large a role in America's future growth as at any time in history.

Overall, then, the U.S. Bureau of the Census projections in Table 3.3 suggest slower rates of growth than in the past; they also suggest that there will be a substantial numerical increase in the total population. Immigration will be the key component of this growth, with immigrants and their descendants being responsible for approximately three-fifths of America's population increase. Population growth in the United States will be increasingly dependent on immigration.

Aging in the Long Term but a Middle-Aged Population in the Near Term

The aging of the population is apparent from Table 3.4. Aging of the population will be substantial over time but will occur most rapidly after the baby-boomers have reached elderly ages. As evident from Table 3.4, in 1990, 12.6 percent of the population was 65 years of age or older. This age distribution changes relatively little by 2000, when (under the middle scenario) only 12.7 percent are 65 years of age or older, or even by 2010, when 13.3 percent would be 65 or older. But by 2030, when all of the baby-boomers born between 1946 and 1964 are 65 years of age or older, 20.2 percent of the population would be at least 65. It is only after 2011,

Table 3.4: U.S. Bureau of the Census' Projections of the Percent of the Population in the United States by Age and Median Age by Race/Ethnicity from 1990-2050 Under Alternative Scenarios

Age Group	Percent of Population by Age and Race/Ethnicity				Total
	Anglo	Black	Hispanic	Other	
1990 Census					
1990					
< 18	23.3	31.9	34.7	30.2	25.6
18-24	10.0	12.3	14.2	12.2	10.7
25-34	16.9	18.0	19.7	19.0	17.4
35-44	15.5	14.0	13.2	16.4	15.1
45-54	10.7	8.7	7.7	9.7	10.1
55-64	9.2	6.6	5.3	6.3	8.5
65-74	8.3	5.1	3.2	4.1	7.3
75-84	4.7	2.6	1.6	1.7	4.1
85+	1.4	0.8	0.4	0.4	1.2
Median Age	34.8	28.0	25.3	29.1	32.9
Low Scenario					
2000					
< 18	22.9	31.5	33.4	29.4	25.4
18-24	8.9	11.1	11.3	10.5	9.5
25-34	12.8	14.5	16.6	16.2	13.5
35-44	16.5	15.9	16.2	16.6	16.5
45-54	14.6	11.8	10.3	12.5	13.6
55-64	9.6	6.8	5.8	7.2	8.8
65-74	7.6	4.9	3.8	4.6	6.7
75-84	5.3	2.6	2.0	2.3	4.5
85+	1.8	0.9	0.6	0.7	1.5
Median Age	38.1	30.3	28.6	31.2	35.8
2010					
< 18	20.3	28.3	29.5	26.4	22.8
18-24	9.6	12.2	12.3	11.2	10.3
25-34	12.3	13.8	14.4	15.3	13.0
35-44	12.9	13.3	14.4	14.9	13.2
45-54	16.0	13.7	13.4	13.4	15.2
55-64	13.6	9.9	8.3	9.5	12.3
65-74	8.2	5.2	4.4	5.4	7.2
75-84	5.0	2.6	2.4	2.8	4.3
85+	2.1	1.0	0.9	1.1	1.7
Median Age	41.0	31.8	30.6	32.9	38.2
2030					
< 18	18.7	25.4	26.2	23.6	21.1
18-24	7.9	10.1	10.0	9.6	8.7
25-34	11.5	13.6	14.0	14.9	12.4
35-44	13.6	14.4	14.1	15.1	13.9
45-54	12.6	11.7	11.1	12.3	12.2
55-64	12.2	10.1	10.3	10.1	11.5
65-74	13.2	9.2	8.7	8.0	11.5
75-84	8.0	4.4	4.3	4.6	6.8
85+	2.3	1.1	1.3	1.8	1.9
Median Age	43.4	35.6	34.9	36.0	40.3

Table 3.4 (Continued)

Age Group	Percent Population by Age and Race/Ethnicity				Total
	Anglo	Black	Hispanic	Other	
			Low Scenario		
2050					
< 18	18.1	24.2	24.8	22.2	20.6
18-24	7.8	9.8	9.8	9.5	8.6
25-34	11.9	13.3	13.6	14.2	12.6
35-44	12.4	13.1	12.7	13.8	12.8
45-54	12.8	12.3	11.7	12.9	12.5
55-64	14.1	12.0	11.0	11.0	12.9
65-74	11.3	8.4	8.0	8.1	10.0
75-84	7.7	4.7	5.6	5.3	6.7
85+	3.9	2.2	2.8	3.0	3.3
Median Age	44.6	37.0	36.4	37.8	41.2
			Middle Scenario		
2000					
< 18	23.1	32.0	33.9	29.6	25.7
18-24	8.8	11.1	11.6	10.7	9.5
25-34	12.8	14.3	17.0	16.6	13.6
35-44	16.4	15.7	15.7	16.5	16.3
45-54	14.5	11.6	9.9	12.0	13.5
55-64	9.6	6.9	5.7	7.1	8.7
65-74	7.6	4.8	3.7	4.6	6.6
75-84	5.3	2.6	1.9	2.2	4.5
85+	1.9	1.0	0.6	0.7	1.6
Median Age	38.4	30.1	28.1	30.9	35.6
2010					
< 18	21.0	30.6	32.0	28.4	24.2
18-24	9.4	11.6	11.9	10.8	10.0
25-34	12.1	13.3	14.9	15.3	12.9
35-44	12.7	12.8	14.2	15.1	13.0
45-54	15.6	13.2	12.2	12.6	14.7
55-64	13.4	9.6	7.6	8.9	11.9
65-74	8.3	5.2	4.1	5.2	7.1
75-84	5.1	2.6	2.3	2.7	4.3
85+	2.4	1.1	0.8	1.0	1.9
Median Age	40.9	31.0	29.2	32.0	37.5
2030					
< 18	19.8	29.6	29.7	26.4	23.4
18-24	8.0	10.6	10.9	10.3	9.1
25-34	11.3	13.0	14.3	14.8	12.3
35-44	12.7	12.6	13.0	14.1	12.9
45-54	11.8	10.3	10.5	11.7	11.4
55-64	11.6	9.3	9.1	9.5	10.7
65-74	13.1	8.7	7.4	7.2	10.9
75-84	8.7	4.4	3.8	4.2	6.9
85+	3.0	1.5	1.3	1.8	2.4
Median Age	43.4	32.8	31.8	33.9	39.0

Table 3.4 (Continued)

Age Group	Percent Population by Age and Race/Ethnicity				
	Anglo	Black	Hispanic	Other	Total
Middle Scenario					
2050					
< 18	19.2	29.4	27.9	24.8	23.2
18-24	7.8	10.4	10.4	9.9	9.0
25-34	11.5	12.9	14.0	14.3	12.5
35-44	11.8	11.9	12.6	13.7	12.2
45-54	11.7	10.4	10.8	11.9	11.4
55-64	12.5	9.7	9.4	9.8	11.1
65-74	11.0	7.5	7.1	7.4	9.2
75-84	8.5	4.6	5.0	5.0	6.8
85+	6.0	3.2	2.8	3.2	4.6
Median Age	44.6	33.2	33.5	35.6	39.3
High Scenario					
2000					
< 18	23.4	32.2	34.1	29.6	26.1
18-24	8.8	11.0	11.9	10.9	9.5
25-34	12.7	14.3	17.4	17.0	13.7
35-44	16.4	15.7	15.4	16.4	16.1
45-54	14.3	11.6	9.7	11.7	13.3
55-64	9.6	6.8	5.5	7.0	8.7
65-74	7.5	4.9	3.6	4.6	6.5
75-84	5.4	2.6	1.8	2.2	4.5
85+	1.9	0.9	0.6	0.6	1.6
Median Age	38.1	30.1	27.7	30.7	35.4
2010					
< 18	22.5	31.3	33.4	29.4	25.6
18-24	9.1	11.3	11.7	10.6	9.9
25-34	11.9	13.2	15.3	15.5	12.8
35-44	12.5	12.9	14.1	15.2	12.9
45-54	15.2	13.1	11.6	12.3	14.2
55-64	13.0	9.4	7.1	8.4	11.5
65-74	8.1	5.2	3.9	5.0	6.8
75-84	5.1	2.6	2.1	2.6	4.3
85+	2.6	1.0	0.8	1.0	2.0
Median Age	40.4	30.9	28.5	31.6	36.7
2030					
< 18	22.5	30.8	32.7	28.5	26.1
18-24	8.6	10.7	11.1	10.6	9.6
25-34	11.3	12.9	14.1	14.6	12.3
35-44	11.8	12.1	12.5	13.5	12.1
45-54	11.0	10.2	10.1	11.3	10.8
55-64	10.8	9.0	8.4	9.1	9.9
65-74	12.0	8.6	6.5	6.7	10.0
75-84	8.3	4.4	3.3	3.8	6.5
85+	3.7	1.3	1.3	1.9	2.7
Median Age	41.4	32.0	29.7	32.6	36.9

Table 3.4 (Continued)

Age Group	Percent Population by Age and Race/Ethnicity				Total
	Anglo	Black	Hispanic	Other	

High Scenario

2050
< 18	22.6	30.7	32.2	27.9	26.5
18-24	8.5	10.6	10.9	10.3	9.6
25-34	11.6	12.9	13.6	14.1	12.6
35-44	11.6	12.0	12.0	13.1	11.9
45-54	10.7	10.1	9.9	11.1	10.5
55-64	10.7	9.1	8.1	8.8	9.6
65-74	9.3	7.2	6.2	6.8	8.0
75-84	7.6	4.8	4.4	4.6	6.1
85+	7.4	2.6	2.7	3.3	5.2
Median Age	41.3	32.1	30.4	33.5	36.3

Zero Immigration Scenario

2000
< 18	23.0	32.0	33.9	30.2	25.5
18-24	8.8	10.9	10.8	9.8	9.3
25-34	12.6	14.1	15.7	14.8	13.2
35-44	16.4	15.8	16.5	16.5	16.4
45-54	14.6	11.7	10.5	13.2	13.7
55-64	9.7	7.0	6.0	7.4	8.9
65-74	7.6	4.8	3.9	4.7	6.7
75-84	5.4	2.7	2.0	2.5	4.7
85+	1.9	1.0	0.7	0.9	1.6
Median Age	38.3	30.3	29.0	31.8	36.3

2010
< 18	20.8	30.4	31.2	27.6	23.6
18-24	9.4	11.5	11.7	11.2	9.9
25-34	11.9	13.1	13.0	13.2	12.3
35-44	12.5	12.6	13.5	13.1	12.7
45-54	15.8	13.4	13.7	13.9	15.1
55-64	13.6	9.8	8.7	10.7	12.4
65-74	8.3	5.3	4.7	5.7	7.4
75-84	5.3	2.7	2.5	3.1	4.5
85+	2.4	1.2	1.0	1.5	2.1
Median Age	41.3	31.4	30.6	33.5	38.6

2030
< 18	19.5	29.4	28.6	26.3	22.5
18-24	7.9	10.5	10.3	9.5	8.7
25-34	11.0	12.7	12.9	13.4	11.7
35-44	12.6	12.4	12.6	13.5	12.5
45-54	11.7	10.2	9.9	10.3	11.2
55-64	11.7	9.4	9.8	9.4	11.0
65-74	13.4	9.1	9.3	9.0	12.0
75-84	9.0	4.7	4.9	5.9	7.7
85+	3.2	1.6	1.7	2.7	2.7
Median Age	44.0	33.3	33.8	35.5	40.6

Table 3.4 (Continued)

Age Group	Percent Population by Age and Race/Ethnicity				Total
	Anglo	Black	Hispanic	Other	
Zero Immigration Scenario					
2050					
< 18	18.9	29.2	27.0	25.1	22.2
18-24	7.7	10.2	9.9	9.7	8.6
25-34	11.3	12.8	13.1	13.8	12.0
35-44	11.5	11.7	11.9	12.2	11.6
45-54	11.6	10.4	10.6	11.1	11.2
55-64	12.7	9.8	10.0	10.2	11.7
65-74	11.1	7.6	7.4	7.2	9.7
75-84	8.7	4.8	6.1	5.6	7.5
85+	6.5	3.5	4.0	5.1	5.5
Median Age	45.4	33.6	35.2	36.2	41.2

Source: See Table 3.2

when baby- boomers begin to enter the elderly ages (those born in 1946 would be 65 years of age in 2011), that the proportion of the population that is elderly increases dramatically. Between now and 2011, it is more correct to refer to the U.S. population as a middle-aged population rather than as an elderly population.

The pervasiveness of the aging of the population is evident in the fact that, in every scenario, both the median age (the age at which one-half of the persons in the population are older and one-half younger) and the proportion of the population 65 years of age or older increase. No matter what, the population will age substantially between now and the end of the third decade of the next century, with the population having a higher median age by 2000, 2030, and 2050 than the 32.9 years in 1990. However, there are clear differences among the scenarios, with the high fertility and high immigration of the high-growth scenario leading to a substantially younger population than in any of the other (nonzero) scenarios. Yet the aging of the population is evident even in the high-growth scenario. Aging is one of the characteristics of the future population of the United States that is unlikely to be altered.

Table 3.4 also points to another important characteristic of the age structure of the population: the substantial difference in the age of Anglo versus minority populations. For example, 14.4 percent of the Anglo population was already 65 years of age or older in 1990 and nearly 26 percent will be 65 years of age or older under the middle scenario in 2050. However, only 5.2 percent of the Hispanic population was 65 years of age or older in 1990 and only 15 percent is projected to be elderly in 2050. This is also evident when median ages are examined (see Fig-

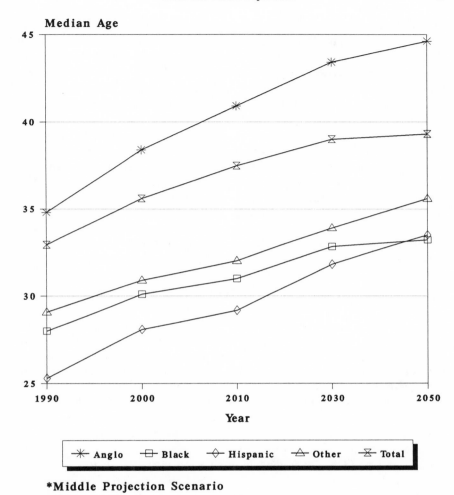

*Middle Projection Scenario

FIGURE 3.2   Median Age of U.S. population by race/ethnicity, 1990–2050.

ure 3.2). In 1990, the median age of Anglos was 34.8 years compared to 28.0 for Blacks, 25.3 for Hispanics, and 29.1 for persons from Other racial/ethnic groups. In 2050 (under the middle scenario), the median age of Anglos would be 44.6 years, but 33.2 years for Blacks, 33.5 years for Hispanics, and 35.6 years for persons from Other racial/ethnic groups. Although both minority and Anglo populations will grow older during the coming decades, the age differences among racial/ethnic groups are projected to remain. As a result, in 2050, the population will be one in which an increasing number of elderly Anglos may be dependent on young minority populations.

The differential effects of mortality among the sexes reflect yet another dimension of the aging of the U.S. population–that is, the differentials among males and females by age and the impacts of aging on the numbers of males relative to females. In 1990, only 10.4 percent of the male population was 65 years of age or older, compared to 14.7 percent of the female population. By 2050, 19.2 percent of the male and 22 percent of the female population (under the middle scenario) would be 65 years of age or older (see Reference Table 3.1).

Although the number of females would continue to exceed the number of males in the future (as at the present time), there would be a substantial narrowing of the differences between the number by sex because the trends in mortality of the 1980s that are assumed to continue into the future decrease male mortality more than female mortality. As a result, the sex ratio for the total population decreases from 105 in 1990 to 104 in 2050, and the number of males 65 years of age and older would increase from 67 percent of the number of females in 1990 to nearly 84 percent of the number of females in 2050 (under the middle scenario). There would be a total of 187 million males and 195 million females by 2050 (under the middle scenario). At 65 years of age and older there would be 36 million males and 43 million females (see Reference Tables 3.1 and 3.2).

Increasing Ethnic Diversity

The increasing ethnic diversity of the population is evident from examining the data by race/ethnicity in Tables 3.2 through 3.5. These tables point to much more rapid growth among minority populations than among the Anglo population. Thus, if the percentage change in population in Table 3.3 is examined, it is evident that, under all of the projected scenarios, minority populations would grow more rapidly than the Anglo population. Under the middle-growth scenario, for example, the Anglo population would increase 7.3 percent from 1990 through 2050 while the Black population would increase 96.2 percent, the Hispanic population 260.9 percent, and the Other population 375.4 percent compared to an increase in total population of 53.9 percent. In the low and zero immigration scenarios, the Anglo population would decline from 1990 to 2050, with declines beginning in the 2000-to-2010 period under the low-growth scenario.

The reason for the rapid growth in minority populations lies in three factors: the younger age structure of minority populations, the higher birth rates of minority populations, and the higher levels of immigration assumed for most minority populations compared to Anglo populations. The younger age structure of minority populations has been examined above, yet is consequential for population growth because it foretells relatively large numbers of persons in the young adult and reproductive ages. The higher birth rates of minority populations can be seen by examining the birth rate assumptions underlying the middle scenario. In 1992, the Census Bureau estimated the total fertility rate (the average number of children per woman) of Anglos to be 1.85, that of Blacks to be 2.45, that of Hispanics to be 2.65, that of Asians to be 2.30, and that of Native Americans to be 2.90. The Census Bureau's projections assume that the rates for all groups except Hispanics and Asians will remain at their 1992 levels through 2050 and that Hispanic fertility will decline to 2.36 and Asian fertility to 2.06 by then. Such differentials lead to differences in rates of future growth among ethnic groups.

Differentials in immigration are as important as differences in fertility in explaining the differentials in rates of growth among racial/ethnic groups. For example, of the 880,000 immigrants projected to enter the United States during each year under the Census Bureau's middle scenario, about 174,000 are assumed to be Anglo (19.8 percent), 60,000 (6.8 percent) to be Black, 324,000 (36.8 percent) Hispanic, and about 323,000 (36.6 percent) are projected to be members of Asian or Other racial/ethnic groups (Day 1992).

In addition, by comparing the projected values under the middle scenario to those in the zero immigration scenario in Table 3.2, one can obtain some indication of how important immigration is to the net growth in each racial/ethnic population and how much migrants and their descendants would contribute to the overall impact of each racial/ethnic group on the total population of the United States. Under the middle scenario, the Anglo population would increase by 13,712,237 from 1990 to 2050, but immigrants and their descendants would account for 14,934,334 persons, meaning that without immigration the Anglo population would decline. Under this same scenario, the total increase in the Black population would be 28,099,295 persons with immigration accounting for 5,954,691 or 21.2 percent of the total increase. For Hispanics, the projected increase is 58,320,953 with immigration accounting for 33,030,726 or 56.6 percent of the net increase. For the Other racial/ethnic group, the total projected growth is 33,831,722 with 27,744,473 or 82.0 percent due to immigration. Examined in terms of the total proportion of the population of each group in 2050 that would result from 1990-to-2050 net immigration, the values suggest that only 7.4 percent of the Anglo population in 2050 would result from 1990-to-2050 net immigration, as opposed to 10.4 percent of the Black population, 40.9 percent of the Hispanic population, and 64.8 percent of the Other population.

Finally, it is evident that growth in minority populations is essential to the total net growth of the population from 1990 to 2050. Under each of the scenarios, the Hispanic population contributes more to the net growth than any other population group and overall minority population growth dominates. For example, under the middle scenario, of the net growth from 1990 through 2050, 10.2 percent would be due to growth in the Anglo population, 21.0 percent to growth in the Black population, 43.5 percent to growth in the Hispanic population, and 25.3 percent to growth in the Other population (see Figure 3.3). In total, nearly 9 of every 10 persons added to the population of the United States between 1990 and

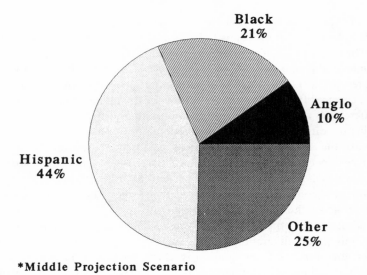

**Black
21%**

**Anglo
10%**

**Hispanic
44%**

**Other
25%**

***Middle Projection Scenario**

FIGURE 3.3   Percent of net U.S. population change by each ethnic group, 1990–2050 (middle projection scenario).

2050 would be members of minority (that is, non-Anglo) groups. This pattern is maintained in the low and high projections as well (see Reference Table 3.3). In the zero immigration scenario, because of the large impact of immigration on the Other population and lower impact on the Black population, the Black population plays a much larger role in the zero immigration scenario than in the other scenarios (see Reference Table 3.3). However examined, it is apparent that population growth in America in the coming decades will largely occur as a result of minority population growth.

These patterns demonstrate that the minority populations of the United States will come to form increasingly larger proportions of the total population. As shown in Table 3.5, the percentage of the total population that is Anglo would decrease under each scenario and the percentage of the population that would be in each minority group increases. For example, under the middle scenario the Anglo population would decrease from 75.7 percent in 1990 to 52.7 percent by 2050. At the same time, the Black population would increase from 11.7 to 15.0 percent, the Hispanic population from 9.0 to 21.1 percent, and the Other population from 3.6 to 11.2 percent (see Figure 3.4). By 2050, the American population is projected to be nearing the point where no single racial/ethnic group will form a majority of the population.

Overall, these data point to an increasingly diverse population in which minority groups, under the middle scenario, will form more than 47 percent of the total population by 2050 and account for nearly 9 of every 10 net additions to the pop-

Table 3.5: U.S. Bureau of the Census' Projections of the Percent of the Population in the United States by Race/Ethnicity from 1990-2050 Under Alternative Scenarios

Year	Anglo	Black	Hispanic	Other
Low Scenario				
1990	75.7	11.7	9.0	3.6
2000	72.4	12.3	10.7	4.6
2010	69.4	12.8	12.2	5.6
2020	66.6	13.2	13.6	6.6
2030	63.6	13.5	15.2	7.7
2040	60.6	13.8	16.8	8.8
2050	57.5	14.1	18.4	10.0
Middle Scenario				
1990	75.7	11.7	9.0	3.6
2000	71.6	12.3	11.1	5.0
2010	67.7	12.8	13.2	6.3
2020	63.9	13.3	15.2	7.6
2030	60.1	13.8	17.2	8.9
2040	56.3	14.4	19.2	10.1
2050	52.7	15.0	21.1	11.2
High Scenario				
1990	75.7	11.7	9.0	3.6
2000	70.9	12.3	11.5	5.3
2010	66.5	12.7	13.9	6.9
2020	62.3	13.1	16.2	8.4
2030	58.5	13.5	18.4	9.6
2040	54.7	13.9	20.6	10.8
2050	51.2	14.3	22.7	11.8
Zero Immigration Scenario				
1990	75.7	11.7	9.0	3.6
2000	73.3	12.5	10.3	3.9
2010	71.1	13.3	11.4	4.2
2020	69.1	14.0	12.5	4.4
2030	66.9	14.9	13.6	4.6
2040	64.6	15.9	14.7	4.8
2050	62.1	17.1	15.8	5.0

Source: See Table 3.2

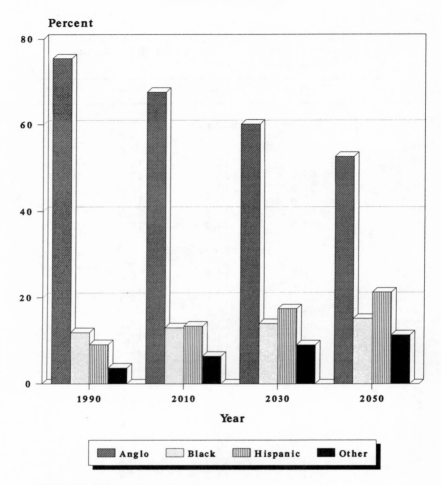

Percent

Year

Anglo   Black   Hispanic   Other

*Middle Projection Scenario

FIGURE 3.4   Percent of the U.S. population by race/ethnicity, 1990–2050 (middle projection scenario).

ulation from 1990 to 2050. America's future will involve an increasingly diverse population.

ALTERNATIVE PROJECTIONS OF THE U.S. POPULATION

How certain can we be that the range of U.S. Bureau of the Census projections will bracket the growth in the future population of the United States? Recently, Ahlburg (1993) reviewed the Census Bureau's projections relative to those from other sources; a table from his work is shown as Table 3.6. This table shows the high and low projections for each of a series of projections from the Census Bureau (both the 1992 projections shown in Tables 3.1–3.5 and those published in 1989) and several other sources. These comparisons show that the low Census Bureau projections from the 1992 set of projections and those by Ahlburg and Vaupel (1990) and Pflaumer (1992) are quite similar. For the high projections, it is evident that the Census Bureau's highest projections are lower than those by either Ahlburg and Vaupel (1990) or Pflaumer (1992), which are higher because they assume lower levels of mortality and higher levels of immigration. Ahlburg points out that the alternative assumptions underlying mortality may be particularly important because they so markedly impact the elderly population. For example, the Census Bureau's middle projection suggests there will be 79 million persons 65 years of age or older in 2050; 18 million of these would be 85 years of age or older. In Ahlburg and Vaupel (1990), however, the number projected to be 65 years of age or older is 110 million, with 37 million of these being 85 years of age or older. Manton et al. (1992) suggest that if there are dramatic decreases in behaviors related to increased health risks, the population over 65 years of age in 2050 could be 140 million, with 60 million being 85 years of age or older. Overall, then, it must be recognized that the projections emphasized in this chapter, and used throughout the analysis in this book, are but one set of projections that must, like all sets of projections, be considered as subject to error.

SUMMARY AND IMPLICATIONS OF FUTURE POPULATION CHANGE IN THE UNITED STATES

The discussion presented in this chapter provides insight into the potential course of demographic change in the United States during the next 60 years. As noted above:

1. Population forecasts are subject to uncertainty and error; they are best used to evaluate the likely direction of future change and to examine what will occur if certain trends continue and not as point estimates of future populations.

2. Because most projections are made using cohort-component projection methods (which project future populations on the basis of assumptions about the demographic processes of fertility, mortality, and migration), the assumptions related to these processes are the key to understanding projections of future populations.

3. Among such cohort-component projections are ones made by the U.S. Bureau of the Census for 1992 through 2050. They report nine separate sets of projections, which combine different high, middle, and low assumptions for each of the processes of fertility, mortality, and migration, and a tenth set that assumes middle levels of fertility and mortality and no immigration so that population change is a result of only natural increase (the excess of births relative to deaths). The scenario producing the highest, lowest, middle, and the zero immigration

Table 3.6: Recent Low and High Projections of the U.S. Population from 2000-2050 (total population in millions)

Year	Low				High			
	Census Bureau 1989	Census Bureau 1992	Ahlburg and Vaupel 1990	Pflaumer 1992	Census Bureau 1989	Census Bureau 1992	Ahlburg and Vaupel 1990	Pflaumer 1992
2000	260	269	---	262	278	282	---	285
2010	264	279	---	270	306	318	---	325
2020	265	286	286	275	335	361	385	370
2030	258	387	---	278	362	406	---	418
2040	246	283	---	277	388	454	---	527
2050	230	276	280	265	414	507	553	713

Source: "The Census Bureau's New Projections of the U.S. Population" by Dennis A. Ahlburg, *Population and Development Review* 19:159-174, 1993.

scenarios are used in this analysis. Under the middle projections, fertility is expected to continue at 1992 levels for all groups except Hispanics and Asians, whose fertility is expected to decline modestly; mortality is projected to decrease at the rate experienced from 1980 to 1990; and immigration is projected to be 880,000 per year for each year during the projection period. This rate of immigration is greater than the 734,000 average number of immigrants per year during the 1980s but less than the 974,000 immigrants recorded for 1992.

4. The Census Bureau's projections show a wide range of projected populations, from a low projection of 276 million in 2050 (only 27 million more than in 1990) to a high projection of 507 million (259 million more than in 1990) by 2050. The middle (termed the most likely) projection scenario projects a population of 383 million by 2050, a 53.9 percent increase from 249 million in 1990.

5. The growth in the U.S. population will be due in large part to immigrants and their descendants. For example, of the 134 million persons who would be added to the population between 1990 and 2050 under the middle projection scenario, nearly 82 million (61 percent) would be due to immigrants and their descendants. The effects of immigration will be as substantial as at any time in the history of the United States.

6. The alternative projection series generally show lower rates of population growth than in the past, with only the highest showing levels of population growth that equal or exceed those of the 1980s. At the same time, the absolute numerical increase is projected to be substantial, with the number of persons added to the population over the 60-year period from 1990 through 2050 under the middle scenario exceeding that from 1930 through 1992. The number added to the population under the high-growth scenario would exceed total population growth since the beginning of the nation. The nation's rate of growth will be reduced from historic levels but numerical growth will nevertheless be extensive.

7. Under every scenario the population will age. Although this aging will be into middle-aged groups from now until 2011 (when the first of the baby-boomers become 65 years of age), by 2030 (when all of the baby-boomers are 65 years of age or older), more than one in five Americans will be at least 65 years old.

8. Women have lower rates of mortality, particularly at older ages, are more numerous than males in the population today, and are projected to remain so in the future. Nonetheless, more rapid decreases in mortality rates are projected for males than for females, so that by 2050 the number of males relative to females will increase from 1990 levels. Whereas there were only 2 males for every 3 females age 65 years and older in 1990, by 2050 there would be 8 males for every 10 females at age 65 years and older.

9. Ethnic diversity will increase substantially. Due to higher rates and levels of immigration, roughly 9 of every 10 net additions to the U.S. population from 1990 through 2050 will be members of minority groups (under the middle scenario). Under the middle scenario, by 2050 the total population is projected to increase by 53.9 percent, but the Anglo population by only 7.3 percent; the Black popula-

tion would increase by 96.2 percent, the Hispanic population by 260.9 percent, and the population in Other racial/ethnic groups by 375.4 percent. From 1990 to 2050, the proportion of the population that is Anglo could decline from 76 percent to 53 percent, while the Black proportion increases from 12 to 15 percent, the Hispanic proportion from 9 to more than 21 percent, and the Other racial/ethnic groups proportion from less than 4 to more than 11 percent.

10. The key to minority population growth, particularly among persons in the Other and Hispanic categories and to a lesser extent among the Black population, lies in extensive immigration. Of the total population projected to be in each racial/ethnic group in the United States in 2050 (under the middle scenario), only 7.4 percent of the Anglo population would be due to immigrants and their descendants; 10.4 percent of the Black population, 40.9 percent of the Hispanic population, and 64.8 percent of the Other population would be due to immigration.

11. Although the Census Bureau's projections are likely to be the most widely used, they are not the only projections of the future population of the United States. Among the most widely used alternatives, there is substantial similarity between the Census Bureau's projections and those from other sources relative to the lowest projected scenario, less so for the highest scenario. Several alternative projections exist that project higher populations than those by the Bureau due to assumptions of higher immigration and lower mortality, particularly lower mortality at older ages. This again suggests that caution should be exercised in using projections, even ones with the wide array of values provided by the Census Bureau's projections.

What does the above suggest about the future population of the United States? Although all projections must be seen as potentially subject to substantial error, it is likely that the population of the United States will increase, that the rate of increase will be slower than in the past, and that the population will age and show increasing ethnic diversity. Of these trends, the greatest certainty is the aging of the population. All of the Census Bureau's projections and those from other sources project the population to age in the coming years. Of somewhat less certainty, due to differentials in both fertility and immigration, is the pattern of increasing ethnic diversity. Increasing diversity is likely under virtually all scenarios, although its extent is highly dependent on rates of immigration and fertility. It is also likely that the rate of population growth will be slower than in the past, not only because larger numerical increases are required to produce the same rate of growth with a larger population base, but also because the aging of the population will result in a reduction in the proportion of persons in childbearing ages.

The most uncertain trends relate to the total numerical increase in the population. Will fertility levels remain at the relatively high levels of the late 1980s and early 1990s? Will immigration continue at levels of nearly 900,000 immigrants per year? How much will longevity increase in the coming years? Numerous factors will impact future fertility, immigration, and mortality levels and are difficult to predict. In sum, the characteristics of the growth that will occur is more easily predicted than the extent of that growth.

Whatever the extent of numerical growth in the future population of the United States, its reduced rate of growth, its aging, and its increasing ethnic diversity will have impacts on America's social and economic structure. In the remainder of this work, these implications are traced for the workforce, for income and wealth, for businesses, and for the goods and services likely to be desired by Americans in the coming century.

PART TWO

The Implications of Population: Change for America's Future

CHAPTER FOUR

The Labor Force: Implications for America's Competitiveness

Perhaps nothing is more important to the long-term economic development of the United States than its labor force. Information about who will be producing America's goods and services in the coming years and how changes in the characteristics of the labor force may impact the economy is critical for examining the future of the country. Examining such patterns has become a major arena for policy analysts (Johnston and Packer 1987; Fullerton 1989, 1991; Mitchell 1993) and is an important consideration in this work. In this chapter, we examine the likely size, gender, age, and race/ethnicity characteristics of the labor force of the United States and suggest some of the implications of such changes for the nation.

The projections of the labor-force presented here were obtained by multiplying labor-force participation rates for persons of different ages, genders, and race/ethnicity by the projected populations in the corresponding age, gender, and race/ethnicity groups shown in Chapter 3. Labor-force participation rates are the proportion of the persons in a given group who are in the labor force and were obtained from projections by the U.S. Bureau of Labor Statistics (1991).[6]

In examining these projections, it is important to note that they are projections of the civilian labor force, not of the total labor force, which includes those in the military. I project the civilian rather than the total labor force because it is nearly impossible to anticipate the size of the military 60 years into the future. The projections are also projections of the entire civilian labor force, not just the number of persons who will be employed. The labor force, as used in this and other analyses, includes both those who are employed and those who are unemployed. I do not attempt to separately project the unemployed and the employed components of the labor force, because unemployment is subject to substantial fluctuation over time due to economic conditions. (I do, however, examine some implications for levels of unemployment in the latter part of the chapter.) Although the

Table 4.1: The Civilian Labor Force of the United States, 1900-1990 (annual averages in thousands)[a]

Year	Labor Force	Change from Preceding Period	Percent Change From Preceding Period
1900	28,376	---	---
1910	36,709	8,333	29.4
1920	41,340	4,631	12.6
1930	48,528	7,188	17.4
1940	55,640	7,112	14.7
1950	62,208	6,568	11.8
1960	69,628	7,420	11.9
1970	82,715	13,087	18.8
1980	106,940	24,225	29.3
1990	124,787	17,847	16.7

[a]Values are annual averages based on Bureau of Labor Statistics Data.

Source: Data for 1900-1970 from *Historical Statistics of the United States: Colonial Times to 1970*, Washington DC: U.S. Bureau of the Census, 1975. Data for 1980 and 1990 from annual averages from *Monthly Labor Review*, November 1991, Washington, DC: U.S. Department of Labor, Bureau of Labor Statistics.

information provided here does not cover all labor-force dimensions, the results suggest much about America's future workforce.

HISTORICAL TRENDS IN THE LABOR FORCE

To understand the future labor force of the United States, it is essential to put it in the context of the past. Therefore, before discussing the characteristics of the future labor force, its history in the United States is examined.

Whether examined in terms of average annual employment, as used by the U.S. Bureau of Labor Statistics (see Table 4.1), or in terms of the labor force as counted by the U.S. Bureau of the Census in the decennial census (see Table 4.2), it is evi-

Table 4.2: Characteristics of the Civilian Labor Force of the United States
from 1970-1990 (decennial census values in thousands)

Characteristic	1970	1980	1990	Percent Change 1970-1980	Percent Change 1980-1990
Total Civilian					
Labor Force	80,051	104,450	123,473	30.5	18.2
Male Labor Force	49,549	59,927	66,986	20.9	11.8
Female Labor Force	30,502	44,523	56,487	46.0	26.9
Percent of					
Population	57.6	61.5	64.9	---	—
Percent of Male					
Population	75.9	74.7	74.0	---	—
Percent of Female					
Population	41.3	49.8	56.7	---	—
White Labor Force	71,177	89,192	101,526	25.3	13.8
Black Labor Force	7,912	10,582	13,095	33.7	23.7
Other Races Labor					
Force	962[a]	4,676	8,853	---[a]	89.3
Hispanic Labor Force	---[b]	5,993	10,022	---[b]	67.2
Percent of White					
Population	57.6	61.9	66.8	---	—
Percent of Black					
Population	57.2	58.8	63.3	---	---
Percent of Other Races					
Population	57.8	63.3	64.9	---	---
Percent of Hispanic					
Population	---[b]	63.0	67.0	---	---

[a]Data for Other Races for 1970 are not comparable to succeeding censuses due to a tendency for Hispanics to report their race as Other in 1980 and 1990.

[b]Data for Hispanics for 1970 are not comparable to those for 1980 and 1990.

Source: Data derived from censuses of Population and Housing for 1970, 1980 and 1990.

dent that the historical growth of the civilian labor force in the United States has been extensive. In 1900, the U.S. labor force was only 28.4 million; by 1990 it was 124.8 million (see Table 4.1). During this same period, the U.S. population increased from 75.9 to 248.7 million. So while the population increased by 227 percent, the labor force increased by nearly 340 percent. This rapid growth rate was primarily caused by the increased participation of women.

In 1900, only 18.8 percent of women 16 years of age or older were in the labor force, but in 1990 56.7 percent of women were. Had the same percentage of women participated in the labor force in 1990 as in 1900, the size of the labor force in 1990 would have been about 85.7 million rather than 124.8 million. Thirty-nine million more women were employed in 1990 than would have been at the rates of labor-force participation of 1900, a number roughly equal to the combined labor forces of California, New York, Texas, and Florida (the four largest states in the nation) in 1990.

When more recent patterns are examined, the importance of increased participation by women is especially apparent (see Table 4.2). Of the roughly 24 million-person net increase in the labor force from 1970 to 1980, 14 million, or more than 57 percent, was due to the increased number of women. Of the more than 19 million net increase from 1980 to 1990, nearly 63 percent was due to the increased number of women.

Analyses of recent trends also suggest that minority labor-force involvement has become increasingly important to the growth of the labor force. Table 4.2, for example, shows from 1970 to 1990 the number of Whites in the civilian labor force increased by more than 30.3 million, which means that, of the 43.4 million persons added to the U.S. labor force, nearly 70 percent were White. However, since nearly 89 percent of the total labor force in 1970 was White, this means that non-White labor-force growth was proportionately greater than that for Whites. This was especially evident in the 1980s, when the White labor force increased by less than 14 percent as the Black labor force increased by nearly 24 percent, the Other racial/ethnic groups' labor force by more than 89 percent, and the Hispanic labor force by more than 67 percent (see Table 4.2).

Increases in female participation in the labor force, the aging of the labor force, and the increasing ethnic diversity of the labor force have impacted the labor force in the past and are projected to continue to do so in the future. Table 4.3 shows Bureau of Labor Statistics (1991) labor-force participation rates for 1975 and 1990 and projections of labor-force participation in the year 2005 for persons with different characteristics. The age, sex, and race/ethnicity-specific versions of these participation rates for 1990 to 2005 are the basis for projections presented later in this chapter.

Table 4.3 shows that the rate of labor-force participation has increased over time for the total population and is expected to continue to increase in the future. However, substantially different patterns exist among groups. One of these is the decreased rate of participation among men. From 1975 to 1990, the proportion of

Table 4.3: Civilian Labor Force Participation Rates by Sex, Age, Race, and Hispanic Origin, 1975 and 1990, and Moderate Growth Projection to 2005, the Civilian Labor Force 1975 and 1990 (in thousands), and Percent Change in the Labor Force, 1975-1990

Group	Participation Rate (Percent)			Civilian Labor Force		% Change in Labor Force
	1975	1990	2005	1975	1990	1975-1990
Total, 16+ Years	61.2	66.4	69.0	93,775	124,787	33.1
Men, 16+	77.9	76.1	75.4	56,299	68,234	21.2
16-19	59.1	55.6	57.7	4,805	3,866	-19.5
20-24	84.5	84.3	86.1	7,565	7,291	-3.6
25-34	95.3	94.2	93.6	14,192	19,813	39.6
35-44	95.6	94.4	93.4	10,398	17,268	66.1
45-54	92.1	90.7	90.3	10,401	11,177	7.5
55-64	75.6	67.7	67.9	7,023	6,785	-3.4
65 +	21.6	16.4	16.0	1,914	2,033	6.2
Women, 16+	46.3	57.5	63.0	37,475	56,554	50.9
16-19	49.1	51.8	54.3	4,065	3,544	-12.8
20-24	64.1	71.6	75.3	6,185	6,552	5.9
25-34	54.9	73.6	79.7	8,673	15,990	84.4
35-44	55.8	76.5	85.3	6,505	14,576	124.1
45-54	54.6	71.2	81.5	6,683	9,316	39.4
55-64	40.9	45.3	54.3	4,323	5,075	17.4
65 +	8.2	8.7	8.8	1,042	1,502	44.4
White, 16+	61.5	66.8	69.7	82,831	107,177	29.4
Men	78.7	76.9	76.2	50,324	59,298	17.8
Women	45.9	57.5	63.5	32,508	47,879	47.3
Black, 16+	58.8	63.3	65.6	9,263	13,493	45.7
Men	71.0	70.1	70.2	5,016	6,708	33.7
Women	48.9	57.8	61.7	4,247	6,785	59.8
Asian and Other, 16+[a]	62.4	64.9	66.4	1,643	4,116	150.5
Men	74.8	74.2	75.0	931	2,226	139.1
Women	51.3	56.7	58.9	712	1,890	165.4
Hispanic, 16+[b]	---[c]	67.0	69.9	---[c]	9,576	---[c]
Men	---[c]	81.2	81.6	---[c]	5,755	---[c]
Women	---[c]	53.0	58.0	---[c]	3,821	---[c]

[a]The "Asian and Other" group includes (1) Asians and Pacific Islanders and (2) American Indians and Alaskan natives.

[b]Persons of Hispanic origin may be of any race.

[c]Data on Hispanics were not available before 1980.

Source: Derived from Table 3 from "Labor Force Projections: The Baby Boom Moves On," by Howard N. Fullerton, Jr., Monthly Labor Review 114(11):31-44, 1991.

men in the labor force decreased and, for all age groups except those 20 to 24 and 55 to 64 years of age, the proportions are projected to continue to decrease from 1990 to 2005. By contrast, female labor-force participation rates increased from 1975 to 1990 and are projected to continue to increase for all age groups from 1990 to 2005. Rates for all racial/ethnic groups are also projected to increase; these increases are projected to disproportionally result from increased participation among women in every racial/ethnic group.

Table 4.3 also suggests that the labor force has become older and is projected to increase most in the older age groups in the future. For example, for men, the fastest percentage increases in the labor force from 1975 to 1990 were for those 25 to 44 years of age. This reflects the aging of the baby-boom generation into these ages. The age data for women show a similar pattern—but also a very noticeable difference. These data show increases for the same ages as shown for men, but the increases are substantially larger for women in all age groups. Noticeable as well is the fact that participation rates are projected to increase substantially for middle-aged women from 1990 to 2005. This reflects the fact that younger women are expected to take their substantially higher rates of participation with them as they age into middle and older age groups.

Finally, Tables 4.2 and 4.3 point to another very important fact about the U.S. labor force. Despite increased participation among women and minority-group members, the labor force has grown more slowly in the most recent decade. Thus, whereas the total labor force increased by 30.5 percent from 1970 to 1980, it increased by only 18.2 percent from 1980 to 1990 (see Table 4.2).

Overall, historical trends suggest that the labor force has begun to grow more slowly and that its growth has increasingly resulted from the higher rates of involvement of women and minorities. In addition, it appears that such patterns may dominate at least the immediate future. The long-term trends are discussed below.

THE FUTURE SIZE AND CHARACTERISTICS
OF THE LABOR FORCE OF THE UNITED STATES

Tables 4.4 and 4.5 and Figure 4.1 show projections of the labor force and of the percentage change in the labor force for selected periods. Several patterns are clear from these data. When Tables 4.4 and 4.5 are compared to Tables 3.2 and 3.3 for the population, it is evident that for every scenario the projected increase in the labor force is less than that for the population. For the low-growth scenario, the total increase in the population from 1990 to 2050 was 10.8 percent (see Table 3.3) but only 8.9 percent for the labor force during the same period. For the middle scenario, the comparable values are 53.9 and 44.3 percent; for the high scenario, 103.7 and 84.9 percent; and for the zero immigration scenario, 21.0 and 12.3 percent. This marked reversal of the historical pattern—in which the labor force increased more rapidly than the population—reflects the fact that the segments of

Table 4.4: Projections of the Labor Force in the United States by Race/Ethnicity from 1990-2050 Under Alternative Scenarios

Year	Labor Force by Race/Ethnicity				Total Labor Force
	Anglo	Black	Hispanic	Other	
Low Scenario					
1990	97,014,837	12,593,868	10,063,810	4,232,330	123,904,845
2000	104,511,572	14,986,523	13,526,500	6,109,364	139,133,959
2010	106,588,918	16,618,995	16,646,635	7,850,316	147,704,864
2020	100,024,053	17,193,571	18,841,121	9,382,053	145,440,798
2030	92,376,836	17,391,771	20,296,787	10,741,278	140,806,672
2040	87,488,673	17,656,898	21,954,460	12,106,770	139,206,801
2050	80,766,587	17,481,666	23,385,813	13,329,660	134,963,726
Middle Scenario					
1990	97,014,837	12,593,868	10,063,810	4,232,330	123,904,845
2000	105,585,064	15,173,000	14,340,132	6,690,729	141,788,925
2010	109,544,881	17,179,335	18,779,673	9,271,667	154,775,556
2020	105,748,790	18,490,335	22,910,004	11,837,590	158,986,719
2030	101,634,932	19,921,729	26,986,752	14,496,123	163,039,536
2040	100,766,494	21,868,892	31,644,514	17,311,243	171,591,143
2050	98,307,000	23,814,749	36,532,465	20,176,728	178,830,942
High Scenario					
1990	97,014,837	12,593,868	10,063,810	4,232,330	123,904,845
2000	106,559,772	15,450,534	15,158,133	7,259,143	144,427,582
2010	112,126,463	17,996,835	20,901,483	10,667,120	161,691,901
2020	111,297,714	20,060,913	26,742,091	14,209,436	172,310,154
2030	112,009,102	22,586,969	33,204,775	18,109,286	185,910,132
2040	117,267,379	25,985,431	40,886,992	22,413,865	206,553,667
2050	122,360,598	29,787,578	49,847,319	27,153,961	229,149,456
Zero Immigration Scenario					
1990	97,014,837	12,593,868	10,063,810	4,232,330	123,904,845
2000	104,556,022	14,884,511	12,716,876	5,061,512	137,218,921
2010	107,141,460	16,493,397	14,964,663	5,586,155	144,185,675
2020	101,821,726	17,360,213	16,478,555	5,855,110	141,515,604
2030	96,213,711	18,311,562	17,624,262	6,077,699	138,227,234
2040	93,976,911	19,767,641	19,314,676	6,495,585	139,554,813
2050	90,155,387	21,190,298	20,976,563	6,845,491	139,167,739

Table 4.5: Percent Change in the Civilian Labor Force for Projections of the Civilian Labor Force in the United States by Race/Ethnicity from 1990-2050 Under Alternative Scenarios

Time Period	Anglo	Black	Hispanic	Other	Total
		Low Scenario			
1990-2000	7.7	19.0	34.4	44.3	12.3
2000-2010	2.0	10.9	23.1	28.5	6.2
2010-2020	-6.2	3.5	13.2	19.5	-1.5
2020-2030	-7.6	1.2	7.7	14.5	-3.2
2030-2040	-5.3	1.5	8.2	12.7	-1.1
2040-2050	-7.7	-1.0	6.5	10.1	-3.0
1990-2050	-16.7	38.8	132.4	214.9	8.9
		Middle Scenario			
1990-2000	8.8	20.5	42.5	58.1	14.4
2000-2010	3.8	13.2	31.0	38.6	9.2
2010-2020	-3.5	7.6	22.0	27.7	2.7
2020-2030	-3.9	7.7	17.8	22.5	2.5
2030-2040	-0.9	9.8	17.3	19.4	5.2
2040-2050	-2.4	8.9	15.4	16.6	4.2
1990-2050	1.3	89.1	263.0	376.7	44.3
		High Scenario			
1990-2000	9.8	22.7	50.6	71.5	16.6
2000-2010	5.2	16.5	37.9	46.9	12.0
2010-2020	-0.7	11.5	27.9	33.2	6.6
2020-2030	0.6	12.6	24.2	27.4	7.9
2030-2040	4.7	15.0	23.1	23.8	11.1
2040-2050	4.3	14.6	21.9	21.1	10.9
1990-2050	26.1	136.5	395.3	541.6	84.9
		Zero Immigration Scenario			
1990-2000	7.8	18.2	26.4	19.6	10.7
2000-2010	2.5	10.8	17.7	10.4	5.1
2010-2020	-5.0	5.3	10.1	4.8	-1.9
2020-2030	-5.5	5.5	7.0	3.8	-2.3
2030-2040	-2.3	8.0	9.6	6.9	1.0
2040-2050	-4.1	7.2	8.6	5.4	-0.3
1990-2050	-7.1	68.3	108.4	61.7	12.3

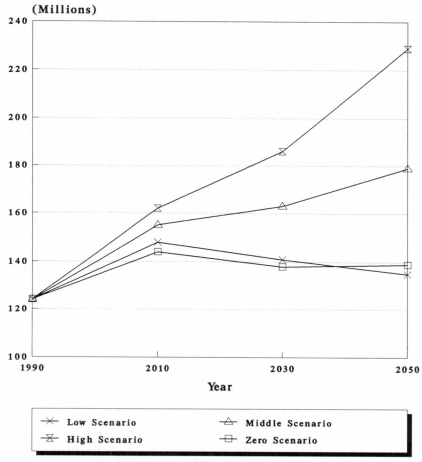

FIGURE 4.1   Projections of the U.S. labor force from 1990–2050.

the population increasing most rapidly are ones with lower rates of labor-force participation and lower proportions of persons who are in the working ages. As a result, growth in employment does not keep pace with the growth in population for the most rapidly increasing segments of the population.

Nevertheless, growth in the labor force could be extensive in numerical terms. From 1990 to 2050, the labor force is projected to increase by 54.9 million under the middle scenario and under the high-growth scenario it would increase by more than 105.2 million (see Table 4.4). The growth in the middle scenario is only slightly larger than the growth in the U.S. labor force for the 30-year period from 1960 to 1990 but is equivalent to the combined labor force of the eight largest states in the nation in 1990. Under the high-growth scenario, the total growth in the labor force would be equal to that experienced by the nation for the entire period from 1880 to 1990.

The projected rate of growth in the labor force is, however, substantially less than that of the past. Even under the high-growth scenario, there is no decade from 1990 to 2050 for which growth in the labor force would be as large as the 18.2-percent rate of growth during the 1980s. In addition, whereas the total labor force of the United States increased by 153.9 percent, from 48.8 million in 1930 to 123.9 million in 1990, the projected rate of growth from 1990 to 2050 is only 84.9 percent for even the high-growth scenario. Slower growth in the labor force is a pervasive pattern in these projections and is brought about by patterns of growth in particular population segments and by the fact that labor-force involvement among women has reached a point of sufficiently high participation so that increases cannot be expected to be as rapid in the future as in the past.

It is also important to note that the labor force is projected to increase at very different rates during different periods in the future. Under all scenarios, the labor force is projected to continue to show strong growth from 1990 to 2000. After that, the rates of growth, except under the high-growth scenario, begin to decline, reaching their lowest levels during the decade 2020 to 2030. The latter is a result of the expected retirement of a large proportion of the baby-boom generation. In fact, under both the low-growth and the zero immigration scenarios, there would be absolute declines in the number of persons in the labor force from 2010 to 2020 and from 2020 to 2030.

Growth in the labor force will be substantially dependent on immigration. A comparison of the middle and zero immigration scenarios, for example, reveals that, of the projected 54.9 million net increase in the labor force in the middle scenario from 1990 to 2050, 39.6 million or 72.1 percent would be due to immigrants and their descendants. An examination of the data for the zero immigration scenario suggests that, without immigration, the number of Anglos in the labor force would decline by nearly 7.0 million; the number of Blacks would increase by nearly 8.6 million, the number of Hispanics by 10.9 million, and the number of workers from Other racial/ethnic groups by 2.6 million. Under the middle scenario, however, the Anglo labor force would *increase* by nearly 1.3 million, the Black labor force by nearly 11.3 million, the Hispanic labor force by 26.5 million, and the Other labor force by nearly 16.0 million. To a large extent, then, the impetus for future growth in the U.S. labor force will be immigrants and their descendants.

Tables 4.4 and 4.5 show especially prominent patterns relative to the impacts of racial and ethnic minorities. Under all but the high-growth scenario, the number of Anglos in the labor force peaks in 2010 and declines thereafter (see Table 4.4). Even in the high-growth scenario, the number of Anglos plateaus by 2010, increasing little until after 2030. For the middle scenario, the number of Anglos in 2050 would be only 1.3 percent higher than in 1990 and, after peaking in 2010, would decline in each of the next four decades.

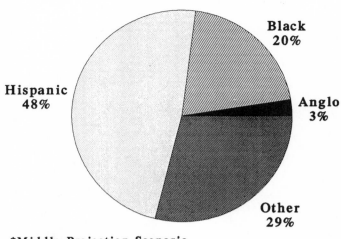

Black 20%

Hispanic 48%

Anglo 3%

Other 29%

*Middle Projection Scenario

FIGURE 4.2   Percent of net U.S. labor force change by each ethnic group, 1990–2050.

The patterns for minority groups show rapid growth. Under the middle scenario, the number of Blacks in the labor force would increase by 89.1 percent from 1990 to 2050, the number of Hispanics by 263.0 percent, and the number of Others by 376.7 percent (see Table 4.5). Of the total net increase of 54.9 million workers between 1990 and 2050 under the middle scenario, only 2.4 percent would be Anglo; 20.4 percent would be Black, 48.2 percent Hispanic, and 29.0 percent would be members of Other racial/ethnic groups (see Figure 4.2). As a result of such changes, under the middle scenario the Anglo proportion of the labor force would decrease from 78.3 percent to 55.0 percent, the Black proportion would increase from 10.2 to 13.3 percent, the Hispanic from 8.1 to 20.4 percent, and the Other race/ethnic groups from 3.4 to 11.3 percent (see Figure 4.3). The rapidly increasing diversity of the population noted in Chapter 3 will also be evident in the labor force.

The general aging of the population is also evident in the labor-force projections. Table 4.6 provides data on the projected age structure of the labor force for various periods under the middle scenario. This table shows the labor force in 1990 was concentrated in the young-adult and early-middle ages but also shows that it will become increasingly older in the coming decades. Thus, in 1990, 53.8 percent of the labor force was 25 to 44 years of age, with only 28.6 percent of the labor force being 45 years of age or older. By 2050, under the middle scenario, 44.8 percent of the labor force would be 25 to 44 years of age and 39.0 percent of the labor force would be 45 years of age or older.

The age structure of the labor force also reflects the differences by ethnicity already noted. The data for the middle scenario (see Table 4.6) show that, although 39 percent of the total labor force would be 45 years old or older in 2050, the pro-

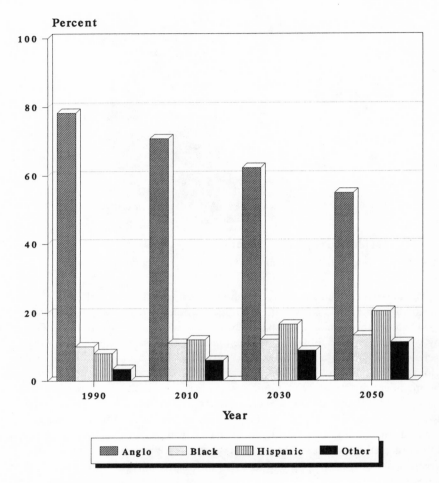

Percent

Year

Legend: Anglo | Black | Hispanic | Other

*Middle Projection Scenario
FIGURE 4.3   Percent of the U.S. labor force by race/ethnicity, 1990–2050.

portion of the Anglo labor force 45 years old or older would be 42.9 percent. However, the proportion of the Hispanic labor force 45 years old or older would be 33.1 percent, the proportion of the Black labor force 45 years old or older would be 34.2 percent, and the proportion of the labor force from Other racial/ethnic groups 45 years old or older would be 36.6 percent. The labor force of the future will not only have a higher proportion of minority workers but will also have a heavier concentration of minority workers at younger ages.

A final and critically important dimension of the future labor force of the United States is the continuing increase in the role played by women. Data related

Table 4.6: Percent of the Civilian Labor Force in the United States by Year, Age, and Race/Ethnicity from 1990-2050 Under the Middle Scenario

Year/ Age Group	Percent of Labor Force by Age and Race/Ethnicity				Total Population
	Anglo	Black	Hispanic	Other	
1990					
16-19	6.0	6.2	7.7	5.4	6.1
20-24	10.8	12.5	16.8	11.9	11.5
25-34	27.4	30.8	33.3	30.3	28.3
35-44	25.6	25.8	22.8	27.3	25.5
45-54	16.9	15.0	12.1	16.1	16.3
55-59	6.0	4.7	3.9	4.8	5.7
60-64	4.1	2.9	2.3	2.7	3.8
65+	3.2	2.1	1.1	1.5	2.8
2000					
16-19	6.0	6.3	7.1	5.4	6.1
20-24	9.1	11.3	13.2	10.3	9.8
25-34	20.4	24.5	28.9	26.3	22.0
35-44	27.2	28.6	27.2	27.9	27.4
45-54	23.2	20.0	15.6	20.0	21.9
55-59	7.2	4.9	4.2	5.5	6.6
60-64	3.8	2.5	2.3	2.9	3.5
65+	3.1	1.9	1.5	1.7	2.7
2030					
16-19	5.8	6.6	6.9	5.2	6.0
20-24	9.3	11.9	13.1	10.6	10.4
25-34	20.0	23.9	25.4	24.4	21.8
35-44	23.4	24.5	23.3	24.8	23.6
45-54	21.2	19.2	17.0	20.5	20.2
55-59	8.4	6.5	6.6	7.2	7.8
60-64	6.0	3.9	4.4	4.2	5.3
65+	5.9	3.5	3.3	3.1	4.9
2050					
16-19	5.6	6.5	6.7	5.0	5.9
20-24	9.2	11.8	12.7	10.3	10.3
25-34	20.5	24.0	24.8	23.8	22.3
35-44	21.8	23.5	22.7	24.3	22.5
45-54	21.0	19.6	17.8	21.0	20.1
55-59	9.6	6.9	7.0	7.5	8.5
60-64	6.2	4.1	4.3	4.4	5.3
65+	6.1	3.6	4.0	3.7	5.1

Table 4.7: Projections of the Labor Force in the United States from 1990-2050 by Sex and Race/Ethnicity Under the Middle Scenario

Year	Labor Force by Race/Ethnicity and Sex				Total Labor Force
	Anglo	Black	Hispanic	Other	
Males by Race/Ethnicity					
1990	53,141,891	6,167,004	6,110,414	2,301,240	67,720,549
2000	55,627,434	7,275,578	8,411,268	3,515,576	74,829,856
2010	57,146,983	8,180,370	10,827,447	4,857,051	81,011,851
2020	55,504,120	8,839,331	13,157,655	6,244,034	83,745,140
2030	53,446,800	9,498,651	15,420,242	7,694,381	86,060,074
2040	52,995,913	10,389,514	18,040,522	9,248,007	90,673,956
2050	51,744,022	11,273,455	20,827,223	10,841,429	94,686,129
Females by Race/Ethnicity					
1990	43,872,946	6,426,864	3,953,396	1,931,090	56,184,296
2000	49,957,630	7,897,422	5,928,864	3,175,153	66,959,069
2010	52,397,898	8,998,965	7,952,226	4,414,616	73,763,705
2020	50,244,670	9,651,004	9,752,349	5,593,556	75,241,579
2030	48,188,132	10,423,078	11,566,510	6,801,742	76,979,462
2040	47,770,581	11,479,378	13,603,992	8,063,236	80,917,187
2050	46,562,978	12,541,294	15,705,242	9,335,299	84,144,813

to this pattern are shown for the middle scenario in Table 4.7. Whereas women made up 45.3 percent of the labor force in 1990, they are projected to account for more than 50 percent of the net increase in the labor force from 1990 to 2050. Overall, the percentage of the labor force made up of women is projected to increase from 45.3 percent in 1990 to 47.1 percent by 2050. The more rapid growth of women's participation appears among every racial/ethnic group, such that the proportion of the labor force that is female would increase from 45.2 percent among Anglos in 1990 to 47.4 percent in 2050, from 51.3 percent to 52.7 percent among Blacks, from 39.3 percent to 43.0 percent among Hispanics, and from 45.6 percent to 46.3 among Other racial/ethnic groups. Thus, although women's participation is not projected to increase as rapidly as in the past, women will move toward greater parity, at least numerically, within the workforce of the United States in the coming decades.

Overall, then, the projections of the future labor force in the United States show a labor force that will grow more slowly than in the past and be increasingly composed of immigrants and their descendants. It will also be a labor force that is older, more female, and more ethnically diverse than at any time in U.S. history. Some of the implications of these patterns for American Society are traced below.

IMPLICATIONS OF FUTURE CHANGES IN THE LABOR FORCE OF THE UNITED STATES

The implications of the labor-force changes noted above are many and only a few of them can be examined here. We concentrate on the implications regarding retirement and pension funds, the likely occupational composition of the labor force, its levels of education and skills, and earnings. In projecting these implications, numerous relatively bold assumptions are made. Foremost is that current differences in occupation, education, and earnings among different age, gender, and racial/ethnic groups are assumed to continue throughout the projection period. In so doing, it is not my intent to imply that certain levels of education or income or occupational attainment are determined by these characteristics. Rather, differential access to socioeconomic opportunities, discriminatory practices, and other factors have created the relationships between certain demographic characteristics and specific labor-force characteristics. Neither is my intent to imply that such differences will never be altered, for such characteristics are likely to change over time. However, examining the implications of current patterns and projecting them into the future allows one to identify what may occur if steps are not taken to alter current differentials in response to future demographic trends.

Before presenting detailed information on the implications noted above, it is useful to note *why* the factors examined may be important and *how* we propose to examine the implications of changes in the labor force for occupational, wage, and income levels. In general, nearly all existing projections suggest that employment growth is likely to occur much more rapidly in some occupations than in others and that those occupations with the most rapid employment growth are ones that generally require more education and provide higher earnings (Silvestri and Lukasiewicz 1991).

Similarly, different age, gender, and racial/ethnic groups have different levels of involvement in different occupations and have different levels of educational attainment. As the numbers of persons in different groups in the labor force change so too will the overall occupational structure, educational level, and earnings of the total labor force—provided that the rate of involvement in different occupations and the levels of education among members of the labor force from different groups remain as they are at the present time. By comparing the current occupational structures, educational levels, and earnings of the total labor force to those of a later date, we can determine some of the implications of the changing composition of the population for these dimensions.

Table 4.8: Civilian Labor Force in the United States by Occupational Group from 1930-1990

Year	Total	Managerial and Professional	Production and Craft	Service	Farming Forestry, and Fishing
1990	115,681	67,252	30,294	15,296	2,839
		58.1	26.2	13.2	2.5
1980	97,639	51,745	30,454	12,629	2,811
		53.0	31.2	12.9	2.9
1970	79,725	37,857	29,169	10,251	2,448
		47.5	36.6	12.9	3.1
1960	64,537	27,028	25,475	7,902	4,132
		41.9	39.5	12.2	6.4
1950	58,999	21,601	24,266	6,180	6,953
		36.6	41.1	10.5	11.8
1940	51,742	16,082	20,597	6,069	8,995
		31.1	39.8	11.7	17.4
1930	48,686	14,320	19,272	4,772	10,321
		29.4	39.6	9.8	21.2

Source: Derived from data from the decennial censuses of population and housing for the years indicated.

Tables 4.8 through 4.12 suggest why some of the differentials noted above are likely to be consequential. Table 4.8 shows historical rates of growth in employment in broad occupational categories. Table 4.9 points to the existence of differentials in the levels of opportunities projected by the U.S. Bureau of Labor Statistics (1991) to occur in different occupations through 2005. Table 4.10 indicates levels of education and median weekly earnings associated with selected occupations. Table 4.11 indicates the involvement of women, Blacks, and Hispanics in these occupational groupings. Table 4.12 shows the levels of educational attainment among members of the labor force from different racial/ethnic groups. Collectively these tables suggest that past growth has been, and is likely to continue to be, most rapid in managerial and managerial-related occupations, which require higher levels of education. They further suggest that women and minorities are

Table 4.9: Projected Job Opportunities in the United States by Occupation from 1990-2005 (employment in thousands)

Occupational Title	1990 Total Employment	Projected Job Openings 1990-2005	Opportunity Ratio[a]
Total, all occupations	122,573	65,743	0.54
Executive, administrative, and managerial	12,451	6,499	0.52
Professional specialty occupations	15,800	9,388	0.59
Engineers, architects, and surveyors	1,755	1,019	0.58
Technicians and related support	4,204	2,751	0.65
Sales occupations	14,088	8,780	0.62
Administrative support, including clerical	21,195	9,722	0.44
Service occupations	19,204	13,233	0.69
Precision production, craft, and repair	14,124	6,832	0.48
Operators, fabricators, and laborers	17,245	7,183	0.42

[a]The opportunity ratio for an occupation is the number of projected job openings in the occupation divided by the total number of persons employed in the occupation.

Source: Derived from Table 9 from "Occupational Employment Projections," by George Silvestri and John Lukasiewicz, *Monthly Labor Review* 114(11):64-94, 1991.

less likely to be involved in such occupations and that minority workers tend to have lower levels of education than nonminority workers. When combined with the labor-force projections presented above these relationships suggest important patterns of potential change in the future labor force of the United States.

The implications of the population's projected slower growth and of changes in its age structure are evident by examining data presented above. The labor force is projected to grow at a slower rate than ever before and to become increasingly older. Under the middle scenario (see Table 4.5 and Table 4.6), growth would not reach the levels of the 1980s during any period in the 60-year projection cycle and the proportion of the workforce under 35 years of age would not regain its 1990 level at any point. Between 1990 and 2010, the labor force would be largely middle-aged and becomes increasingly older thereafter.

One of the implications of the aging of the workforce is that an increasing number of persons will be entering retirement ages, thereby increasing costs for social security and other pension programs. Although prevailing analyses suggest that the social security trust fund is now sufficient to meet the needs of retirees for the foreseeable future (Wilkin et al. 1984; Burtless 1993), the impacts of the ag-

Table 4.10: Selected Occupational Groups Ranked by 1990-2005 Projected Percentage Rate of Employment Growth and Levels of Educational Attainment and Median Weekly Earnings in 1990 in the United States

Occupational Title	1990-2005 Rates of Employment Change	Levels of Educational Attainment (Percent of Occupational Employment)				Median Weekly Earnings
		Less than High School	High School	1-3 Years of College	4+ Years of College	
Total, all occupations	20	15	39	22	24	$415
Executive, administrative, and managerial	27	4	27	24	45	604
Supervisors, administrative support	22	4	42	29	24	497
Transportation and material moving	21	26	54	15	4	413
Construction trades	21	25	51	18	6	479
Mechanics and repairers	16	19	54	22	6	476
Mail and message distributing	15	8	50	31	11	514
Handlers, equipment cleaners, helpers, and laborers	8	35	48	14	3	298
Farming, forestry, and fishing	5	37	41	14	8	257
Private household workers	-29	50	36	10	4	172

Source: Derived from Table 11 from "Occupational Employment Projections," by George Silvestri and John Lukasiewicz, *Monthly Labor Review* 114(11):64-94, 1991.

Table 4.11: Projected Percent Change in Employment for Selected Occupations in the
United States from 1990-2005

Occupational Title	Percent Change 1990-2005	Percent in 1990 Composed of Women	Blacks	Hispanics
Total, all occupations	20	45	10	8
Executive, administrative, and managerial	27	40	6	4
Professional specialty occupations	32	51	7	3
Engineers	26	9	3	3
Mathematical and computer scientists	73	37	7	3
Natural scientists	26	26	3	4
Health diagnosing occupations	29	18	3	4
Health assessment and treating occupations	43	86	7	3
Teachers, college and university	19	38	5	3
Teachers, except college and university	30	74	9	4
Lawyers and judges	34	21	3	3
Technicians and related support	37	49	9	4
Health technologists and technicians	42	84	14	5
Engineering and related technologists and technicians	23	20	7	5
Sales occupations	24	49	6	5
Administrative support, including clerical	13	80	11	7
Supervisors, administrative support	22	58	12	7
Computer equipment operators	13	66	13	7
Secretaries, stenographers, and typists	9	98	9	5
Financial records processing	-4	92	6	5
Mail and message distributing	15	45	25	5
Service occupations	29	60	17	11
Private household	-29	60	17	11
Protective service	32	15	17	6
Food preparation and service	30	60	12	13
Health service	44	90	26	6
Cleaning and building service	18	44	22	17
Personal service	44	82	12	7
Precision production, craft, and repair	13	9	8	9
Mechanics and repairers	16	4	8	7
Construction trades	21	2	7	9
Operators, fabricators, and laborers	4	26	15	12
Machine operators, assemblers, and inspectors	-9	40	14	14
Transportation and material moving	21	9	15	9
Handlers, equipment cleaners, helpers, and laborers	8	18	16	13
Farming, forestry, and fishing	5	16	6	14

Source: Derived from Table 13 from "Occupational Employment Projections," by George Silvestri and John Lukasiewicz, *Monthly Labor Review* 114(11):64-94, 1991.

Table 4.12: Percent of Persons 25 Years of Age or Older by Educational Level
and Race/Ethnicity, 1990 (numbers in thousands)

Education Level	White	Black	Hispanic	Other	Total
< 9 Years of School	8.9	13.8	30.7	23.9	11.7
9-11 Years of School	13.2	23.1	19.5	15.7	14.8
High School	31.0	27.9	21.5	20.5	29.5
1-3 Years of College	25.4	23.8	14.3	14.5	24.6
4 Years of College	13.9	7.5	10.7	18.2	12.5
Graduate	7.6	3.8	3.3	7.2	6.9
Total Persons	132,023	16,761	11,227	10,084	170,095

Source: Derived from the Summary Tape File 3A from the 1990 Census of
Population and Housing.

ing of the labor force are extensive. Table 4.13 illustrates this point. In this table, the number of persons 55 to 64 years of age at a preceding decade period (for example, the number 55 to 64 years of age in 1980) are assumed to retire by the beginning of the next decade (that is, by 1990). The monthly costs of these new retirees under the monthly retirees average compensation level in 1990 (Social Security Administration 1993) are assumed to be the costs for their retirement. Obviously this table presents a simplistic view because some of these persons will die before reaching 65 years of age, some will delay retirement, some will not be covered by the social security system, and the average monthly payment will change over time, among other factors. Although based on numerous assumptions, the results are nevertheless useful in exemplifying the significant effects of the aging workforce on retirement and pension funds.

Table 4.13 suggests that the increase in net monthly costs attributed to the increasing number of retirees would be extensive during the coming decades, particularly during the decade from 2020 to 2030, when a majority of the baby-boom generation reaches retirement age. Thus, total monthly social security expenditures would increase by more than 103 percent between 1990 and 2030. An older workforce will require increased retirement expenditures.

Some of the effects of the changing race/ethnicity and gender composition of the future labor force can be seen by looking at their implications for the occupational composition of the labor force. Table 4.14 shows the distribution of the labor force by occupational groups in 1990 and 2050 under the middle scenario, as-

Table 4.13: Number of Labor Force Members Reaching 65 Years of
Age During Each Decade and Approximate Monthly
Retirement Costs by Decade, 1980-2050

Decade	Number of Labor Force Members Reaching 65 During the Decade[a]	Approximate Monthly Costs for Social Security Retirement Payments[b]
1980-1990	12,091,450	$7,285,824,000
1990-2000	11,746,333	7,077,870,000
2000-2010	14,233,736	8,576,680,000
2010-2020	21,098,885	12,713,340,000
2020-2030	24,559,599	14,798,630,000
2030-2040	21,292,369	12,829,930,000
2040-2050	22,222,430	13,390,350,000

[a]Assuming no mortality between age 55 and 65.

[b]Assuming all persons retire at age 65 + and 1990 levels of benefits for
retired workers of $602.56 per month as noted in *Annual Statistical
Supplement to the Social Security Bulletin, 1992,* Washington DC: Social
Security Administration, 1993.

suming that the proportion of each racial/ethnic group and gender in each
occupational category remains constant.

Comparing data in Table 4.14 for 1990 to data for 2050 shows that, in all occupational categories, the proportion of the labor force that will be minority is projected to increase. Anglos, who formed a majority of all employed workers in
every occupational group in 1990, would constitute less than 50 percent of all service, farming, and operator and laborer jobs by 2050; the proportion of all
workers who are minority would increase in every occupational category. For example, from 1990 to 2050, the proportion of all managers and professionals of
Black heritage would increase from 6.8 to 9.5 percent; the proportion of Hispanics
would increase from 4.2 to 11.6 percent, and Other racial/ethnic groups from 3.8
percent to 13.3 percent. Similar changes are found for all other occupations.
Equally important, however, is the fact that, because of the higher rates of minority unemployment, and minority employment in lower-paying service and laborer positions, the patterns of occupational employment of 1990, if continued to

Table 4.14: Percent of Labor Force in the United States by Sex and Race/Ethnicity in Each Occupation in 1990 and Projected for 2050 Under the Middle Scenario

Occupational Title	All Persons			Anglo			Black			Other			Hispanic		
	Total	Male	Female	Total	Male	Female	Total	Male	Female	Total	Male	Female	Total	Male	Female
							Distribution in 1990								
Total	100.0	54.3	45.7	77.9	42.6	35.3	10.4	4.9	5.4	3.5	1.9	1.6	8.1	4.8	3.3
Managerial and professional	100.0	51.7	48.3	85.2	44.8	40.4	6.8	2.6	4.2	3.8	2.1	1.7	4.2	2.1	2.1
Technical, sales, and administrative support	100.0	36.8	63.2	80.5	30.0	50.5	9.5	2.9	6.6	3.6	1.5	2.1	6.5	2.5	4.0
Service	100.0	41.8	58.2	67.5	27.3	40.0	17.1	6.9	10.1	4.1	1.9	2.2	11.4	5.6	5.7
Farming, forestry, and fishing	100.0	83.7	16.3	74.2	62.0	12.3	6.4	5.5	0.9	2.4	1.9	0.5	17.0	14.3	2.7
Precision production, craft, and repair	100.0	90.5	9.5	80.7	73.9	6.8	7.3	6.2	1.1	2.8	2.2	0.6	9.2	8.2	1.0
Operators, fabricators, and laborers	100.0	73.7	26.3	70.4	53.1	17.3	14.2	9.8	4.4	3.2	2.0	1.2	12.2	8.8	3.4
Unemployed, no recent civilian work	100.0	44.6	55.4	44.5	19.5	25.0	31.1	14.2	17.0	5.4	2.5	2.9	19.0	8.5	10.5

Table 4.14 (Continued)

Occupational Title	All Persons			Anglo			Black			Other			Hispanic		
	Total	Male	Female	Total	Male	Female	Total	Male	Female	Total	Male	Female	Total	Male	Female
						Distribution in 2050									
Total	100.0	52.9	47.1	55.0	28.9	26.0	13.3	6.3	7.0	11.3	6.1	5.2	20.4	11.6	8.8
Managerial and professional	100.0	49.9	50.1	65.6	33.2	32.5	9.5	3.6	5.9	13.3	7.5	5.9	11.6	5.6	5.9
Technical, sales, and administrative support	100.0	35.6	64.4	58.9	20.8	38.1	12.5	3.7	8.7	11.6	4.9	6.7	17.0	6.2	10.8
Service	100.0	42.3	57.7	43.1	16.5	26.5	19.6	7.9	11.6	11.6	5.5	6.1	25.7	12.3	13.4
Farming, forestry, and fishing	100.0	82.7	17.3	46.9	38.6	8.3	7.5	6.4	1.1	6.9	5.6	1.3	38.6	32.0	6.6
Precision production, craft, and repair	100.0	88.6	11.4	57.4	52.2	5.2	9.7	8.2	1.5	9.4	7.5	1.9	23.6	20.8	2.8
Operators, fabricators, and laborers	100.0	71.0	29.0	45.4	33.5	11.9	16.9	11.7	5.2	9.4	5.9	3.5	28.3	19.9	8.4
Unemployed, no recent civilian work	100.0	43.7	56.3	23.1	9.7	13.5	29.1	13.2	15.9	12.5	5.7	6.8	35.2	15.1	20.1

2050, would mean that 57 percent of service workers, 55 percent of all laborers, and 77 percent of the unemployed would be minorities.

The increased importance of women in the labor force is also evident from Table 4.14. Women, who accounted for a majority of workers only in the technical, sales, and administrative support and service occupations in 1990, would hold a slight majority of managerial and professional jobs by 2050. Women's proportion would increase in every occupational category except services from 1990 to 2050 and, for every racial/ethnic group, it would increase more rapidly than that of men.

The levels of change shown in Table 4.14 must be examined relative to expected occupational opportunities and the wage levels of different occupational groups (see Tables 4.9 and 4.10). Clearly, women and minorities would remain disproportionately concentrated in occupations with poor levels of compensation and in areas where job opportunities are likely to be less prevalent.

The occupational implications of future demographic change can also be examined using the information provided in Table 4.15. This table shows that the occupational composition of the labor force will be impacted by the changing racial/ethnic composition of the workforce. Two sets of projections for 2050 are presented. In one set (shown in column 2), the rate of labor-force involvement by occupation for each racial/ethnic group in 1990 is applied to the number of persons projected to be in each racial/ethnic group in 2050, under the middle scenario. In the second set of projections (shown in column 3), the total population was assumed to be of the same size as projected for 2050 under the middle scenario, and occupational patterns by race/ethnicity are assumed to remain as in 1990, but it was also assumed that the proportion of persons by race/ethnicity in the population in 2050 would be as it was in 1990. Differences in the values shown in the two columns are due to differences in the distribution of workers among different racial/ethnic groups.

The fourth column in Table 4.15 shows the percentage difference in the number of workers by occupation. For example, the number of private household workers would be 21.7 percent higher because of the projected racial/ethnic composition of the population (assuming that involvement in occupations by race/ethnicity group remains in 2050 as it was in 1990). The last column shows the percentage change in each occupational group based on projected growth under the middle scenario, this time with the 2050 composition of the population by race/ethnicity assumed to prevail. The percentage change projected under the assumption that the 1990 race/ethnicity composition of the population prevails in 2050 are not shown because the percentage change for all occupations from 1990 to 2050 are the same as that for the total change in the labor force, that is, 44.8 percent. This is because the assumption of the same composition in 2050 as in 1990 leads to uniform change across all categories. However, it is nevertheless useful to compare

Table 4.15: Civilian Labor Force in the United States by Occupation in 1990 and Projected for 2050 Assuming 1990 Race/Ethnicity Composition and Race/Ethnicity Composition Under the Middle Scenario in 2050

Occupational Title	1990 Composition	Projections for 2050 Assuming Middle Scenario Composition	Projections for 2050 Assuming 1990 Composition	Percent Difference	Percent Change 1990-2050 (Middle Scenario)
Total	123,473,450	178,830,944	178,830,944	0.0	44.8
Managerial and professional	31,266,845	43,921,593	45,284,872	-3.0	40.5
Executive, admin., managerial	14,619,157	19,973,108	21,173,439	-5.7	36.6
Professional specialty	16,647,688	23,948,485	24,111,433	-0.7	43.9
Technical, sales, and admin. support	38,525,740	55,453,151	55,798,183	-0.6	43.9
Technicians and related support	4,387,408	6,778,638	6,354,438	6.7	54.5
Sales	14,432,769	20,067,557	20,903,486	-4.0	39.0
Admin. support	19,705,563	28,606,956	28,540,259	0.2	45.2
Service	16,567,557	26,271,476	23,995,375	9.5	58.6
Private household	563,918	993,587	816,743	21.7	76.2
Protective service	2,084,775	2,876,096	3,019,452	-4.7	38.0
Service, except protective	13,918,864	22,401,793	20,159,180	11.1	60.9
Farming, forestry, and fishing	3,105,395	4,308,111	4,497,653	-4.2	38.7
Farm operators and managers	1,087,365	1,228,414	1,574,869	-22.0	13.0
Other agricultural and related	1,809,415	2,772,416	2,620,640	5.8	53.2

Table 4.15 (Continued)

Occupational Title	1990 Composition	Projections for 2050 Assuming Middle Scenario Composition	Projections for 2050 Assuming 1990 Composition	Percent Difference	Percent Change 1990-2050 (Middle Scenario)
Forestry and logging	148,023	202,469	214,387	-5.6	36.8
Fishers, hunters, and trappers	60,592	104,812	87,757	19.4	73.0
Precision production, craft, and repair	14,031,300	18,961,451	20,322,026	-6.7	35.1
Mechanics and repairers	4,271,166	5,598,099	6,186,080	-9.5	31.1
Construction trades	5,318,000	6,865,568	7,702,246	-10.9	29.1
Extractive	192,862	234,984	279,329	-15.9	21.8
Precision production	4,249,272	6,262,800	6,154,371	1.8	47.4
Operators, fabricators, and labor	18,976,662	28,041,238	27,484,567	2.0	47.8
Machine operators, assemblers	8,635,504	13,514,298	12,507,105	8.1	56.5
Transportation and material moving	5,098,974	6,847,457	7,385,023	-7.3	34.3
Handlers, equip. cleaners, helper	5,242,184	7,679,483	7,592,439	1.1	46.5
Unemployed, no recent civilian work	99,951	1,873,924	1,448,264	29.4	87.4

the rates of percentage change in the last column, which show the rate of change expected under the middle scenario to 44.8 percent. Such a comparison indicates in which occupations the projected change in race/ethnicity composition leads to fewer persons than would otherwise be expected to be employed in that occupation (indicated by a value less than 44.8 percent) and in which occupations the number would be greater than expected (indicated by a value greater than 44.8 percent) because of the racial/ethnic composition of the population projected for 2050.

In general, Table 4.15 suggests that if minority involvement by occupation and/ or the proportion of the minority labor force do not change, the result will be more rapid increases in the number employed in technical support, service, and operator and laborer positions and less growth in managerial, professional, and other occupations. These projected patterns may be problematic because projected growth is greatest in those occupations that are expected to show the smallest increases in opportunities over the coming decades. This is poignantly indicated by the fact that the largest differences between the two distributions (in columns 2 and 3) in Table 4.15 are in the number of unemployed workers: The number of unemployed would be 29.4 percent higher and would increase nearly twice as fast as the overall labor force (by 87.4 percent compared to 44.8 percent) under the projected patterns.

Such changes have further implications for earning power. Table 4.16 shows differences in earnings by occupation, again assuming two different patterns, one in which the race/ethnicity composition of the labor force in 1990 remains constant through 2050 and one in which the composition is that projected to actually prevail in 2050 under the middle scenario. The values in this table were obtained by assuming that average weekly earnings by occupation in 1990 would prevail for each occupational group in 2050.

Table 4.16 points to a significant loss in weekly earnings due to different patterns of occupational participation among different racial/ethnic groups and the projected differences in rates of growth among different racial/ethnic groups. Weekly earnings would be reduced by more than $2.1 billion, with losses occurring in managerial and professional, technical, and precision production occupations. Although there are increases in aggregate earnings in other occupations, these are lower-paying occupations and do not adequately compensate for the reductions. The overall result is a net loss in aggregate income. The change in the composition of the population, if not addressed by change in the occupational involvement of different racial/ethnic groups, would significantly impact the earning power of the labor force.

The economic returns to given occupations are in part, of course, a function of the skills and education required to perform the tasks associated with them. Table 4.17 shows the distribution of the labor force by level of educational attainment.

Table 4.16: Aggregate Weekly Income for Civilian Labor Force in the United
States in 2050 Assuming 1990 Distribution and Projected
Distribution Under the Middle Scenario (numbers in thousands)

Occupational Title	Projections for 2050 Assuming 1990 Distribution	Projections for 2050 Assuming Middle Scenario	Difference
Managerial and professional	$29,023,150	$26,441,700	$-2,581,450
Technical, sales, and administrative support	22,090,940	21,475,632	-615,308
Service	6,546,877	7,333,462	786,585
Farming, forestry, and fishing	1,161,263	1,260,990	99,727
Precision production, craft, and repair	9,657,519	9,217,947	-439,572
Operators, fabricators, and laborers	9,673,194	10,307,440	634,246
Total	78,152,843	76,037,175	-2,115,668

This projection uses the same two scenarios used in the previous analysis. The
first scenario is based on the 2050 middle scenario projection of the racial/ethnic
composition; the second assumes that the racial/ethnic composition of 1990 will
continue throughout the projection period. If the current educational levels of
minorities are not increased, the projected patterns of future growth would lead
to a decrease in the proportion of workers with higher levels of education. For example, under the pattern projected to occur (that is, the middle scenario), the
proportion of workers with less than a high school education is 31.8 percent in
2050 compared to 26.5 percent under a scenario based on 1990 patterns. Given
that employment opportunities requiring higher levels of education are projected
to increase most, this finding suggests that extensive changes in current trends
may be necessary if the skill level of the labor force is not to deteriorate at the very
time demands for higher levels of education and training increase.

Table 4.17: Civilian Labor Force in the United States by Education Level in 2050 Assuming 1990 Race/Ethnicity Composition by Educational Attainment and Under the Middle Scenario (numbers in thousands)

Level of Educational Attainment	Assuming Middle Scenario Race/Ethnicity Composition		Assuming 1990 Race/Ethnicity Composition	
	Number	%	Number	%
< 9 Years	28,104	15.7	20,938	11.7
9-11 Years	28,729	16.1	26,412	14.8
High School	49,114	27.5	52,826	29.5
Some College	31,311	23.3	43,899	24.6
4 Year Degree	30,474	11.2	22,416	12.5
Graduate	11,094	6.2	12,341	6.9
Total Labor Force	178,831	100.0	178,831	100.0

SUMMARY AND IMPLICATIONS OF FUTURE LABOR-FORCE CHANGE IN THE UNITED STATES

The findings presented in this chapter have several implications for the future of America's workforce. These findings include:

1. The labor force of the United States has increased rapidly, with the rate of increase exceeding that for the population. Historically, the growth of the labor force has resulted from increased participation of women, and more recently results from the increased participation of both women and of minorities.

2. Projections of the future labor force suggest that it will be 178.8 million persons in 2050 (under the middle scenario), an increase of 44.3 percent from the 123.9 million in 1990. This rate of growth is less than that for the population (53.9 percent), however, and is slower than historical trends.

3. The projected labor force will be older and more ethnically diverse than today's. The proportion of the labor force 45 years old or older would increase from 28.6 percent in 1990 to 39.0 percent in 2050. By 2050, the proportion of the Anglo labor force would decline to 55.0 percent (under the middle scenario) compared to 78.3 percent in 1990. The percentage of Blacks in the labor force in 2050 would be 13.3 percent, Hispanics 20.4 percent, and Other racial/ethnic groups 11.3 percent. Of the 54.9-million net increase in the labor force from 1990 to 2050, 97.6 percent would be due to growth in the minority labor force.

4. Women will also continue to increase as a proportion of the labor force, from 45.7 percent in 1990 to 47.1 percent in 2050. The net increase in the labor force in every racial/ethnic group would be disproportionately due to the participation of women. However, the facts that women's participation is already high for some groups and that those groups with lower rates of female participation are projected to grow most rapidly reduce the rate of increase of women in the labor force from historical levels.

5. There are marked differences in the levels of involvement in different occupations among age, race/ethnicity, and gender groups. This, coupled with differentials in education, will result in differential labor-force patterns for such groups. Examining how the projected patterns of growth in the labor force will impact occupational involvement and the levels of education of the workforce allows one to identify some of the implications of future demographic patterns for labor and the returns to labor.

6. If the levels of education and the occupational involvement of women and minorities are not enhanced from current levels, the projected patterns will likely increase the proportion of the labor force in low-skill and low-wage occupations and reduce the educational skills and the earnings of the workforce relative to historical patterns. The projected patterns suggest that the competitive characteristics of the labor force could be negatively impacted by future demographic change unless steps are taken in the coming decades to alter the historical relationships between age, gender, and race/ethnicity and labor-force involvement and education in the United States.

The patterns noted above have both public- and private-policy implications. The decreased proportion of young workers, the increase in retirees, and the aging of the large cohort of baby-boomers through the middle years of their working lives are likely to have numerous effects that could require difficult decisions. For example, the smaller proportion of young workers is likely to require that employers dependent on young workers either alter their labor requirements or seek to hire older workers, who traditionally command higher wages.

Equally important, however, is the fact that the labor force should be more stable as a result of its aging, because middle-aged and older workers are less likely to change jobs. Middle-aged workers are also among the most productive. Therefore the aging of the United States labor force should create the potential for increased productivity. However, the large number of workers in the baby-boom ages has caused reduced rates of mobility, especially to upper-level positions, and decreased rates of growth in employee compensation. Many workers in the baby-boom generation may be destined to retire from middle management positions. This, in turn, has implications for retirement strategies. On the one hand, if retirement programs are relatively attractive, and mobility and compensation are limited, workers may opt to retire early. On the other hand, if retirement plans and options are not attractive, given the limited compensation from which to save for retirement, workers may remain active in the labor force at older ages. Thus there is a major policy consideration for the public and private sectors in the coming decades: knowing how to balance the rewards of the workplace and those of retirement so as to maintain a motivated, productive workforce and not create an atmosphere in which competition is so extensive, and advancement so limited, as to make early retirement too attractive.

The data on occupational patterns, earnings, and levels of education in the workforce have several implications. One is that the projected patterns are not conducive to maintaining the competitiveness of the labor force of the United States. Increases in the proportions of women and minorities in the workforce could lead to reduced levels of growth in critical occupational areas, to decreased compensation for workers (resulting in decreased income for purchasing goods and services), and to a workforce that is not as well educated in crucial skills.

The potential problem is not, of course, the growth of women and minorities in the workforce. Rather, it is the levels of occupational involvement, compensation, and education that are accessible to, and acquired by, women and minorities. Patterns of discrimination, limited access to social and economic opportunities, and cultural differences have all played a role in the development of such differences. It is apparent, however, that the level of involvement in the labor force of both women and minorities must be enhanced, through improved access to all occupations and to higher levels of education. Unless this is done, the United States may find itself with a labor force that is declining in competitiveness at a time when the world's labor market has become larger and more competitive. Given that all projections suggest that minority population growth and increased participation of women in the labor force are essential to the overall growth of the entire U.S. labor force in the coming years, it is evident that development of human capital—that is the education, training, and skills—is critical to the ability of the United States to compete in the coming decades. However, given the magnitude of educational and other human-capital differentials among groups, the upgrading of the labor force of the United States is likely to present a major and costly challenge. Achieving this capital enhancement will not be easy, and it will not be inexpensive.

CHAPTER FIVE

Population Change, Household Structure, and Income and Poverty in America

Population change and characteristics, such as the age and race/ethnicity composition of a population, play central roles in the distribution of a society's resources, particularly its distribution of income and the incidence of poverty. The number of people and their characteristics impact the magnitude and distribution of income and other resources. Of particular importance to income generation are the characteristics of how we group ourselves into units for living, or households.

Technically, there are two types of households: family and nonfamily. Family households include units of two or more persons related by kinship, marriage, or adoption. Nonfamily households are units with a single person or two or more persons who are not related to one another but who live in a common living area. The significance of these household types for the analysis of income and other resources lies in the fact that households are the basic unit for consumption, resource sharing and accumulation, and the level of resources in a household varies by type of household. Thus, in examining the implications of demographic change for income and poverty in America, it is essential to do so relative to the number and characteristics of household units as well as the population.

In this chapter, we examine the characteristics of future populations and households and the implications of change in these characteristics for the growth of resources in the population of the United States. As in previous chapters, it is essential to note that in delineating the importance of demographic and household change for income and poverty, I do not intend to imply that population dimensions alone determine income growth and change. Clearly, economic trends in the world and national economies are major factors that determine the total amount of income growth and resources in a society. What I attempt to show is only that demographic change will likely play a role in the future income patterns of Americans if relationships between demographic characteristics and income and poverty are not altered from historical patterns.

THE LINKAGES BETWEEN DEMOGRAPHIC AND ECONOMIC FACTORS

How does demographic change impact economic factors? The effects of population growth are perhaps the most apparent. As populations increase they require more goods and services, which in turn generate a need for more resources. Provided the basic natural resources, labor, and capital are available, a growing population is one in which additional income is also generated for each new person. However, if income and other resources grow less rapidly than population, or if income is distributed to only a few persons in the population, then the number of persons in poverty may increase. Whether income growth or increased poverty is the result, population change plays a role in the development of both the level and the distribution of a society's resources.

The effects of population characteristics on income and poverty are less direct. Data for 1990 demonstrate some of the relationships among age, race/ethnicity, household composition, and income and poverty (see Reference Tables 5.1 through 5.4). These data show that household incomes tend to be largest for those households with a householder (what is more commonly referred to as a household head) who is middle-aged. Thus, the median income for households whose householder was less than 25 years of age was $17,376 in 1989, but it was $42,607 for those with a householder 45 to 54 years of age and $13,150 for those with a householder 75 years of age or older. Similarly, income varies by race/ethnicity. The median household income of Whites in the United States in 1989 was $31,687 but it was $20,082 for Blacks; $24,284 for Hispanics; $20,317 for American Indians, Eskimos, and Aleuts; and $37,169 for Asian and Pacific Islanders. It is also evident that income varies with household composition, with married-couple households having median incomes of more than $48,000 in 1989, but with single-adult households with a female householder with children having a median household income of only $16,568.

Poverty reflects patterns opposite to those shown for income, but data also show that age, race/ethnicity, and household composition markedly impact the incidence of poverty. Poverty is higher for children (more than 18 percent) and the elderly (10–14 percent) and less evident among young and middle-aged adults (7–9 percent). Poverty is highest for Blacks (28.2 percent in 1990) and Hispanics (24.2 percent) and lowest for Whites (9.5 percent). It is higher for one-adult households, particularly those with a female householder; whereas only 5.5 percent of married-couple family households were in poverty in 1990, 31.1 percent of families with a female householder lived in poverty. Finally, it is evident that differentials by age, race/ethnicity, and household type often interact to accentuate or mitigate resource differences (for example, the poorest households include those with young children headed by minority women without a spouse present in the household).

With such differentials in income and poverty by age, race/ethnicity, and household composition, it is apparent that a population composed primarily of middle-aged adults, majority-group members, and households composed of married couples have higher levels of income (all other things being the same) than populations with persons and households with other characteristics. The existence of such interrelationships between demographic and economic patterns, given the projected patterns of population change discussed in Chapter 3, suggests that the future economic resources of the population of the United States may be markedly impacted by demographic change.

These interrelationships are important not only because they point to important existing patterns, but also because they are changing in ways that promise to make many future demographic trends even more likely to alter the economic characteristics of the nation. Thus, nearly all analyses suggest that, whereas the economic conditions of the elderly have improved, those for children have declined over time (Ahlburg and De Vita 1992). Existing evidence also suggests that the trends are away from two-parent families and toward an increasing range of nontraditional household forms, which may reflect increased individual freedom but often have negative economic implications (Bumpass 1990). It is apparent that both the earning power of households and the well-being of children within households have been negatively impacted by trends away from two-parent (and two-earner) households; the number of persons in poverty has been substantially impacted by these patterns (Galston 1993; Eggebeen and Lichter 1991). A preponderance of the available evidence also suggests that inequality in income between majority- and minority-group members has increased in the last several decades (Karoly 1992; Bluestone and Harrison 1986; Bradbury 1986). The suggestion is that trends that accentuate forms of growth likely to increase the number and proportion of single-adult households, the relative proportion of children, and the relative proportion of minority group members are also likely to impact the resource base of the nation.

FUTURE PATTERNS OF HOUSEHOLD CHANGE

Having examined the patterns of projected population change in Chapter 3, it is not necessary to repeat that analysis here. However, it is essential to briefly examine projections of future change in households. These projections were completed by multiplying householder rates (the proportion of persons in a group who are householders) by the projections of population shown in Chapter 3. In these projections, householder rates by age, sex, and race/ethnicity from the 1990 Census were multiplied by the age, sex, and race/ethnicity projections of the population. That is, householder rates for 1990 were assumed to prevail for the entire projection period.

The number of households projected under the alternative projection scenarios are shown in Table 5.1 and Figure 5.1; Table 5.2 shows the percentage change for selected periods by race/ethnicity. These data indicate that household growth is projected to exceed population growth under each scenario. Under the low-growth scenario, the number of households would increase by 23.0 percent from 1990 to 2050 as population increased only 10.8 percent. Under the middle scenario, household increase would be 63.8 percent as population increased 53.9 percent. For the high-growth scenario, the corresponding values are 104.5 percent for households and 103.7 percent for population, and for the zero immigration scenario they are 33.8 percent for households and 21.0 percent for population.

The increase in the number of households would be substantial in numerical terms but lower than recent rates of household growth. Under the middle scenario, the 58.6-million increase in the number of households from 1990 to 2050 would be only 5 million less than the total number of households in the nation in 1970 and, under the high-growth scenario, the increase in the number of households would be 5.0 million greater than the total number of households in the nation in 1990. However, the rate of increase is slower for each decade during the projection period than for the 1980s, except for the 1990-to-2000 decade under the high-growth scenario.

It is also apparent for households, as for the population, that immigration is important to future increases. For example, a comparison of the number of households in the middle and zero immigration scenarios shows that, by 2050, there would be an additional 28 million households resulting from immigrants and their descendants. In fact, under the zero immigration scenario, the number of households added for the entire 60-year period would be only slightly more than the number of households added between 1970 and 1990 (see Table 2.7) and the rate of growth would be less than one-half that for the 1980s.

As for the projections of population, the data on household growth project much more rapid increases in minority households than in majority households. In fact, as indicated in Figure 5.2 (for the middle scenario), the increase in households from 1990 to 2050 would mostly be due to increases in minority households. Roughly 75 percent of the net number of new households added to the population under the middle scenario would be due to increases among minority households. As a result of such patterns, the proportion of Anglo households is reduced to less than 60 percent of all households by 2050 in both the middle- and high-growth scenarios (see Table 5.3, and for the middle scenario see Figure 5.3).

Households also reflect the aging of the population. Table 5.4 displays households by age of householder for the middle scenario. The data in this table suggest that there is likely to be a substantial overall aging of households coupled with substantial differences in aging among racial/ethnic groups. By 2050, 32.6 percent of all households would be headed by a person over the age of 65 compared to 21.7 percent in 1990. However, the 2050 proportion of households with a head over 65 years of age would be 37.4 percent for Anglos, 27.5 for Blacks, 26.0 percent for the

Table 5.1: Projections of Households in the United States from 1990-2050 by
Race/Ethnicity Under Alternative Scenarios

Year	Anglo	Black	Hispanic	Other	Total
			Low Scenario		
1990	73,633,749	9,766,771	6,001,718	2,545,172	91,947,410
2000	78,049,046	11,500,672	8,367,694	3,701,794	101,619,206
2010	80,399,194	13,023,126	10,584,073	4,865,181	108,871,574
2020	81,746,674	14,454,701	12,869,277	6,085,226	115,155,878
2030	80,085,209	15,336,813	14,913,055	7,258,105	117,593,182
2040	75,496,498	15,716,973	16,571,555	8,337,164	116,122,190
2050	69,978,292	15,849,231	17,922,138	9,326,060	113,075,721
			Middle Scenario		
1990	73,633,749	9,766,771	6,001,718	2,545,172	91,947,410
2000	79,075,660	11,669,403	8,780,030	4,034,064	103,559,157
2010	83,490,865	13,583,055	11,788,209	5,723,360	114,585,489
2020	87,747,024	15,662,429	15,216,856	7,585,391	126,211,700
2030	90,039,719	17,595,191	18,941,957	9,593,312	136,170,179
2040	89,909,083	19,416,416	22,834,764	11,703,146	143,863,409
2050	88,487,070	21,367,923	26,845,356	13,878,080	150,578,429
			High Scenario		
1990	73,633,749	9,766,771	6,001,718	2,545,172	91,947,410
2000	79,917,126	11,870,717	9,190,540	4,357,109	105,335,492
2010	85,914,459	14,222,004	12,969,298	6,560,113	119,665,874
2020	92,368,700	16,937,762	17,433,492	9,040,300	135,780,254
2030	98,296,772	19,822,440	22,635,151	11,840,398	152,594,761
2040	103,379,835	22,874,686	28,604,258	14,966,961	169,825,740
2050	107,984,331	26,269,564	35,395,931	18,405,798	188,055,624
			Zero Immigration Scenario		
1990	73,633,749	9,766,771	6,001,718	2,545,172	91,947,410
2000	78,541,049	11,504,524	7,973,318	3,122,269	101,141,160
2010	82,154,779	13,157,770	9,733,781	3,558,457	108,604,787
2020	85,435,087	14,912,526	11,583,275	3,976,293	115,907,181
2030	86,594,821	16,452,355	13,341,210	4,326,397	120,714,783
2040	85,220,566	17,823,503	14,905,892	4,625,845	122,575,806
2050	82,517,934	19,282,141	16,300,459	4,888,644	122,989,178

(Millions)

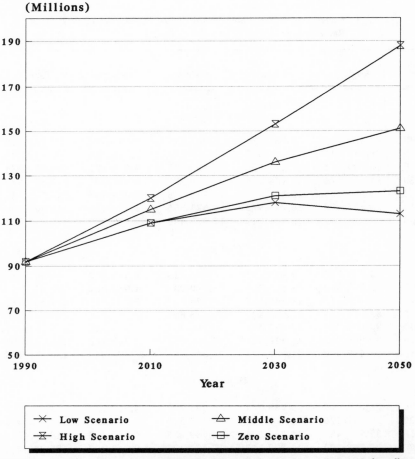

FIGURE 5.1   Projections of households in the United States, 1990–2050 under all scenarios.

Hispanic racial/ethnic group, and 23.7 percent for Others. In 1990, 27.1 percent of all households had a householder under 35 years of age, 37.8 percent of households had householders 35 to 54 years of age, and 35.2 percent had householders 55 years of age or older. By 2050, only 18.3 percent of householders would be less than 35 years, 32.7 percent would be 35 to 54 years of age, and 49 percent would be 55 years of age or older. A substantial aging of households is evident.

Projections for households can be extended to include *types* of households. For purposes of this analysis, the proportion of households by type for each racial/ethnic group in 1990 was multiplied by the total number of households projected to be in each racial/ethnic group. Rates for Whites were assumed to apply to An-

Table 5.2: Percent Change for Selected Time Periods in the Projected Number of Households in the United States by Race/Ethnicity Under Alternative Scenarios

Time Period	Anglo	Black	Hispanic	Other	Total
Low Scenario					
1990-2000	6.0	17.8	39.4	45.4	10.5
2000-2010	3.0	13.2	26.5	31.4	7.1
2010-2020	1.7	11.0	21.6	25.1	5.8
2020-2030	-2.0	6.1	15.9	19.3	2.1
2030-2040	-5.7	2.5	11.1	14.9	-1.3
2040-2050	-7.3	0.8	8.2	11.9	-2.6
1990-2050	-5.0	62.3	198.6	266.4	23.0
Middle Scenario					
1990-2000	7.4	19.5	46.3	58.5	12.6
2000-2010	5.6	16.4	34.3	41.9	10.6
2010-2020	5.1	15.3	29.1	32.5	10.1
2020-2030	2.6	12.3	24.5	26.5	7.9
2030-2040	-0.1	10.4	20.6	22.0	5.6
2040-2050	-1.6	10.1	17.6	18.6	4.7
1990-2050	20.2	118.8	347.3	445.3	63.8
High Scenario					
1990-2000	8.5	21.5	53.1	71.2	14.6
2000-2010	7.5	19.8	41.1	50.6	13.6
2010-2020	7.5	19.1	34.4	37.8	13.5
2020-2030	6.4	17.0	29.8	31.0	12.4
2030-2040	5.2	15.4	26.4	26.4	11.3
2040-2050	4.5	14.8	23.7	23.0	10.7
1990-2050	46.7	169.0	489.8	623.2	104.5
Zero Immigration Scenario					
1990-2000	6.7	17.8	32.9	22.7	10.0
2000-2010	4.6	14.4	22.1	14.0	7.4
2010-2020	4.0	13.3	19.0	11.7	6.7
2020-2030	1.4	10.3	15.2	8.8	4.1
2030-2040	-1.6	8.3	11.7	6.9	1.5
2040-2050	-3.2	8.2	9.4	5.7	0.3
1990-2050	12.1	97.4	171.6	92.1	33.8

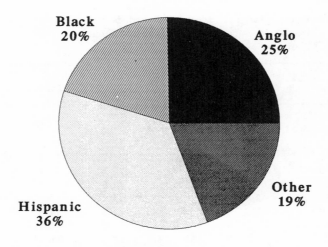

Black
20%

Anglo
25%

Other
19%

Hispanic
36%

*Middle Projection Scenario

FIGURE 5.2   Percent of net household change by each ethnic group, 1990–2050.

glos and rates for the Other group were computed from combined data for the Asian and Pacific Islander and the American Indian, Eskimo, and Aleut racial groups. These proportions for 1990 were assumed to prevail throughout the projection period.

Tables 5.5 and 5.6 show the results of this analysis for 1990 and 2050 for the middle scenario. These tables demonstrate that the differences in household type by race/ethnicity, coupled with the substantial differentials in rates of population growth among different types of households, result in marked changes in the types of households that would exist in 2050 compared to 1990. The total number of households would increase by 63.8 percent; family household types would increase by 67.9 percent and nonfamily households by only 53.7 percent. This is a marked reversal of recent historical patterns, in which nonfamily households have grown substantially faster than family households. This reversal is a function of the much higher rate of family households among Hispanic and Other populations and the faster growth in households projected for these groups. Within family households, the data point to a continuation of the pattern of faster growth for single-adult households than for married-couple households, with faster rates of increase for both male and female householders than for married-couple households. Also important is the reversal from recent patterns: family households with children (whether married couples, male or female householder families) are projected to grow more rapidly than families without children. Although these differences are not substantial, the fact that they reverse past patterns is important. Again, minority populations, with relatively high proportions of households with children, are projected to increase most rapidly and account for this reversal.

Table 5.3: Projections of the Percent of Total Households in the United States by Race/Ethnicity from 1990-2050 Under Alternative Scenarios

Year	Anglo	Black	Hispanic	Other
Low Scenario				
1990	80.1	10.6	6.5	2.8
2000	76.9	11.3	8.2	3.6
2010	73.8	12.0	9.7	4.5
2020	70.9	12.6	11.2	5.3
2030	68.1	13.0	12.7	6.2
2040	65.0	13.5	14.3	7.2
2050	62.0	14.0	15.8	8.2
Middle Scenario				
1990	80.1	10.6	6.5	2.8
2000	76.3	11.3	8.5	3.9
2010	72.8	11.9	10.3	5.0
2020	69.5	12.4	12.1	6.0
2030	66.2	12.9	13.9	7.0
2040	62.5	13.5	15.9	8.1
2050	58.8	14.2	17.8	9.2
High Scenario				
1990	80.1	10.6	6.5	2.8
2000	75.9	11.3	8.7	4.1
2010	71.8	11.9	10.8	5.5
2020	68.0	12.5	12.8	6.7
2030	64.4	13.0	14.8	7.8
2040	60.9	13.5	16.8	8.8
2050	57.4	14.0	18.8	9.8
Zero Immigration Scenario				
1990	80.1	10.6	6.5	2.8
2000	77.6	11.4	7.9	3.1
2010	75.6	12.1	9.0	3.3
2020	73.7	12.9	10.0	3.4
2030	71.7	13.6	11.1	3.6
2040	69.5	14.5	12.2	3.8
2050	67.0	15.7	13.3	4.0

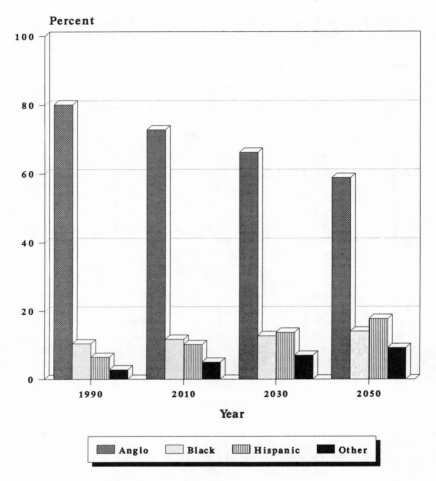

*Middle Projection Scenario

FIGURE 5.3   Percent of households in the United States by race/ethnicity, 1990–2050 (middle projection scenario).

It is also evident that the importance of minority populations for different types of households varies. A comparison of the two panels of Table 5.6 suggests that minority populations would come to form increasing proportions of all types of households, particularly one-parent family households with children. Under these projections, by 2050 more than 60 percent of all one-adult households with children would be composed of minority householders compared to between 35 and 45 percent in 1990.

Table 5.4: Percent of the Households in the United States by Age and Race/Ethnicity in 1990 and Projection of the Percent of the Households in the United States by Age, Year, and Race/Ethnicity for 2000, 2030, and 2050 Under the Middle Scenario

Year/Age of Householder	Anglo	Black	Hispanic	Other	Total
1990					
15-24	5.1	6.6	8.7	6.3	5.5
25-34	20.5	23.9	29.2	25.5	21.6
35-44	21.6	23.7	24.7	28.1	22.2
45-54	15.5	15.8	15.2	18.1	15.6
55-64	13.8	12.9	11.0	11.2	13.5
65-74	13.4	10.4	7.1	7.0	12.5
75+	10.1	6.7	4.2	3.7	9.2
2000					
15-24	4.6	5.9	6.9	5.6	5.0
25-34	15.1	18.5	23.6	21.3	16.4
35-44	22.3	25.6	27.6	27.0	23.3
45-54	20.3	20.7	18.4	21.6	20.3
55-64	14.0	12.8	10.9	12.0	13.5
65-74	12.0	9.6	7.6	7.6	11.2
75+	11.7	6.8	5.0	4.8	10.3
2030					
15-24	3.8	5.3	5.8	5.0	4.4
25-34	12.4	15.7	17.8	17.9	13.9
35-44	16.0	19.0	20.5	21.6	17.4
45-54	15.4	17.1	17.4	19.8	16.2
55-64	15.6	16.2	15.8	15.1	15.7
65-74	19.2	16.2	13.6	11.2	17.5
75+	17.5	10.5	9.1	9.4	14.9
2050					
15-24	3.7	5.2	5.4	4.7	4.3
25-34	12.5	15.5	16.7	16.7	14.0
35-44	14.7	17.9	19.1	20.4	16.5
45-54	15.1	17.1	17.4	19.5	16.2
55-64	16.7	16.7	15.5	15.0	16.4
65-74	15.9	13.7	12.5	11.2	14.5
75+	21.5	13.8	13.5	12.5	18.1

Table 5.5: Number of Households by Type in the United States and Percent Change in the Number of Households by Type, from 1990-2050 Under the Middle Scenario

	Number		Percent
Household Type	1990	2050	Change
Family households:	65,329,955	109,660,675	67.9
Married couple:			
With own children	24,512,124	42,690,107	74.2
Without own children	27,155,876	40,521,533	49.2
Male householder with no spouse present:			
With own children	1,331,025	2,674,385	100.9
Without own children	1,729,275	3,385,195	95.8
Female householder with no spouse present:			
With own children	6,031,320	12,089,964	100.5
Without own children	4,570,335	8,299,491	81.6
Nonfamily households:	26,617,456	40,917,753	53.7
Total households:	91,947,411	150,578,428	63.8

The projections of total households, households by race/ethnicity, households by age of householder, and households by type suggest that household growth will be slower than in the past and lead to increasingly older and more ethnically diverse households. Such projections also suggest a partial reversal of recent patterns of decline in the number of family households, particularly those with children.

IMPLICATIONS OF POPULATION CHANGE FOR INCOME AND POVERTY IN AMERICA

What do projected income and poverty patterns mean for the level and distribution of economic resources in America? The implications are shown in the tables and figures presented in this section. In these tables, the proportion of households by income and poverty levels, by age and/or race/ethnicity, and by household type for 1990 were assumed to prevail throughout the projection period and were multiplied by the number of households projected under the middle sce-

Table 5.6: Number and Percent of Households in the United States by Type of Household and Race/Ethnicity of Householder in 1990 and Projected for 2050 Under the Middle Scenario

Household Type	Total		Anglo		Black		Hispanic		Other	
	Number	%	Number	%	Number	%	Number	%	Number	%
					1990					
Family households:	65,329,955	100.0	51,553,499	78.9	6,930,822	10.6	4,881,551	7.5	1,964,083	3.0
Married couple:										
With own children	24,512,124	100.0	19,472,945	79.4	1,832,718	7.5	2,249,983	9.2	956,478	3.9
Without own children	27,155,876	100.0	23,782,882	87.6	1,626,652	6.0	1,163,465	4.3	582,877	2.1
Male householder with no spouse present:										
With own children	1,331,025	100.0	867,013	65.2	214,553	16.1	201,220	15.1	48,239	3.6
Without own children	1,729,275	100.0	1,168,642	67.6	265,244	15.3	214,498	12.4	80,891	4.7
Female householder with no spouse present:										
With own children	6,031,320	100.0	3,297,011	54.7	1,867,635	31.0	698,011	11.5	168,663	2.8
Without own children	4,570,335	100.0	2,965,006	64.9	1,124,020	24.6	354,374	7.7	126,935	2.8
Nonfamily households:	26,617,456	100.0	22,080,250	83.0	2,835,950	10.6	1,120,168	4.2	581,088	2.2
Total households:	91,947,411	100.0	73,633,749	80.1	9,766,772	10.6	6,001,719	6.5	2,545,171	2.8

Table 5.6 (Continued)

2050

Household Type	Total Number	%	Anglo Number	%	Black Number	%	Hispanic Number	%	Other Number	%
Family households:	109,660,675	100.0	61,952,816	56.5	15,163,379	13.8	21,834,905	19.9	10,709,575	9.8
Married couple:										
With own children	42,690,107	100.0	23,401,006	54.8	4,009,654	9.4	10,064,051	23.6	5,215,396	12.2
Without own children	40,521,533	100.0	28,580,339	70.5	3,558,819	8.8	5,204,114	12.8	3,178,261	7.9
Male householder with no spouse present:										
With own children	2,674,385	100.0	1,041,906	38.9	469,403	17.6	900,045	33.7	263,031	9.8
Without own children	3,385,195	100.0	1,404,380	41.5	580,306	17.1	959,436	28.4	441,073	13.0
Female householder with no spouse present:										
With own children	12,089,964	100.0	3,962,081	32.8	4,086,046	33.8	3,122,164	25.8	919,673	7.6
Without own children	8,299,491	100.0	3,563,104	42.9	2,459,151	29.6	1,585,095	19.1	692,141	8.4
Nonfamily households:	40,917,753	100.0	26,534,254	64.9	6,204,544	15.2	5,010,451	12.2	3,168,504	7.7
Total households:	150,578,428	100.0	88,487,070	58.8	21,367,923	14.2	26,845,356	17.8	13,878,079	9.2

nario. Because 1990 income levels are used in the analysis, all monetary values are shown in 1990 dollars.

The aging of the population could have important implications for the level and distribution of income. The projected patterns (see Reference Table 5.5) are likely to lead to much more rapid growth in low-income households than in high-income households. The patterns are also likely to lead to the largest increases in income for those in middle and older age groups. For all age groups the highest percentage increases from 1990 to 2050 are for the lowest income categories. However, no matter which income level is examined, growth is likely to be largest among those households with a householder who is middle-aged or elderly. On the one hand, from 1990 to 2050 growth in the number of households in the below-$5,000 category is projected to be 45.9 percent for householders less than 25 years of age and 33.2 percent for householders 25 to 34 years of age. But the increase is expected to be more than 100 percent for households with householders 45 years of age or older. On the other hand, the increase in the number of households with incomes of more than $100,000 will be less than 25 percent for all groups where the householder is less than 45 years of age, but greater than 50 percent for all categories where the householder is 45 years of age or older. Aging will clearly impact the rate of growth in income and the distribution of income.

Aggregate income would also be increasingly concentrated in households headed by an older householder. Thus, as shown in Figure 5.4, although the proportion of aggregate income accounted for by households with a householder less than 55 years of age would decline, the proportion would increase for households with a householder 55 years of age or older.

The effects of change in the race/ethnicity composition of households on income are indicated in the data in Tables 5.7 and 5.8 and Figure 5.5. In these tables, the middle projection scenario is compared to the zero immigration scenario in order to identify the effects of immigration. Projections are also shown in which the projected total number of households from the middle projection scenario is used but the distribution of households by race/ethnicity in 1990 is applied to that total. By comparing the values that assume the 1990 distribution by race/ethnicity in 2050 to those for the middle scenario, the effects of the projected change in the racial/ethnic composition of the population from 1990 to 2050 can be identified.

Table 5.7 indicates that change in racial/ethnic composition will increase the rate of growth in low-income households more rapidly than those of middle- and upper-income households. Equally important, this table shows that immigrants will contribute significantly to the growth in households across all income levels. In fact, for every income category, the difference in the percentage change is at least 26 percent between the middle and zero immigration scenarios, suggesting that immigrants and their descendants will increase the number of households at every income level.

Table 5.7 also suggests that the distribution projected for 2050 would result in a reduction in the number of higher-income households and an increase in the

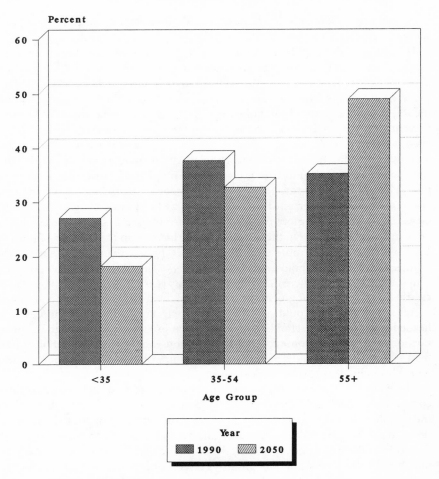

Percent

*Middle Projection Scenario

FIGURE 5.4   Percent of aggregate household income by age for the United States, 1990–2050 (middle projection scenario).

number of lower-income households relative to those that would exist if the distribution of 1990 prevailed in 2050. For every income category above $25,000 the number of households is lower, and for every category less than $25,000 the number of households is larger, assuming the middle scenario projection rather than the 1990 distribution.

Table 5.8 and Figure 5.5 indicate that income would increasingly be accounted for by minority households and that immigrants would play a major role in the growth of income. The table shows annual aggregate income for all households in

Table 5.7: Income Distribution in 1990 and Projected for 2050 for Middle and Zero Immigration Scenarios Assuming Projected Race/Ethnicity Composition in 2050 and Assuming 1990 Distribution by Race/Ethnicity

	Number of Households				Percent Change, 1990-2050		
Income Category	1990	Middle Scenario, 2050	Zero Immigration Scenario, 2050	Assuming 1990 Composition in 2050	Middle Scenario	Zero Immigration Scenario	1990 Distribution
$< 5,000	5,792,385	11,040,892	8,772,689	9,305,746	90.6	51.5	60.7
$5,000-$9,999	8,594,574	14,773,789	12,049,484	13,958,620	71.9	40.2	62.4
$10,000-$14,999	8,198,059	13,943,085	11,317,278	13,311,133	70.1	38.0	62.4
$15,000-$24,999	16,197,042	26,973,535	22,003,986	26,396,398	66.5	35.9	63.0
$25,000-$34,999	14,569,512	23,597,404	19,361,858	23,851,623	62.0	32.9	63.7
$35,000-$49,999	16,346,494	25,850,283	21,294,543	26,893,307	58.1	30.3	64.5
$50,000-$74,999	13,651,173	21,302,204	17,483,883	22,556,648	56.0	28.1	65.2
$75,000-$99,999	4,640,768	7,180,888	5,853,892	7,694,557	54.7	26.1	65.8
$100,000+	3,957,400	5,916,332	4,851,558	6,610,380	49.5	22.6	67.0
Total	91,947,407	150,578,412	122,989,171	150,578,412	63.8	33.8	63.8

Table 5.8: Aggregate and Average Per-Household Income by Race/Ethnicity of the Householder in 1990 and Projected for 2050 Under Middle and Zero Immigration Scenarios and Projected for 2050 Assuming 1990 Race/Ethnicity Composition (aggregate income in thousands)

	1990		Middle Scenario, 2050		Zero Immigration Scenario, 2050		Assuming 1990 Composition in 2050		Percent Change, 1990-2050		
	Aggregate Income	%	Aggregate Income	%	Aggregate Income	%	Aggregate Income	%	Middle Immigration Scenario	Zero Immigration Scenario	1990 Composition
Anglo	$2,967,995,019	85.0	$3,566,695,797	65.8	$3,326,094,630	74.1	$4,861,681,783	84.7	20.2	12.1	63.8
Black	252,684,462	7.2	552,827,760	10.2	498,864,715	11.1	412,951,090	7.2	118.8	97.4	63.4
Hispanic	181,860,688	5.2	813,452,899	15.0	493,927,353	11.0	343,035,735	5.9	347.3	171.6	88.6
Other	89,202,918	2.6	486,397,473	9.0	171,336,675	3.8	127,754,955	2.2	445.3	92.1	43.2
Total	3,491,743,087	100.0	5,419,373,929	100.0	4,490,223,373	100.0	5,745,423,563	100.0	55.2	28.6	64.5
Average per-household income	$37,975	--	$35,990	--	$36,509	--	$38,156	--	-5.2	-3.9	0.5

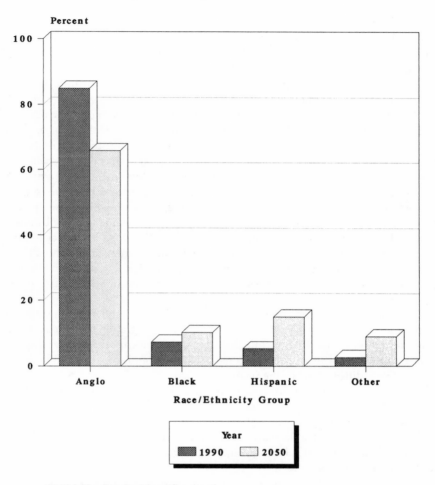

*Middle Projection Scenario

FIGURE 5.5   Percent of aggregate income for households by race/ethnicity (middle projection scenario).

1990 and that projected for 2050, assuming that average per-household incomes by race/ethnicity for 1990 prevail in 2050. All values are in 1990 dollars.

The proportion of total income accounted for by minority populations would increase from 15 percent in 1990 to nearly 35 percent by 2050 (under the middle scenario). Of the more than $5.4 trillion dollars in aggregate income projected for 2050, Hispanics would account for 15 percent in 2050 compared to only 5.2 percent in 1990; the share accounted for by Blacks would increase from 7.2 percent to 10.2 percent and the share accounted for by Others from 2.6 to 9.0 percent. In percentage terms, under the middle scenario, the rate of increase in aggregate income would be 445.3 percent for Others, 347.3 percent for Hispanics, and 118.8 percent for Blacks, but only 20.2 percent for Anglos. The impact of immigrants on total income is also apparent. A comparison of the zero immigration and middle scenarios shows that immigrants and their descendants would contribute nearly an additional $1 trillion to the economy in 2050.

Aggregate income will be markedly impacted by the projected ethnic patterns. Comparing the data for 2050 in Table 5.8, assuming the 1990 distribution and that projected for 2050 under the middle scenario, suggests that the distribution of dollars of income among racial/ethnic groups will likely shift due to changes in the racial/ethnic composition of the population. The total income accounted for by Anglo households would decline by $1.3 trillion, that of Black households would increase by nearly $140 billion, that of Hispanics would increase by more than $470 billion, and that of Other racial/ethnic groups would increase by nearly $360 billion compared to amounts that would prevail in 2050 if the racial/ethnic composition of 1990 was to remain unchanged. Thus, if there are no shifts in the relative incomes of racial/ethnic groups in the future, the growth of minority populations will lead to substantial changes in the amount of income attributable to different groups.

The data on average per-household income in Table 5.8 show that the effect of the projected patterns under the middle and zero immigration scenarios is to reduce overall per-household income by 5.2 and 3.9 percent respectively; the 1990 composition would increase the average per household income by only 0.5 percent. Unless differentials in the income opportunities of minorities are altered, the projected patterns will likely lead to reduced average incomes for American households.

The effects of changes in household composition on income are addressed in Table 5.9. This table also compares the middle scenario projections for 2050, the zero immigration scenario for 2050, and values for 2050 assuming the proportion of households by type in 1990.

A comparison of the middle and zero immigration scenarios in Table 5.9 suggests that immigration would nearly double the total household income that would occur if there were no immigration. A comparison of the middle scenario and the values assuming the 1990 distribution of households in 2050 shows that the effect of the likely projected household structure is to reduce the net increase in income by $37 billion ($5.727 trillion versus $5.690 trillion). Particularly evident is the fact that, because there will be more family households among those groups most likely to dominate future growth, increases in income are projected to be highest on an aggregate basis for families with children, regardless of whether these are couples or single-parent households. Overall, as suggested by average per-household income, the effect of the expected patterns under the middle and the zero immigration scenarios is to reduce per-household income whereas 1990 patterns would lead to virtually no change in household incomes.

Table 5.9: Aggregate and Average Per-Household Income by Household Type in the United States in 1990 and Projected for 2050 Under the Middle and Zero Immigration Scenarios and Assuming 1990 Composition in 2050 (aggregate income in thousands)

Household Type	Aggregate Income				Percent Change, 1990-2050		
	1990	Middle Scenario, 2050	Zero Immigration Scenario, 2050	Assuming 1990 Composition in 2050	Middle Scenario	Zero Immigration Scenario	Assuming 1990 Composition
Family households:	$2,855,005,107	$4,703,923,880	$3,803,594,641	$4,664,244,577	64.8	33.2	63.4
Married couple:							
With own children							
< 18 yrs of age	1,198,151,214	2,086,689,980	1,632,038,766	1,937,960,024	74.2	36.2	61.8
Without own children	1,318,102,419	1,966,849,851	1,657,260,758	2,184,593,062	49.2	25.7	65.7
Male householder with no spouse present:							
With own children							
< 18 yrs of age	36,725,787	73,791,923	56,132,394	57,751,160	100.9	52.8	57.3
Without own children	65,552,783	128,324,849	97,469,865	103,887,898	95.8	48.7	58.5
Female householder with no spouse present:							
With own children							
< 18 yrs of age	99,928,608	200,309,927	159,084,298	159,167,185	100.5	59.2	59.2
Without own children	136,544,296	247,957,350	201,608,561	220,885,248	81.6	47.7	61.8
Nonfamily households:	641,474,038	986,107,622	831,481,842	1,062,916,570	53.7	29.6	65.7
Total households:	3,496,479,145	5,690,031,502	4,635,076,483	5,727,161,147	62.7	32.6	63.8
Average per-household income	$38,027	$37,788	$37,687	$38,034	-0.6	-0.9	0.1

Note that Tables 5.8 and 5.9 illustrate a difference in average household incomes. Whereas average per-household incomes under the middle and zero immigration scenarios decrease by 5.2 and 3.9 percent respectively in Table 5.8, they decrease by less than 1 percent in Table 5.9. This reflects the fact that minority households, which are projected to show the largest increase in the number of households during the projection period, also have patterns of household composition that generally place them in those types of households that have higher income levels. Because these patterns of household composition are not reflected in Table 5.8 but are in Table 5.9, the values in Table 5.9 show a smaller decline in household income. In particular, the tendency for Hispanics to be in married-couple households with higher incomes partially offsets the otherwise low income received by this group.

Finally, the implications of the changes in family composition for poverty levels are demonstrated in Table 5.10 and Figure 5.6. The data in the table show that the projected patterns of future population and household change are ones that could lead to increases in rates of poverty for all types of households and to increases in the total number of households in poverty. Increases in the number of households in poverty exceed 100 percent between 1990 and 2050 for all but one household type. The projected patterns would not only make households generally poorer (as suggested by Tables 5.8 and 5.9), but would also result in nearly 8 million more households being in poverty in 2050.

Overall, the projected patterns are ones that lead to reduced income levels and increased poverty. Unless the incomes of minority populations are increased, and their rates of poverty decreased, the projected patterns are ones that could lead to a substantial reduction in income growth. Although projected patterns suggest substantial increases in the number of households, these households will be ones with relatively modest resources.

SUMMARY AND IMPLICATIONS OF DEMOGRAPHIC CHANGE FOR INCOME AND POVERTY

Changes in income and poverty are likely to be impacted by changes in populations and in households. Specifically, the data suggest that:

1. Age, racial/ethnic composition, and type of household impact income and other resources. In general, middle-aged persons, majority-group members, and married-couple households have higher incomes and lower rates of poverty than younger or older persons, minority-group members, and households with only one adult.

2. The projected growth in households reflects the changes shown in Chapter 3 for population. That is, it is likely that households, although continuing to grow faster than population, will increase less rapidly than in the past, show a marked aging, and reflect a substantial increase in the number of minority householders. By 2050, the number of households is projected to be 150.6 million under the mid-

Table 5.10: Number and Percent of Families in Poverty by Family Type in 1990 and Projected for 2050 Under the Middle Scenario

Family Type	1990		2050		Percent Change 1990-2050
	Number	%	Number	%	
Married couple	3,025,963	5.9	6,536,629	7.9	116.0
With children < 5 yrs of age	390,682	7.2	877,944	9.5	124.7
With children 5 to 17 yrs of age	850,686	6.3	1,926,450	8.4	126.5
With children < 5 and 5-17 yrs of age	688,416	12.5	1,736,869	16.6	152.3
No children < 18 yrs of age	1,096,179	4.0	1,995,366	4.9	82.0
Male householder with no spouse present	409,086	13.4	953,631	15.7	133.1
With children < 5 yrs of age	74,296	22.6	172,186	24.7	131.8
With children 5 to 17 yrs of age	126,406	15.8	278,293	18.7	120.2
With children < 5 and 5-17 yrs of age	64,607	31.7	171,810	35.3	165.9
No children < 18 yrs of age	143,777	8.3	331,342	9.8	130.5
Female householder with no spouse present	3,093,965	29.2	6,823,513	33.5	120.5
With children < 5 yrs of age	528,720	50.7	1,108,456	53.2	109.7
With children 5 to 17 yrs of age	1,272,828	33.8	2,754,777	38.1	116.4
With children < 5 and 5-17 yrs of age	784,174	63.9	1,846,954	66.5	135.5
No children < 18 yrs of age	508,243	11.1	1,113,326	13.4	119.1
Total households	6,529,014	10.0	14,313,773	13.1	119.2

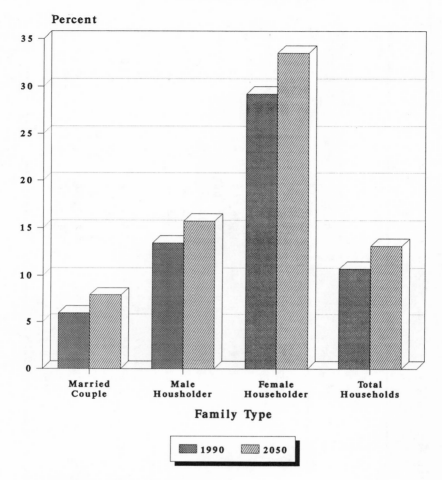

Percent

Family Type

1990   2050

*Middle Projection Scenario

FIGURE 5.6   Percent below poverty by family type, 1990 and 2050 (middle projection scenario).

dle scenario, an increase of 63.8 percent from the 91.9 million households in 1990. The percentage of all households accounted for by Anglos would be 58.8 percent, compared to 14.2 percent for Blacks, 17.8 percent for Hispanics, and 9.2 percent for Other racial/ethnic groups. Of the net increase of 58.6 million households from 1990 to 2050, more than 75 percent would be due to growth in minority households.

3. Households would also change in form if the projected patterns occur and the relationship between age, race/ethnicity, and type of household that existed in

1990 continue into the future. Because the minority households expected to increase most rapidly are ones in which children are more likely to be present, the projected increase in households with children is substantial. In fact, the pattern of faster growth of nonfamily rather than family households and of households without children rather than those with children (both of which have characterized recent change in households) would reverse as a result of the faster growth of minority households. Family growth would be most rapid among one-parent households with children.

4. The patterns projected for population and for households show that income growth will be greatest among middle-aged and older households, with an increasing share of all income being concentrated in middle and elderly households. For nearly all income categories, the rates of growth in households with a householder 45 years of age or older is nearly twice that in households with a householder less than 45 years of age.

5. The projected pattern of income distribution is one of faster growth among lower-income households compared to higher-income households and one of reduced income growth compared to what would exist if the 1990 race/ethnicity distribution were to prevail in the future. Thus, the highest rates of growth would be in households with incomes of less than $25,000 (in 1990 dollars), with slower growth in higher-income households. Aggregate annual income would increase but would be $325 billion less in 2050 if the patterns projected under the middle scenario prevail than if the patterns of 1990 were to continue.

6. Aggregate income will also shift markedly toward greater concentration in minority households. The proportion of all household income in Anglo households in 1990 was 85 percent, but would be only 66 percent by 2050. The aggregate income in Anglo households would increase by only 20.2 percent from 1990 to 2050, but would increase by 118.8 percent for Black households, 347.3 percent for Hispanic households, and 445.3 percent for households of Other racial/ethnic groups.

7. Because of the lower incomes of minority households and their more rapid numerical increases during the projection period, the projected patterns of population and household growth lead to generally reduced household income and increased poverty in the future. Average annual per-household income could decline from 1990 levels by more than 5 percent by 2050 and the proportion of all households in poverty could increase by roughly 3 percent. Although the higher proportion of minority populations living in family household types that generally have higher household incomes will partially offset such patterns, it is evident that, if the relationships between resources and minority status do not change, the projected patterns of change will lead to general stagnation in household income in the United States and to increased rates of poverty.

These patterns have profound implications for the public and private sectors in America. The image of more-but-poorer households and more impoverished households is a sobering one. For the private sector, the reduced growth in household incomes and the increase in the number of households with modest incomes suggest that the projected increase in households may bring more modest markets and profits. This may also mean more complex markets.

Thus, the data in this chapter suggest the potential existence of two very different market segments. One segment, composed of middle-aged and elderly persons, is likely to control increasing amounts of income. Because of the disparity in age structure and household composition between majority and minority groups, this segment is also likely to have a larger proportion of majority-group members than the population as a whole and to contain households with relatively few children. Given current distributions of income by age and race/ethnicity, this could be a relatively affluent market with interest in upscale and more expensive products and services. A second and larger market segment may be composed of minority-group members living in households with children and households with more limited resources. This second market segment will nevertheless account for an increasing part of the total income base of the nation. These are two very different market segments that are likely to require very different marketing and other approaches. This suggests that it will be increasingly difficult to develop products and services for all households. Targeting the middle may mean that one will miss a very large proportion of the total market.

For the public sector, these projected patterns suggest that the future is likely to result in populations with higher proportions of persons with service and other needs that cannot be met without assistance. On the one hand, an increasing number of elderly households, more households that are poor and/or in poverty, are predicted under the projected patterns. On the other hand, the income necessary to pay for increased service needs may not be available. This suggests that the current financial difficulties of public services and treasuries may continue and may even become more acute.

The patterns projected here could be reversed, however, by altering the relationships between certain age, race/ethnicity, and household structures and socioeconomic resources. Additional education, training, and other assistance aimed at increasing the competitiveness of American workers were discussed in Chapter 4. But the need for such investments is made even more apparent by the data presented in this chapter. Although it is not easy to discern how much investment in human capital should be made, it is evident that if the human capital of youth, minority, immigrant, and nontraditional households is not increased, the negative impacts on the socioeconomic welfare of the nation may be profound. This investment may be difficult to make because of the likely immediate service and other needs of the projected population, but it is perhaps one of the few means by which the relationship between resources and certain demographic characteristics can be altered and the level of unmet need ultimately reduced.

CHAPTER SIX

Demographic Change
and Business in America

The demographic changes discussed in the preceding chapters have substantial implications for business in America. An extensive literature has demonstrated that demographic trends in aging (Leventhal 1991; Crone 1990; Clark and Lempert 1993), ethnic change (Foot 1992; Chatterjee 1991; Dunn 1991; Morrison 1987; Gruen 1992), and household composition (Wacker 1992) will impact the overall trends in markets in the United States. In addition, such changes have been shown to impact housing patterns (Sternlieb and Hughes 1986; Mills 1991), catalog sales (Jasper and Lan 1992), transportation patterns (Wolfe 1989), savings levels (Meyer 1992; Heller 1989), recreation (Murdock et al. 1991b), new product and service demands (Clark 1991; Brody 1993), and numerous other factors (Pol 1987).

The implications of demographic change for American business are thus extensive, and no one chapter can attempt to examine more than a small number of these implications. First, how factors basic to business activity—the magnitude and characteristics of consumer expenditures and discretionary income—are likely to change as a result of demographic change is examined. The implications of demographic change are then examined in three specific sectors: asset accumulation and net worth; housing markets; and demands for different forms and types of recreation. These areas were selected because they display different aspects of demographic change that are expected to impact business and are sufficiently diverse to suggest how widespread the implications of demographic change are likely to be.

IMPLICATIONS FOR CONSUMER EXPENDITURES
AND DISCRETIONARY INCOME

One of the keys to the impacts of demographic change on business is the effect that such change is likely to have on consumer expenditures. Although it is difficult to know how much money might be available for consumers to spend in the coming years, much can be learned by simply examining how the demographics of tomorrow will impact spending, if patterns of spending by demographic characteristics remain as they are today. Thus, the tables on consumer expenditures that follow were prepared by multiplying consumer expenditures for 1990 for various categories of expenditures and for households categorized by specific demographic characteristics by the number of households as projected in Chapter 5. The per capita consumer expenditures used in these projections were taken from the 1990 Consumer Expenditure Survey conducted by the U.S. Bureau of Labor Statistics (1991).

Impacts on Consumer Expenditures

Table 6.1 projects consumer expenditures by category for selected years from 1990 through 2050; Table 6.2 shows the percentage change in expenditures by decade and for the total period from 1990 through 2050. Although the percentage change in expenditures between categories is often similar, due to the fact that per capita measures were applied to a common base of projected population, we can nevertheless expect extensive consumer expenditures. Expenditures are projected to increase from $2.5 trillion in 1990 to more than $3.7 trillion in 2050.

The immigration base of future population growth will be important in determining the level of consumer expenditures. Total expenditures would be $700 billion less in 2050 if growth were restricted to that which would occur if the population experienced no immigration (see Reference Table 6.1). Overall, there would be 19.5 percent fewer dollars of consumer expenditures by 2050 if growth through immigration did not occur (comparing values in Reference Table 6.1 to those in text Table 6.1). These results suggest that the projected population growth will result in substantial growth in the volume of purchasing activity and that immigrants will be essential to developing significant growth in consumer expenditures.

The impact of changes in ethnicity and age on consumer expenditures is extensive as well. Data on patterns of expenditures among ethnic groups point to markedly different patterns of change among ethnic groups (see Reference Table 6.2). Under the middle scenario, the 1990-to-2050 pattern shows an increase of 12.0 percent for total Anglo expenditures, 108.9 percent for Blacks, 309.9 percent for Hispanics, and 441.5 percent for Other racial/ethnic groups. Clearly, growth in expenditures will reflect population change and be most extensive among minority groups.

As a result of such disparate rates of growth in expenditures among ethnic groups, the proportion of all expenditures accounted for by Anglo households would decline and that accounted for by minority groups would increase from 1990 to 2050. From 1990 to 2050, the proportion of expenditures accounted for by Anglos would decline from roughly 84 to 63 percent. However, the proportion accounted for by Blacks would increase from 7 to 10 percent, the proportion accounted for by Hispanics would increase from less than 6 to more than 15 percent,

Table 6.1: Consumer Expenditures by Category in the United States in 1990 and Projected to 2050 Under the Middle Scenario

Year	Total	Food	Housing	Alcohol	Apparel
1990	$2,501,623,506,367	$404,766,038,877	$772,538,459,292	$23,029,673,659	$121,750,975,098
2000	2,849,030,655,233	464,375,724,811	875,977,328,109	25,100,465,311	139,209,032,352
2030	3,458,705,913,078	585,116,176,714	1,076,181,788,916	28,401,299,066	163,644,501,268
2050	3,735,982,547,633	641,251,172,516	1,172,525,516,078	29,817,488,998	176,440,373,468

Year	Transportation	Health	Entertainment	Personal	Reading
1990	$469,243,143,552	$131,825,339,365	$124,651,509,578	$22,776,234,120	$14,347,121,878
2000	533,324,819,394	150,306,636,670	140,197,528,493	26,118,965,576	16,144,525,010
2030	634,154,059,269	203,534,250,566	159,562,396,788	33,579,856,070	19,439,557,494
2050	679,809,073,134	220,041,829,611	167,345,108,215	36,476,536,005	20,414,264,611

Year	Education	Tobacco	Miscellaneous	Cash	Insurance
1990	$33,841,482,389	$25,197,642,415	$37,634,450,034	$77,372,781,504	$242,648,654,606
2000	40,034,688,216	28,250,794,167	42,428,825,316	90,912,384,993	276,648,936,815
2030	45,123,287,650	32,936,664,231	51,656,431,192	114,178,093,612	311,197,550,242
2050	49,372,161,824	34,603,976,770	54,756,658,344	121,636,714,607	331,491,673,452

Table 6.2: Percent Change in Consumer Expenditures by Category in the United States for Selected Time Periods from 1990-2050 Under the Middle Scenario

Time Period	Total	Food	Alcohol	Housing	Apparel	Transportation	Health	Entertainment
1990-2000	13.9	14.7	9.0	13.4	14.3	13.7	14.0	12.5
2000-2010	9.0	10.2	6.5	8.7	8.0	8.9	11.3	7.4
2010-2020	6.4	8.0	4.4	7.2	4.9	5.3	11.6	4.0
2020-2030	4.7	5.9	1.7	5.5	3.7	3.7	9.0	1.9
2030-2040	4.0	4.7	2.2	4.5	3.6	3.5	4.7	2.0
2040-2050	3.9	4.7	2.8	4.3	4.0	3.5	3.3	2.8
1990-2050	49.3	58.4	29.5	51.8	44.9	44.9	66.9	34.3

Time Period	Personal	Reading	Education	Tobacco	Miscellaneous	Cash	Insurance
1990-2000	14.7	12.5	18.3	12.1	12.7	17.5	14.0
2000-2010	11.1	8.0	10.2	9.0	8.3	10.0	7.8
2010-2020	9.1	6.7	0.0	5.1	7.6	6.4	3.2
2020-2030	6.1	4.5	2.2	1.8	4.5	7.3	1.1
2030-2040	4.1	2.4	5.7	2.0	2.5	4.7	2.8
2040-2050	4.3	2.6	3.5	3.0	3.5	1.8	3.7
1990-2050	60.2	42.3	45.9	37.3	45.5	57.2	36.6

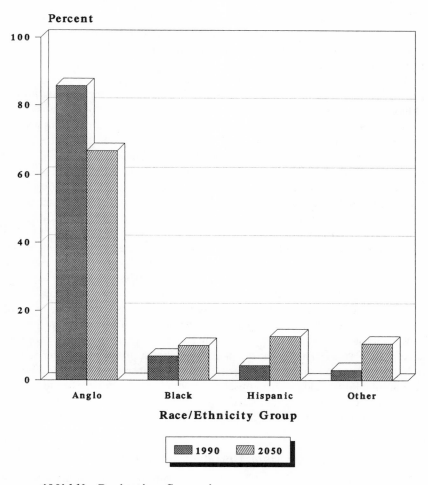

Percent

*Middle Projection Scenario

FIGURE 6.1   Consumer expenditures in the United States by race/ethnicity, 1990 and 2050.

and the proportion accounted for by Other racial/ethnic groups would increase from roughly 3 to roughly 12 percent (see Figure 6.1).

The level of expenditures by race/ethnicity also varies substantially among expenditure categories (see Reference Table 6.2). The proportion of expenditures more closely follows the relative population size of race/ethnicity groups for expenditures for basic items such as food and housing whereas Anglo dominance is greater for more discretionary items such as entertainment. These results suggest not only that overall population change is a key determinant of growth in expenditures, but also that differentials in expenditures by race/ethnicity are likely to create very different markets for basic necessity and discretionary items.

The data on expenditures by age of householder indicate that expenditures will be increasingly concentrated among older age groups (see Reference Table 6.3). From 1990 to 2050, expenditures among households with a householder who is 15 to 24 years of age are projected to increase by 22.8 percent, those among householders 25 to 34 years of age by 2.6 percent, those among 35- to 44-year-olds by 14.4 percent, those among 45- to 54-year-olds by 63.9 percent, those among 55- to 64-year-olds by 96.1 percent, those among 65- to 74-year-olds by 80.3 percent, and those among householders 75 years of age or older by 206.0 percent.

The proportion of all expenditures accounted for by older households increases rapidly. In 1990, 28.3 percent of all expenditures were among households with a householder 55 years of age or older but, by 2050, the figure reaches 39.9 percent (see Table 6.3). This pattern is especially apparent for specific categories of expenditures. For example, as might be expected, persons 55 years of age or older accounted for 48.0 percent of all health care expenditures in 1990; this would increase to 62.6 percent by 2050. Food expenditures show a very rapid increase among older consumers as well. In 1990, 23.3 percent of all food expenditures were to households with a householder under 35 years of age whereas 30.3 percent were to households with a householder who was 55 years of age or older. However, by 2050, these figures change markedly, to 16 and 42 percent respectively. Even for education, a category in which expenditures are generally concentrated among younger persons, substantial growth occurs among older households. In 2050, more than 57.7 percent of all expenditures for education would occur among households with a householder who is 45 years of age or older compared to 44.3 percent in 1990. In nearly all expenditure categories, there will be a substantial shift toward a larger proportion of aggregate expenditures occurring among older households.

Impacts on Discretionary Income

Businesses must also pay close attention to the amount of discretionary income among consumers. Recently, T. G. Exter (1993) estimated the proportion of households with discretionary income and the total level of discretionary income among households of different types. By subtracting average costs for housing, food, clothing, health, and other basic items from total income, he was able to estimate the proportion of households with discretionary income and average levels of discretionary income among all households and households categorized by the age and race/ethnicity of the householder. For this analysis, Exter's averages were multiplied by the projections of the number of households to project the number of households with discretionary income and the aggregate level of discretionary income among households by type. These results are presented in Table 6.4.

This table shows that discretionary income was highest among Anglos and among households with a householder of middle age in 1990. By 2050, although

Table 6.3: Percent of Consumer Expenditures by Category and Age of Householder in the United States in 1990 and Projected for 2050 Under the Middle Scenario

1990

Age of Householder	Total	Food	Alcohol	Housing	Apparel	Transportation	Health	Entertainment
15-24	3.2	3.3	7.0	3.0	4.1	3.7	1.4	3.2
25-34	21.1	20.0	28.1	22.8	21.4	22.5	13.6	22.1
35-44	27.3	26.8	26.2	27.9	30.4	26.5	20.4	28.9
45-54	20.1	19.6	16.7	18.6	20.8	21.4	16.5	20.7
55-64	13.9	14.2	12.2	13.0	13.2	13.7	16.1	14.4
65-74	9.3	10.6	7.1	9.1	7.1	8.4	18.3	8.0
75+	5.1	5.5	2.7	5.7	3.0	3.8	13.7	2.7

Age of Householder	Personal	Reading	Education	Tobacco	Miscellaneous	Cash	Insurance
15-24	2.9	2.6	11.5	4.2	2.6	1.0	2.0
25-34	17.8	18.6	17.4	21.5	18.7	10.5	22.6
35-44	24.7	27.0	25.7	25.5	29.5	23.2	31.3
45-54	19.0	18.6	29.6	20.4	17.4	24.4	22.9
55-64	15.6	14.2	13.1	16.0	14.6	14.6	15.2
65-74	13.1	12.4	1.2	9.4	11.8	13.8	5.1
75+	7.0	6.7	1.4	3.0	5.5	12.5	0.9

Table 6.3 (Continued)

Age of Householder	Total	Food	Alcohol	Housing	Apparel	Transportation	Health	Entertainment
				2050				
15-24	2.6	2.8	5.9	2.6	3.6	2.8	1.0	2.8
25-34	14.5	13.6	20.6	15.6	15.6	16.1	8.2	15.7
35-44	20.9	20.0	22.6	21.6	24.1	21.0	13.3	23.4
45-54	22.1	21.6	18.9	20.8	23.3	23.5	14.9	22.7
55-64	18.3	18.2	16.5	17.1	18.6	18.6	18.3	19.3
65-74	11.2	12.8	8.9	11.0	8.5	10.3	19.5	9.8
75+	10.4	11.1	6.6	11.6	6.4	7.7	24.9	6.4

Age of Householder	Personal	Reading	Education	Tobacco	Miscellaneous	Cash	Insurance
15-24	2.5	2.2	8.6	3.4	1.9	0.9	1.8
25-34	11.9	12.3	12.6	14.8	12.1	6.6	16.1
35-44	18.2	20.1	21.1	20.7	23.0	15.6	24.3
45-54	20.5	19.7	34.8	21.4	20.2	24.0	26.9
55-64	19.0	17.6	18.6	21.2	19.1	16.5	21.7
65-74	14.9	14.2	1.6	11.6	13.0	14.2	6.9
75+	13.0	14.0	2.7	7.0	10.7	22.2	2.4

Table 6.4: Projected Discretionary Income for Households in the United States and Proportion of Discretionary Income by Race/Ethnicity and Age of Householder, 1990 and 2050, Under the Middle Scenario

	1990	2000	2030	2050
Total Discretionary Income	638,154,178,448	706,755,961,721	886,187,630,225	945,191,927,820
Percent Distribution by Race/Ethnicity of Householder				
Anglo	88.3	85.6	77.7	71.6
Black	5.8	6.2	7.5	8.5
Hispanic	3.1	4.1	7.1	9.4
Other	2.8	4.1	7.7	10.5
Percent Distribution by Age of Householder				
15-24	2.8	2.5	2.3	2.3
25-34	19.4	14.4	12.8	12.9
35-44	24.7	25.4	19.9	18.9
45-54	21.4	27.2	22.8	22.9
55-64	17.2	16.9	20.5	21.6
65-74	9.6	8.3	13.7	11.5
75+	4.9	5.3	8.0	9.9

these general patterns would continue, there would be a substantial shift in discretionary income as a result of increases in the minority population and the aging of the population. The proportion of discretionary income accounted for by Anglos would shift from 88 percent in 1990 to 72 percent in 2050. Discretionary income among those households with a householder under the age of 35 would decline from more than 22 percent in 1990 to 15 percent in 2050, and the proportion accounted for by households with a householder 65 years of age or older would increase from 15 percent to 21 percent.

The data on discretionary income also suggest, however, that discretionary income will not show as large a shift toward minority households as total consumer spending. In 2050, whereas 67 percent of all expenditures would be by Anglos, they would hold nearly 72 percent of discretionary income. The proportions of total consumer expenditures and discretionary income by age tend to be closer, suggesting a counterbalancing of young and old age effects on nondiscretionary income. Whether examined in terms of total expenditures or discretionary income, it is evident that future demographic patterns will likely have substantial impacts on consumer spending patterns.

IMPLICATIONS FOR SELECTED BUSINESS SECTORS

Implications for Asset Accumulation

Changing demographics have received extensive attention as factors differentially impacting savings, spending, and other financial characteristics of nations across the world (Kotlikoff 1989; Masson and Tryon 1990; Heller and Hemming 1986; Heller 1989; Meyer 1992). One area likely to be so impacted is the level of asset accumulation and changes in net worth that occur in the population as a whole and among specific population segments. To examine these implications, data on average assets by age and race/ethnicity of households were obtained from the U.S. Bureau of the Census' Survey of Income and Program Participation for 1988 (Eargle 1990) and adjusted for inflation using the Consumer Price Index to obtain 1990 values. This adjustment makes the values consistent with the other 1990 base data used in this work.

Tables 6.5 and 6.6 suggest that asset accumulation may be substantially impacted by change in the race/ethnicity composition of the population if the assets of minority populations do not increase. Table 6.5 shows the projected change in net worth and assets for 1990 and 2050 and the percentage change in total aggregate net worth and assets by category. It is essential to note that the total increase in the number of households from 1990 to 2050 was 63.8 percent. This is important because percentage changes in asset items larger than 63.8 percent suggest that the projected changes in ethnic characteristics will lead to asset increases larger than those resulting simply from the increase in the number of households;

Table 6.5: Projected Net Worth and Assets in the United States in 1990 and 2050 Assuming Race/Ethnicity Effects Under the Middle Scenario

Categories of Assets	1990	2050	Percent Change 1990-2050
Net Worth	$9,042,991,426,100	$13,174,581,948,614	45.7
Interest-earning assets	5,190,634,937,132	7,164,169,611,051	38.0
Regular checking accounts	103,505,322,751	160,883,675,465	55.4
Stocks and mutual fund shares	2,481,460,823,513	3,554,559,821,608	43.2
Equity in business or profession	6,065,479,014,870	8,981,522,881,154	48.1
Equity in motor vehicles	612,064,804,729	951,951,103,102	55.5
Equity in own home	6,149,315,566,184	9,697,378,573,533	57.7
Rental property equity	7,820,506,512,591	12,069,365,865,808	54.3
Other real estate equity	3,627,037,217,872	5,684,664,293,424	56.7
U.S. Savings Bonds	282,522,043,017	417,702,768,790	47.9
IRA or KEOGH accounts	1,519,132,926,591	2,308,621,259,386	52.0
Other assets	3,553,982,819,305	4,775,651,579,465	34.4

percentage changes smaller than this value would suggest that the impact of compositional change was to cause assets to not keep pace with household growth.

An examination of the data in Table 6.5 suggests that the projected changes in asset accumulation would not keep pace with the overall level of growth in households. The percentage changes in all asset categories from 1990 to 2050 are smaller than the 63.8-percent increase in the number of households, suggesting that the increase in minority households, given a continuation in the limited assets of minorities, would lead to a decrease in average per-household assets. The average assets per household would decline from roughly $98,300 in 1990 to $87,500 in 2050.

The low levels of growth in assets are particularly evident in interest-earning assets, for which the projected growth of 38.0 percent is 26 percent less than that in the projected number of households, and in stocks and mutual funds, for which the growth is 43.2 percent compared to 63.8 percent for households (see Table 6.6). These are assets concentrated in Anglo households and thus are substantially impacted by the slower growth in Anglo households and faster growth in minority households because minority households have low average assets in these categories.

In these asset categories and in all others, however, there is a marked increase in the proportion of all assets held by minority populations. As shown in Table 6.6, the total amount of net worth held by minority populations would increase from 8.9 percent in 1990 to nearly 25 percent in 2050. For all asset types the proportion held by minorities increases by at least 10 percent from 1990 to 2050, with the largest increases being in the equity and real estate asset categories.

Table 6.6: Proportion of Net Worth and Assets in the United States by Race/Ethnicity of Householder, 1990 and 2050, Under the Middle Scenario

Year and Race/ Ethnicity	Net Worth	Interest-Earning Assets	Regular Checking Accounts	Stocks and Mutual Fund Shares	Equity in Business or Profession	Equity in Motor Vehicles
1990						
Anglo	91.1	94.9	84.9	92.8	89.2	85.2
Black	2.8	0.9	7.5	1.6	4.5	7.0
Hispanic	2.9	0.9	4.7	2.4	3.2	4.9
Other	3.2	3.3	2.9	3.2	3.1	2.9
Total	100.0	100.0	100.0	100.0	100.0	100.0
2050						
Anglo	75.2	82.6	65.6	77.9	72.4	65.8
Black	4.2	1.4	10.5	2.4	6.6	9.9
Hispanic	8.8	3.0	13.6	7.5	9.6	14.0
Other	11.8	13.0	10.3	12.2	11.4	10.3
Total	100.0	100.0	100.0	100.0	100.0	100.0

Year and Race/ Ethnicity	Equity in Own Home	Rental Property Equity	Other Real Estate Equity	U.S. Savings Bonds	IRA or KEOGH Accounts	Other Assets
1990						
Anglo	84.9	86.7	86.3	89.8	88.4	96.7
Black	6.5	5.3	4.9	3.9	3.9	0.0
Hispanic	5.7	5.0	5.8	3.2	4.6	0.0
Other	2.9	3.0	3.0	3.1	3.1	3.3
Total	100.0	100.0	100.0	100.0	100.0	100.0
2050						
Anglo	64.7	67.5	66.2	73.0	69.9	86.4
Black	9.0	7.6	6.8	5.7	5.7	0.0
Hispanic	16.2	14.3	16.6	9.9	13.4	0.0
Other	10.1	10.6	10.4	11.4	11.0	13.6
Total	100.0	100.0	100.0	100.0	100.0	100.0

Table 6.7: Projected Net Worth and Assets in the United States, 1990 and 2050, Assuming Age Effects Under the Middle Scenario

Categories of Assets	1990	2050	Percent Change 1990-2050
Net Worth	$9,373,494,783,431	$17,547,939,740,723	87.2
Interest-earning assets	5,235,656,381,965	10,268,220,057,485	96.1
Regular checking accounts	107,106,833,710	191,304,476,539	78.6
Stocks and mutual fund shares	2,596,439,889,567	5,088,614,328,322	96.0
Equity in business or profession	6,400,043,254,895	11,229,088,878,734	75.5
Equity in motor vehicles	627,975,123,211	1,047,001,639,120	66.7
Equity in own home	5,892,276,950,985	10,455,590,022,391	77.5
Rental property equity	7,352,749,678,410	12,901,801,593,793	75.5
Other real estate equity	3,605,560,317,639	6,046,913,185,073	67.7
U.S. Savings Bonds	321,579,028,239	660,262,297,812	105.3
IRA or KEOGH accounts	1,554,844,906,413	2,916,029,986,746	87.5
Other assets	3,666,812,173,446	6,998,328,080,738	90.9

Tables 6.7 and 6.8 show patterns for assets related to the age of householders. These data show that the aging of the population will have the effect of increasing assets relative to what would be produced under other age structures. Thus, when the percentage-change values in Table 6.7 are examined, it is evident that for all types of assets and for net worth, the percentage-change values are larger than the 63.8-percent increase projected for households from 1990 to 2050. Changes are particularly rapid for interest-earning assets, stocks and mutual funds, and savings bonds, with projected levels of increase nearing or exceeding 100 percent for each of these asset categories.

Table 6.8 also suggests that assets and net worth will be increasingly concentrated in older households. Whereas 53.5 percent of aggregate net worth was held by households with a householder 55 years of age or older in 1990, by 2050, that figure rises to 65 percent. Some assets would be particularly concentrated among the elderly. More than 73 percent of interest-earning assets, 73 percent of stocks and mutual funds, and 81 percent of assets in U.S. savings bonds would be held by persons 55 years of age or older in 2050.

Overall, the projected patterns suggest that the aging of the population should increase the volume of per-household savings relative to today. Thus, the average number of dollars of net worth per household increases from $101,944 in 1990 to $116,537 in 2050, the average in interest-earning assets increases from $56,942 to $68,192, the average assets in stocks and mutual funds increases from $28,238 to $33,794, and the average assets in savings bonds increases from $3,497 to $4,384.

The values for net worth and assets by race/ethnicity and age of householder shown above were projected by using average net worth and asset values for 1990

Table 6.8: Proportion of Net Worth and Assets in the United States in 1990 and 2050 by Age of Householder Under the Middle Scenario

Age	Net Worth	Interest-Earning Assets	Stocks and Regular Checking Accounts	Equity in Mutual Fund Shares	Equity Business or Profession	Equity in Motor Vehicles
			1990			
<35	7.8	10.2	17.9	7.5	16.7	20.7
35-44	18.5	13.8	17.9	15.4	19.9	23.3
45-54	20.2	14.1	16.4	15.2	19.2	19.1
55-64	21.5	17.9	18.2	19.8	18.6	16.8
65+	32.0	44.0	29.6	42.1	25.6	20.1
Total	100.0	100.0	100.0	100.0	100.0	100.0

Age	Equity in Own Home	Rental Property Equity	Other Real Estate Equity	U.S. Savings Bonds	IRA or KEOGH Accounts	Other Assets
<35	14.1	16.3	21.4	6.9	12.6	7.7
35-44	21.7	18.4	23.1	10.1	17.2	12.8
45-54	18.7	22.6	17.0	11.0	14.4	27.1
55-64	17.9	18.3	16.7	22.5	19.6	17.9
65+	27.6	24.4	21.8	49.5	36.2	34.5
Total	100.0	100.0	100.0	100.0	100.0	100.0

that were race/ethnicity-specific and age of householder-specific. Rates were not available that were both age- and race/ethnicity-specific. As a result, the sum of values across age groups does not equal the sum across race/ethnicity groups. Unfortunately, there is no way to resolve this problem with the data that are readily available. However, it nevertheless is possible to identify clear age and race/ethnicity effects on net worth and assets. In Table 6.9, net worth and asset values are examined relative to what they would be in 2050 assuming the number of households projected under the middle scenario for 2050 but age and race/ethnicity distributions as they were in 1990. A comparison of these values for 2050 to those projected for 2050 under the middle scenario allows one to identify the impacts of race/ethnicity and age effects on future net worth and assets.

On one hand the values in Table 6.9 show that the projected race/ethnicity structure in 2050 (see Panel A of Table 6.9) decreases net worth and interest-earning assets, stock and mutual fund holdings, equity in businesses, holdings in U.S. savings bonds, and assets in the "other" categories relative to what they would be if the 1990 distribution continued through 2050. For all other asset categories, the

Table 6.8 (Continued)

Age	Net Worth	Interest-Earning Assets	Regular Checking Accounts	Stocks and Mutual Fund Shares	Equity in Business or Profession	Equity in Motor Vehicles
			2050			
<35	4.6	5.8	11.1	4.2	10.5	13.7
35-44	12.0	8.6	12.2	9.6	13.8	17.0
45-54	18.4	12.2	15.6	13.2	18.7	19.5
55-64	22.9	18.1	20.3	20.1	21.1	20.1
65+	42.1	55.3	40.8	52.9	35.9	29.7
Total	100.0	100.0	100.0	100.0	100.0	100.0

Age	Equity in Own Home	Rental Property Equity	Other Real Estate Equity	U.S. Savings Bonds	IRA or KEOGH Accounts	Other Assets
<35	8.8	10.3	14.1	3.7	7.5	4.5
35-44	14.9	12.7	16.7	6.0	11.1	8.2
45-54	18.0	22.0	17.3	9.2	13.1	24.2
55-64	20.1	20.8	19.8	21.8	20.8	18.6
65+	38.2	34.2	32.1	59.3	47.5	44.5
Total	100.0	100.0	100.0	100.0	100.0	100.0

projected distribution leads to larger values than would exist under the 1990 distribution. Although having effects on some assets and net worth, these data suggest that the ethnicity effects are relatively small overall.

On the other hand, the projected age composition (see Panel B of Table 6.9) will increase assets substantially by 2050 compared to what they would be under the age structure of 1990. The 1990 distribution extended to 2050 would produce 21 percent less net worth than is projected for 2050 and all assets under the 1990 distribution are 11 to 28 percent less than projected. The aging of the population into middle age, where levels of savings are greater, leads to a substantial increase in assets and net worth.

Overall, Table 6.9 suggests that the projected race/ethnicity composition of the population will decrease some forms of assets and net worth in the future unless minority assets increase. The aging of households increases assets and net worth beyond what they would be otherwise. The effects of age are substantially larger than for race/ethnicity, suggesting that the pervasive effects of age will increase the levels of assets and net worth in the coming years despite rapid growth in mi-

Table 6.9: Projected Net Worth and Assets by Category in the United States in 2050 by Race/Ethnicity and Age of Householder Under the Middle Scenario and Assuming 1990 Distribution in 2050

Panel A: Race/Ethnicity of Householder

Categories of Assets	Assuming 1990 Distribution in 2050	Middle Scenario in 2050	Numerical Difference	Percent Difference
Net Worth	$13,402,107,662,925	$13,174,581,948,614	-227,525,714,311	-1.7
Interest-earning assets	7,692,747,343,054	7,164,169,611,051	-528,577,732,003	-7.4
Regular checking accounts	153,399,402,236	160,883,675,465	7,484,273,229	4.7
Stocks and mutual fund shares	3,677,633,158,213	3,554,559,821,608	-123,073,336,605	-3.5
Equity in business or profession	8,989,304,418,655	8,981,522,881,154	-7,781,537,501	-0.1
Equity in motor vehicles	907,106,733,066	951,951,103,102	44,844,370,036	4.7
Equity in own home	9,113,533,843,857	9,697,378,573,533	583,844,729,676	6.0
Rental property equity	11,622,780,474,854	12,069,365,865,808	446,585,390,954	3.7
Other real estate equity	5,375,427,333,821	5,684,664,293,424	309,236,959,603	5.4
U.S. Savings Bonds	418,709,988,681	417,702,768,790	-1,007,219,891	-0.2
IRA or KEOGH accounts	2,251,421,247,366	2,308,621,259,386	57,200,012,020	2.5
Other assets	5,267,157,529,205	4,775,651,579,465	-491,505,949,740	-10.3

Table 6.9 (Continued)

Panel B: Age of Householder

Categories of Assets	Assuming 1990 Distribution in 2050	Middle Scenario in 2050	Numerical Difference	Percent Difference
Net Worth	$13,891,928,051,909	$17,547,939,740,723	3,656,011,688,814	20.8
Interest-earning assets	7,759,471,087,704	10,268,220,057,485	2,508,748,969,781	24.4
Regular checking accounts	158,736,998,542	191,304,476,539	32,567,477,997	17.0
Stocks and mutual fund shares	3,848,037,148,399	5,088,614,328,322	1,240,577,179,923	24.4
Equity in business or profession	9,485,143,212,888	11,229,088,878,734	1,743,945,665,846	15.5
Equity in motor vehicles	930,686,518,913	1,047,001,639,120	116,315,120,207	11.1
Equity in own home	8,732,611,406,548	10,455,590,622,391	1,722,979,215,843	16.5
Rental property equity	10,897,095,680,548	12,901,801,593,793	2,004,705,913,245	15.5
Other real estate equity	5,343,597,631,056	6,046,913,185,073	703,315,554,017	11.6
U.S. Savings Bonds	476,594,144,075	660,262,297,812	183,668,153,737	27.8
IRA or KEOGH accounts	2,304,347,958,879	2,916,029,986,746	611,682,027,867	21.0
Other assets	5,434,375,552,586	6,998,328,080,738	1,563,952,528,152	22.3

nority populations that may inhibit the accumulation of assets because of the lack of resources available to minority households.

Implications for Housing Markets

Housing markets have shown substantial expansion in past decades as the baby-boom generation entered key household-formation ages. The impetus for much of this growth was the increase in the number of households and the change in the characteristics of such households that are described in Chapter 5. But what are the implications of such patterns for housing markets? In this section, we examine impacts on two dimensions of housing: the impacts of demographic change on housing tenure (that is, the number of owners and renters) and the impacts on total expenditures for owner and renter housing. The projections of the number of households by tenure were completed by multiplying the proportion of owners and renters by age and race/ethnicity in the 1990 Census by the projections of households shown in Chapter 5. The expenditures of owners and renters were projected by multiplying the consumer expenditures for owner and renter housing from the 1990 Consumer Expenditure Survey by the number of owner and renter households.

Tables 6.10 through 6.13 show the number of owner and renter households projected under the middle scenario. They suggest that demographic change will markedly impact tenure patterns, but more in terms of the characteristics of owners and renters than in terms of the total proportion of owner and renter households. Thus, the total ownership rate changes only slightly over the projection period, from 64.2 percent in 1990 to 63.0 percent in 2050.

Ownership rates are markedly higher among Anglos than among minority-group members. Whereas more than 69 percent of Anglo households were owner households in 1990, less than 44 percent of Black households, 42 percent of Hispanic households, and 53 percent of Other households were (see Table 6.11). Anglos are overrepresented among owners and underrepresented among renters: Anglos made up 86 percent of all homeowners and 69 percent of all renters in 1990 compared to 80 percent of all households (see Table 6.12). By 2050, Anglos would still account for 67 percent of owners but only 45 percent of renters. Given that Anglos would account for roughly 59 percent of all households in 2050, this suggests that Anglos will continue to be overrepresented among owners and underrepresented among renters in 2050 as they were in 1990, but that the overall increase in the minority population will lead to a larger proportion of both minority owners and minority renters.

It is important to note, however, that the ownership rate is projected to increase across time among all racial/ethnic groups. Ownership rates increase from roughly 69 percent in 1990 to 72 percent in 2050 among Anglos, from 44 percent to 49 percent among Blacks, from 42 to 48 percent among Hispanics, and from 53 to 56 percent among Other racial/ethnic groups (see Table 6.11). Roughly 64 percent of the net change in the number of owner households and 91 percent of the

Table 6.10: Projections of the Number of Households in the United States by Race/Ethnicity from 1990 to 2050 Under the Middle Scenario

Year	Anglo	Black	Hispanic	Other	Total
Total					
1990	73,633,749	9,766,771	6,001,718	2,545,172	91,947,410
2000	79,075,660	11,669,403	8,780,030	4,034,064	103,559,157
2010	83,490,865	13,583,055	11,788,209	5,723,360	114,585,489
2020	87,747,024	15,662,429	15,216,856	7,585,391	126,211,700
2030	90,039,719	17,595,191	18,941,957	9,593,312	136,170,179
2040	89,909,083	19,416,416	22,834,764	11,703,146	143,863,409
2050	88,487,070	21,367,923	26,845,356	13,878,080	150,578,429
Owner					
1990	50,860,725	4,276,707	2,545,584	1,341,795	59,024,811
2000	55,921,542	5,315,291	3,898,268	2,195,813	67,330,914
2010	59,834,712	6,390,261	5,431,597	3,169,200	74,825,770
2020	63,325,477	7,496,718	7,171,462	4,227,457	82,221,114
2030	64,987,024	8,506,299	9,043,736	5,365,854	87,902,913
2040	64,641,919	9,413,232	10,968,194	6,569,706	91,593,051
2050	63,721,547	10,397,110	12,972,537	7,818,680	94,909,874
Renter					
1990	22,773,024	5,490,064	3,456,134	1,203,377	32,922,599
2000	23,154,118	6,354,112	4,881,762	1,838,251	36,228,243
2010	23,656,153	7,192,794	6,356,612	2,554,160	39,759,719
2020	24,421,547	8,165,711	8,045,394	3,357,934	43,990,586
2030	25,052,695	9,088,892	9,898,221	4,227,458	48,267,266
2040	25,267,164	10,003,184	11,866,570	5,133,440	52,270,358
2050	24,765,523	10,970,813	13,872,819	6,059,400	55,668,555

net change in the number of renter households from 1990 to 2050 would be due to increases in minority households (see Figure 6.2). The fact that the proportion of minorities with lower overall rates of ownership increases faster than the Anglo population accounts for the apparent paradox that, although ownership increases within each ethnic group, the overall level of home ownership changes relatively little. This highlights the importance of analyzing patterns by demographic characteristics rather than only in terms of aggregate averages.

The impacts of aging are pervasive, leading to substantial increases in both the number of older owners and renters. As shown in Table 6.13, although renters would continue to be younger than owners, both owners and renters would age

Table 6.11: Projections of the Percent of Households in the United
States for Selected Years by Housing Tenure and
Race/Ethnicity Under the Middle Scenario

Year	Anglo	Black	Hispanic	Other	Total
Owner					
1990	69.1	43.8	42.4	52.7	64.2
2020	70.7	45.6	44.4	54.4	65.0
2010	71.7	47.1	46.1	55.4	65.3
2020	72.2	47.9	47.1	55.8	65.2
2030	72.2	48.3	47.7	55.9	64.6
2040	71.9	48.5	48.0	56.1	63.7
2050	72.0	48.7	48.3	56.3	63.0
Renter					
1990	30.9	56.2	57.6	47.3	35.8
2000	29.3	54.5	55.6	45.6	35.0
2010	28.3	53.0	53.9	44.6	34.7
2020	27.8	52.1	52.9	44.3	34.9
2030	27.8	51.7	52.3	44.1	35.5
2040	28.1	51.5	52.0	43.9	36.3
2050	28.0	51.3	51.7	43.7	37.0

rapidly over the projection period. On the one hand, more than 26 percent of owners and 17 percent of renters were 65 years of age or older in 1990, but by 2050, nearly 39 percent of owners and 32 percent of renters would be. On the other hand, 16.6 percent of owners and 45.7 percent of renters were under 35 years of age in 1990; by 2050, only 9.8 percent of owners and 32.4 percent of renters would be. Substantial differences would appear among racial/ethnic groups, with minority owners and renters remaining younger than Anglo owners and renters, but the households of both renters and owners in all racial/ethnic groups would age substantially.

The changing demographic characteristics of owners and renters would substantially impact the amount of funds likely to be spent on owner and renter housing. Tables 6.14 through 6.16 show the projected annual expenditures for owner and renter households, assuming 1990 per-household averages. These tables indicate that annual expenditures on housing will increase substantially for both owner and renter housing. Annual expenditures for owner-related housing would increase from $174 billion in 1990 to $259 billion in 2050, while expenditures for renter housing would increase from $52 billion to $92 billion.

Table 6.12: Projections of the Percent of Total Households in the United States by Race/Ethnicity of Householder and Housing Tenure from 1990-2050 Under the Middle Scenario

Year	Anglo	Black	Hispanic	Other
Total				
1990	80.1	10.6	6.5	2.8
2000	76.4	11.3	8.5	3.9
2010	72.9	11.9	10.3	5.0
2020	69.5	12.4	12.1	6.1
2030	66.1	12.9	13.9	7.1
2040	62.5	13.5	15.9	8.1
2050	58.8	14.2	17.8	9.2
Owner				
1990	86.2	7.3	4.3	2.3
2000	83.1	7.9	5.8	3.3
2010	80.0	8.5	7.3	4.2
2020	77.0	9.1	8.7	5.1
2030	73.9	9.7	10.3	6.1
2040	70.6	10.3	12.0	7.2
2050	67.1	11.0	13.7	8.2
Renter				
1990	69.2	16.7	10.5	3.7
2000	63.9	17.5	13.5	5.1
2010	59.5	18.1	16.0	6.4
2020	55.5	18.6	18.3	7.6
2030	51.9	18.8	20.5	8.8
2040	48.3	19.1	22.7	9.8
2050	44.5	19.7	24.9	10.9

Equally important to the magnitude of change, however, is the change that would occur among different ethnic and age groups. For example, as shown in Table 6.15, nearly 92 percent of all expenditures for owner housing were among Anglo households in 1990 but, by 2050, that proportion would decline to roughly 78 percent. Although 65 percent of all expenditures in renter households were in Anglo households in 1990, this would be reduced to less than 40 percent by 2050. Minority households would expend a majority of the resources for renter housing

Table 6.13: Percent of the Households in the United States by Age
and Race/Ethnicity in 1990 and the Projected Percent
of the Households in the United States by Age and
Race/Ethnicity for 2050 Under the Middle Scenario

Age Group	Anglo	Black	Hispanic	Other	Total
Total					
1990					
15-24	5.1	6.6	8.7	6.3	5.5
25-34	20.5	23.9	29.2	25.5	21.6
35-44	21.6	23.7	24.7	28.1	22.2
45-54	15.5	15.8	15.2	18.1	15.6
55-64	13.8	12.9	11.0	11.2	13.5
65-74	13.4	10.4	7.1	7.0	12.5
75+	10.1	6.7	4.2	3.7	9.2
Owner					
1990					
15-24	1.4	1.4	2.3	1.6	1.5
25-34	15.2	12.9	19.9	17.3	15.2
35-44	22.4	23.5	26.5	30.7	22.9
45-54	17.9	20.1	19.7	23.0	18.3
55-64	16.7	18.1	16.0	14.6	16.7
65-74	15.9	14.7	10.1	8.6	15.4
75+	10.5	9.3	5.5	4.2	10.1
Renter					
1990					
15-24	13.2	10.6	13.4	11.6	12.7
25-34	32.5	32.6	36.1	34.6	33.0
35-44	19.7	23.8	23.3	25.2	20.9
45-54	10.0	12.5	11.8	12.7	10.7
55-64	7.4	8.9	7.3	7.4	7.6
65-74	8.0	7.1	4.8	5.2	7.4
75+	9.2	4.6	3.2	3.3	7.6

by 2050 and increase their share of owner-related expenditures by 14 percent from 1990 to 2050.

Similarly, when examined by age, it is evident that expenditures would shift to older households over time (see Table 6.16). In fact, 46 percent of expenditures among owner households were among households with a householder less than 45 years of age in 1990 but, by 2050, this proportion would decline to less than 33 percent; for persons 45 years of age or older the increase would be from 54 percent in 1990 to 67 percent in 2050. For renter households, the proportion of expendi-

Table 6.13 (Continued)

Age Group	Anglo	Black	Hispanic	Other	Total
Total					
2050					
15-24	3.7	5.2	5.4	4.7	4.3
25-34	12.5	15.5	16.7	16.7	14.0
35-44	14.7	17.9	19.1	20.4	16.5
45-54	15.1	17.1	17.4	19.5	16.2
55-64	16.7	16.7	15.5	15.0	16.4
65-74	15.9	13.7	12.5	11.2	14.5
75+	21.5	13.8	13.5	12.5	18.1
Owner					
2050					
15-24	1.0	1.0	1.2	1.1	1.0
25-34	8.8	7.5	10.0	10.6	9.0
35-44	14.7	16.0	18.0	20.9	15.8
45-54	16.7	19.6	19.8	23.2	18.0
55-64	19.4	21.1	19.8	18.3	19.5
65-74	18.0	17.4	15.7	12.9	17.2
75+	21.4	17.3	15.5	13.0	19.5
Renter					
2050					
15-24	10.6	9.1	9.3	9.2	9.8
25-34	21.8	23.1	22.9	24.5	22.6
35-44	14.8	19.8	20.0	19.8	17.6
45-54	10.8	14.8	15.1	14.8	13.1
55-64	9.9	12.6	11.5	10.7	10.9
65-74	10.5	10.2	9.5	9.0	10.0
75+	21.6	10.4	11.6	11.8	15.9

tures among householders less than 45 years of age decreases from nearly 82 percent in 1990 to 69 percent in 2050; the proportion among households with a householder 45 years of age or older increases from 19 percent to 31 percent. Particularly pronounced is the increase in expenditures among those persons 65 years of age or older. The proportion of owner-related expenditures accounted for by those 65 years of age or older would increase from 16 percent in 1990 to 23 percent in 2050 and the proportion of renter-related expenditures would increase from 7 to 15 percent. Although owner expenditures would continue to be concen-

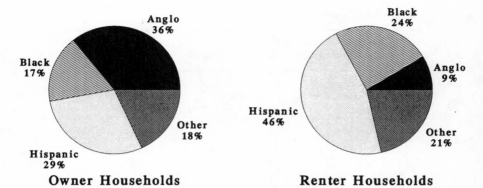

Owner Households   Renter Households

*Middle Projection Scenario

FIGURE 6.2   Net change of owners and renters by each ethnic group, 1990–2050 (middle projection scenario).

trated among older households and renter expenditures among younger households, there would be a marked shift toward a larger proportion of all expenditures being among older households.

Table 6.17 allows one to assess the overall effects of race/ethnicity and age of householders on owner and renter expenditures. In this table, the effects of race/ethnicity are examined separately from those for age because of the inability to obtain data that were both age- and race/ethnicity-specific so that the total projected expenditures differ for race/ethnicity and age effects. These data suggest that the projected race/ethnicity composition would increase expenditures for renter-related housing and decrease expenditures for owner-related housing compared to what they would be if the composition of 1990 prevailed in 2050. The projected effects of age are pervasive across both owner and renter households and would decrease the levels of household expenditures for both owner and renter households below what they would be if the 1990 distribution prevailed in 2050. Clearly, recent population conditions have been favorable for real estate expenditures although future patterns of minority population growth and the aging of the population may be less positive.

Impacts on Recreation

Recreational involvement has increased substantially over recent decades as both the number of participants and the range of recreational activities expand substantially (Clawson 1985; Kelly 1987). Recreational activities have been found to be related to demographic characteristics (Loomis and Ditton 1988; Murdock et al. 1990, 1991b, 1992) and demographic characteristics are projected to be increasingly important to recreational activities in the coming years (Murdock et al. 1993).

Table 6.14: Projected Aggregate Annual
Expenditures for Housing in the
United States by Housing
Tenure from 1990-2050 Under
the Middle Scenario

Year	Total
	Owner
1990	$174,234,747,876
2000	196,300,338,974
2010	215,438,510,888
2020	233,855,248,580
2030	246,813,415,960
2040	253,584,346,486
2050	258,910,528,142
	Renter
1990	$52,448,143,745
2000	58,247,193,569
2010	64,391,644,089
2020	71,710,835,769
2030	79,142,023,353
2040	86,206,678,844
2050	92,405,589,451

Tables 6.18 through 6.20 show projections for various recreational activities by the race/ethnicity of the participants. They were completed by multiplying recreational participation rates by age, sex, and race/ethnicity developed from various sources (Market Opinion Research 1986; Texas Parks and Wildlife 1986; Murdock et al. 1993) by the projections of population noted in Chapter 3. These values refer to persons participating in an activity at least once a year. They do not indicate total days of participation but simply the number of persons involved in a given activity annually.

Participation in some recreational activities tends to be associated with the larger personal resource bases necessary to afford participation in such activities. Since financial resources are more limited for minorities, the more rapid growth projected for minority populations and the slower growth in Anglo populations leads to generally slower increases in participation than in population growth. The total population is projected to increase by 53.9 percent from 1990 to 2050 but, as Table 6.19 suggests, only one recreational activity is projected to increase

Table 6.15: Projected Percent of Annual Expenditures for Housing in the United States by Race/Ethnicity and Housing Tenure from 1990-2050 Under the Middle Scenario

Year	Anglo	Black	Hispanic	Other
Owner				
1990	92.0	3.5	2.1	2.4
2000	89.7	3.9	2.9	3.5
2010	87.5	4.3	3.6	4.6
2020	85.3	4.6	4.4	5.7
2030	82.9	5.0	5.2	6.9
2040	80.3	5.3	6.2	8.2
2050	77.5	5.8	7.2	9.5
Renter				
1990	64.7	19.6	12.3	3.4
2000	59.2	20.4	15.7	4.7
2010	54.7	20.9	18.5	5.9
2020	50.7	21.3	21.0	7.0
2030	47.1	21.5	23.4	8.0
2040	43.6	21.7	25.8	8.9
2050	39.9	22.2	28.1	9.8

by that amount. Thus, one major finding from this analysis is that growth in recreational industries could be decreased relative to historical levels unless minority levels of participation increase.

Because of the different rates of involvement of racial/ethnic groups in these activities, and the differences projected in rates of population growth among racial/ethnic groups, involvement in activities that are most dependent on Anglo involvement tend to grow particularly slowly during the projection period. This is accentuated when the activities are ones that largely involve younger persons because of the more rapid aging of the Anglo population. Such activities as backpacking, which increases by only 23.1 percent from 1990 to 2050; tennis, which increases by 27.2 percent; and golf, which increases by 29.7 percent, are among those activities with the slowest growth. Whereas growth in recreational activities will be slower than overall population growth in all but one recreational area, it will be particularly slow for some recreational activities.

Table 6.16: Projected Proportion of Annual Expenditures for Housing in the United
States from 1990-2050 by Age of Householder Under the Middle
Scenario

Year	15-24	25-34	35-44	45-54	55-64	65-74	75+
			Total				
1990	4.4	21.7	28.4	19.3	12.6	8.5	5.0
2000	4.0	16.3	29.3	24.9	12.5	7.5	5.5
2010	4.2	15.4	23.2	26.8	16.9	8.0	5.6
2020	3.8	16.1	22.2	21.8	18.7	11.2	6.2
2030	3.9	15.0	23.3	21.1	15.4	12.6	8.6
2040	3.9	15.2	21.9	22.5	15.2	10.6	10.8
2050	3.9	15.4	22.1	21.2	16.2	10.5	10.7
			Owner				
1990	0.2	14.2	31.7	23.1	15.4	10.3	5.2
2000	0.1	10.1	31.7	28.9	14.8	8.7	5.6
2010	0.1	9.4	24.7	30.9	20.0	9.3	5.7
2020	0.1	9.8	23.6	25.1	22.1	13.0	6.3
2030	0.1	8.9	24.9	24.4	18.3	14.7	8.8
2040	0.1	9.0	23.4	26.1	18.1	12.4	11.0
2050	0.1	9.0	23.6	24.6	19.4	12.4	10.9
			Renter				
1990	18.0	45.5	18.1	7.4	3.8	3.1	4.2
2000	17.7	38.1	21.2	10.6	4.2	3.1	5.1
2010	18.5	36.7	17.8	12.2	5.9	3.4	5.4
2020	16.8	38.3	17.1	10.3	6.8	4.8	5.9
2030	16.7	35.7	18.1	10.1	5.8	5.5	8.1
2040	16.4	35.5	17.1	10.7	5.7	4.7	10.0
2050	15.8	35.6	17.4	10.3	6.2	4.7	10.0

Tables 6.18 and 6.19 also suggest that for all recreational activities there will be an increase in the total number of participants but that increased participation will be most extensive for minority populations. In fact, for 13 of the 16 recreational activities examined here, the number of Anglo participants decreases during the total projection period from 1990 to 2050, while minority involvement increases for all recreational activities.

As a result of these changes, the proportion of all participants who would be minority increases for all recreational activities. For example, from 1990 to 2050 (see Table 6.20), the proportion of all participants in softball who would be minority increases by 26.2 percent, the proportion in basketball increases by 24.7 percent, and the proportion in baseball increases by 26 percent. By 2050, minority

Table 6.17: Projected Annual Expenditures for Housing by Tenure for the United States in 2050
Assuming Projected Patterns by Race/Ethnicity and Age of Householder Under the
Middle Scenario and Assuming 1990 Distributions in 2050

Housing Tenure	Assuming 1990 Distribution in 2050	Middle Scenario in 2050	Numerical Difference	Percent Difference
	Race/Ethnicity of Householder			
Owner	$280,163,505,960	$258,910,528,142	$-21,252,977,818	-8.2
Renter	85,354,839,807	92,405,589,451	7,050,749,644	7.6
Total	365,518,345,757	351,316,117,593	-14,202,228,174	-4.0
	Age of Householder			
Owner	$296,239,701,332	$274,516,462,189	$-21,723,239,143	-7.9
Renter	98,507,320,536	86,386,827,398	-12,120,493,138	-14.0
Total	394,747,021,868	360,903,289,587	-33,843,732,281	-9.4

populations would account for a majority of participants for 7 of 16 activities and
for at least 40 percent of all participants for all but three activities. Minority participation will be increasingly important to the recreational industry in the coming years.

Tables 6.21 and 6.22 highlight the impact of the aging of the population on recreational activities. They show that some activities are largely activities of the
young but also that, even for these activities, there is likely to be an aging of the
population of participants in the coming decades. Activities such as backpacking,
jogging, softball, baseball, football, basketball, and tennis were young-adult activities in 1990. For all activities, however, the largest percentage increases in the
number of participants over the projection period are for persons 50 years of age
or older, with particularly large increases being evident among those who are 70
years of age or older. As a result of these patterns, the proportion of all participants who are older increases for all activities, with such activities as birdwatching, walking, golf, and nature studies having more than 30 percent of their
participants being 50 years of age or older in 2050. Not only will activities concentrated in younger populations grow more slowly, but it is also evident that even
for such activities the number of older participants will increase.

Table 6.23 provides a final means of examining the implications of demographic change for recreational participation. This table shows projections of the
number of persons participating in each recreational activity in 2050 under the
middle scenario and the number that would participate if the age and race/eth-
nicity distribution of 1990 were to prevail in 2050. The data indicate those areas in
which involvement is higher and those areas in which it is lower as a result of demographic change. Backpacking, birdwatching, hunting, camping, walking, ten-

Table 6.18: Projections of the Number of Participants in Selected Recreational Activities in the United States in 1990 and 2050 by Race/Ethnicity of Participant Under the Middle Scenario

Recreational Activity	Anglo	Black	Hispanic	Other	Total
		1990			
Backpacking	41,060,827	3,648,260	3,636,569	2,045,900	50,391,556
Bird-watching	61,690,707	9,258,313	6,893,836	2,767,626	80,610,482
Hunting	44,009,424	4,767,367	2,865,839	2,188,263	53,830,893
Camping	62,141,865	7,629,690	6,245,874	3,289,098	79,306,527
Walking	155,466,606	24,345,507	18,545,385	7,306,973	205,664,471
Bicycling	49,850,621	9,863,118	7,477,871	2,673,402	69,865,012
Jogging	29,801,158	7,921,725	6,715,260	1,614,923	46,053,066
Softball	26,249,705	6,272,142	5,119,624	1,415,127	39,056,598
Baseball	12,961,812	3,395,500	3,456,948	722,251	20,536,511
Football	14,604,455	3,702,372	3,336,114	820,491	22,463,432
Basketball	21,434,166	7,247,715	4,460,951	1,183,414	34,326,246
Tennis	23,137,559	2,584,925	2,434,050	1,228,406	29,384,940
Golf	22,365,390	978,352	1,144,322	1,078,969	25,567,033
Nature Studies	25,266,978	1,616,268	2,246,690	1,204,280	30,334,216
Freshwater Fishing	65,726,693	6,719,856	5,079,794	3,249,598	80,775,941
Saltwater Fishing	19,567,567	2,331,114	3,266,332	954,710	26,119,723

Table 6.18 (Continued)

Recreational Activity	Anglo	Black	Hispanic	Other	Total
		2050			
Backpacking	36,213,750	6,398,805	10,950,535	8,480,447	62,043,537
Bird-watching	68,748,963	18,703,438	26,240,914	14,081,349	127,774,664
Hunting	43,643,842	8,895,148	9,441,333	9,922,304	71,902,627
Camping	56,293,134	13,988,806	20,020,889	13,838,184	104,902,627
Walking	164,206,045	47,250,382	66,337,727	35,266,746	313,060,900
Bicycling	45,436,771	17,174,223	22,900,799	11,326,259	96,838,052
Jogging	25,969,836	13,842,798	20,636,880	6,701,168	67,150,682
Softball	22,642,065	10,957,869	15,707,154	5,822,639	55,129,727
Baseball	11,405,798	5,981,652	10,288,434	2,983,017	30,658,901
Football	12,619,228	6,369,568	9,773,993	3,356,068	32,118,857
Basketball	18,574,465	12,335,633	13,240,349	4,891,334	49,041,781
Tennis	20,466,974	4,293,683	7,434,596	5,179,971	37,375,224
Golf	22,113,755	2,151,674	3,928,983	4,960,540	33,154,952
Nature Studies	26,263,443	3,140,016	7,699,792	5,712,566	42,815,817
Freshwater Fishing	64,736,691	13,256,161	17,043,374	14,755,512	109,791,738
Saltwater Fishing	19,295,289	4,808,712	11,121,391	4,381,683	39,607,075

Table 6.19: Percent Change in the Number of Participants in Selected Recreational Activities in the United States from 1990 to 2050 by Race/Ethnicity of the Participant Under the Middle Scenario

Recreational Activity	Anglo	Black	Hispanic	Other	Total
Backpacking	-11.8	75.4	201.1	314.5	23.1
Bird-watching	11.4	102.0	280.6	408.8	58.5
Hunting	-0.8	86.6	229.4	353.4	33.6
Camping	-9.4	83.3	220.5	320.7	31.3
Walking	5.6	94.1	257.7	382.6	52.2
Bicycling	-8.9	74.1	206.2	323.7	38.6
Jogging	-12.9	74.7	207.3	315.0	45.8
Softball	-13.7	74.7	206.8	311.5	41.2
Baseball	-12.0	76.2	197.6	313.0	49.3
Football	-13.6	72.0	193.0	309.0	43.0
Basketball	-13.3	70.2	196.8	313.3	42.9
Tennis	-11.5	66.1	205.4	321.7	27.2
Golf	-1.1	119.9	243.3	359.7	29.7
Nature Studies	3.9	94.3	242.7	374.4	41.1
Freshwater Fishing	-1.5	97.3	235.5	354.1	35.9
Saltwater Fishing	-1.4	106.3	240.5	359.0	51.6

nis, golf, nature studies, and freshwater fishing all have fewer participants under the projected patterns than would be the case under the 1990 distribution. This is because these are activities with higher percentages of Anglo and young participants and Anglo populations are projected to grow more slowly and age more rapidly than minority populations. The fact that a larger proportion of future participants is projected to be both minority-group members and older will impact recreational markets.

SUMMARY AND IMPLICATIONS OF DEMOGRAPHIC CHANGE FOR AMERICAN BUSINESS

American business will be markedly affected by the demographic changes that will occur in the nation in the coming decades. Although only a few of the many implications are examined in this chapter, analyses of the potential effects of demographic change relative to consumer expenditures and discretionary income, asset accumulation and net worth, housing, and recreational activity suggest the following:

1. Consumer expenditures will increase substantially during the projection period as a result of population growth. The aggregate increase in annual consumer expenditures would be from $2.5 trillion in 1990 to $3.7 trillion in 2050.

Table 6.20: Projections of the Proportion of Participants in Selected
Recreational Activities in the United States in 1990 and 2050 by
Race/Ethnicity of the Participant Under the Middle Scenario

Recreational Activity	Anglo	Black	Hispanic	Other
1990				
Backpacking	81.5	7.2	7.2	4.1
Bird-watching	76.5	11.5	8.6	3.4
Hunting	81.7	8.9	5.3	4.1
Camping	78.4	9.6	7.9	4.1
Walking	75.6	11.8	9.0	3.6
Bicycling	71.4	14.1	10.7	3.8
Jogging	64.7	17.2	14.6	3.5
Softball	67.2	16.1	13.1	3.6
Baseball	63.2	16.5	16.8	3.5
Football	64.9	16.5	14.9	3.7
Basketball	62.5	21.1	13.0	3.4
Tennis	78.7	8.8	8.3	4.2
Golf	87.5	3.8	4.5	4.2
Nature Studies	83.3	5.3	7.4	4.0
Freshwater Fishing	81.4	8.3	6.3	4.0
Saltwater Fishing	74.9	8.9	12.5	3.7

Recreational Activity	Anglo	Black	Hispanic	Other
2050				
Backpacking	58.4	10.3	17.6	13.7
Bird-watching	53.9	14.6	20.5	11.0
Hunting	60.7	12.4	13.1	13.8
Camping	54.1	13.4	19.2	13.3
Walking	52.4	15.1	21.2	11.3
Bicycling	47.0	17.7	23.6	11.7
Jogging	38.7	20.6	30.7	10.0
Softball	41.0	19.9	28.5	10.6
Baseball	37.2	19.5	33.6	9.7
Football	39.4	19.8	30.4	10.4
Basketball	37.8	25.2	27.0	10.0
Tennis	54.7	11.5	19.9	13.9
Golf	66.6	6.5	11.9	15.0
Nature Studies	61.4	7.3	18.0	13.3
Freshwater Fishing	59.0	12.1	15.5	13.4
Saltwater Fishing	48.7	12.1	28.1	11.1

Table 6.21: Percent Change in the Number of Participants in Selected Recreational Activities in the United States from 1990 to 2050 by Age of Participant Under the Middle Scenario

Recreational Activity	Total	< 30	30-39	40-49	50-59	60-69	70+
Backpacking	23.1	19.5	1.8	34.6	91.7	88.2	181.7
Bird-watching	58.5	31.0	14.8	42.8	99.3	90.9	181.3
Hunting	33.6	18.9	4.1	30.4	84.7	87.2	201.1
Camping	31.3	23.0	5.1	38.6	106.1	137.2	204.5
Walking	52.2	31.0	14.8	42.8	99.4	91.6	182.4
Bicycling	38.6	35.7	13.1	42.6	108.4	77.6	186.1
Jogging	45.8	41.5	23.6	55.7	147.0	145.0	318.3
Softball	41.2	37.5	16.6	61.7	127.4	162.7	245.2
Baseball	49.3	47.7	30.2	62.4	187.0	158.7	153.7
Football	43.0	40.7	27.6	80.9	177.1	195.8	178.4
Basketball	42.9	40.2	24.9	68.5	151.7	157.5	159.0
Tennis	27.2	24.2	10.5	31.9	98.3	106.0	148.8
Golf	29.7	10.9	0.6	28.9	77.7	80.4	188.3
Nature Studies	41.1	22.8	7.7	36.0	88.4	80.5	157.2
Freshwater Fishing	35.9	20.5	6.7	33.1	88.1	85.5	199.1
Saltwater Fishing	51.6	34.1	20.4	51.4	110.7	97.6	227.5

2. Through its impact on population growth, immigration will play a major role in the growth of expenditures. Immigrants and their descendants would account for nearly $700 billion in consumer spending in 2050.

3. Anglos accounted for 84 percent of consumer expenditures in 1990 but would account for only 63 percent by 2050, a proportional decline of 21 percent. The increase in expenditures from 1990 to 2050 among Blacks would be 109 percent, among Hispanics 310 percent, and among Other racial/ethnic groups 442 percent.

4. Differentials in the proportion of expenditures accounted for by different racial/ethnic groups is most extensive for nonbasic items such as entertainment; expenditures for items such as food and housing more closely reflect the size of the populations involved.

5. The aging of the population will also impact consumer expenditures. By 2050, 40 percent of all expenditures would be made by persons 55 years of age or older compared to 28 percent in 1990. By contrast, the proportion of all spending accounted for by households with a householder under 35 years of age would decline from 24 percent in 1990 to 17 percent in 2050.

6. Discretionary income will also be affected by change in ethnicity and age. Although discretionary income is more concentrated among Anglos and middle-aged adult households than are expenditures, the proportion of discretionary income involving minority households would increase from 12 to 28 percent from 1990 to 2050 and the proportion of all discretionary income accounted for by those 65 years of age or older would increase from 14 to 21 percent.

7. Asset accumulation and the net worth of households will also reflect demographic changes shifting toward larger proportions of net worth and assets going

Table 6.22: Projections of the Proportions of Participants in Selected Recreational Activities in the United States in 1990 and 2050 by Age of Participant Under the Middle Scenario

Recreational Activity	<30	30-39	40-49	50-59	60-69	70+
			1990			
Backpacking	67.03	17.99	9.07	2.88	1.65	1.38
Bird-watching	38.81	17.24	13.28	10.11	10.06	10.50
Hunting	54.95	16.14	11.09	8.55	5.89	3.38
Camping	62.08	19.29	9.64	4.41	2.51	2.06
Walking	45.20	17.47	12.35	9.07	8.49	7.41
Bicycling	68.55	16.25	7.73	3.50	2.31	1.66
Jogging	67.24	18.30	9.42	3.12	1.38	0.54
Softball	66.68	20.57	7.42	3.16	1.43	0.74
Baseball	75.36	15.26	6.78	1.51	0.44	0.64
Football	81.49	12.38	4.65	1.06	0.24	0.18
Basketball	74.04	16.50	6.50	1.76	0.96	0.25
Tennis	59.66	21.98	12.24	3.71	1.65	0.76
Golf	42.46	22.69	14.71	8.08	7.71	4.35
Nature Studies	45.18	18.39	13.15	8.48	7.89	6.91
Freshwater Fishing	48.93	19.67	12.97	8.04	6.59	3.79
Saltwater Fishing	45.05	20.17	16.20	8.68	6.41	3.49

Recreational Activity	<30	30-39	40-49	50-59	60-69	70+
			2050			
Backpacking	65.04	14.88	9.92	4.48	2.53	3.15
Bird-watching	32.08	12.48	11.97	12.71	12.12	18.64
Hunting	48.90	12.57	10.83	11.83	8.25	7.61
Camping	58.14	15.44	10.18	6.92	4.54	4.78
Walking	38.92	13.17	11.59	11.88	10.69	13.75
Bicycling	67.14	13.26	7.95	5.26	2.97	3.43
Jogging	65.27	15.52	10.06	5.29	2.32	1.54
Softball	64.95	16.99	8.50	5.09	2.66	1.81
Baseball	74.56	13.31	7.38	2.90	0.76	1.09
Football	80.17	11.05	5.88	2.05	0.51	0.35
Basketball	72.63	14.43	7.66	3.09	1.74	0.46
Tennis	58.26	19.10	12.69	5.78	2.67	1.49
Golf	36.30	17.61	14.62	11.07	10.72	9.67
Nature Studies	39.30	14.03	12.66	11.32	10.09	12.60
Freshwater Fishing	43.37	15.45	12.70	11.13	9.00	8.35
Saltwater Fishing	39.85	16.02	16.17	12.07	8.35	7.54

Table 6.23: Projected Number of Participants in Selected Recreational Activities in the United States in 2050 Under the Middle Scenario and Assuming 1990 Race/Ethnicity and Age of Householder Distributions in 2050

Activity	Assuming 1990 Distribution in 2050	Middle Scenario in 2050	Numerical Difference	Percent Difference
Backpacking	67,659,814	62,043,537	-5,616,277	-9.1
Bird-watching	128,177,581	127,774,664	-402,917	-0.3
Hunting	77,707,853	71,902,627	-5,805,226	-8.1
Camping	108,449,773	104,902,627	-3,547,146	-3.4
Walking	313,512,352	313,060,900	-451,452	-0.1
Bicycling	96,094,899	96,838,052	743,153	0.8
Jogging	61,521,884	67,150,682	5,628,798	8.4
Softball	51,732,717	55,129,727	3,397,010	6.2
Baseball	27,821,024	30,658,901	2,837,877	9.3
Football	29,968,340	32,118,857	2,150,517	6.7
Basketball	45,641,922	49,041,781	3,399,859	6.9
Tennis	39,261,302	37,375,224	-1,886,078	-5.0
Golf	36,984,188	33,154,952	-3,829,236	-11.5
Nature Studies	45,825,560	42,815,817	-3,009,743	-7.0
Freshwater Fishing	116,848,663	109,791,738	-7,056,925	-6.4
Saltwater Fishing	37,833,178	39,607,075	1,773,897	4.5

to minority and older households. For example, the proportion of aggregate net worth accounted for by minorities increases from about 9 percent in 1990 to 25 percent in 2050; households with a householder 55 years of age or older controlled 54 percent of all net worth in 1990 but would control 65 percent by 2050. Because of the small size of assets among minority populations and the larger proportion of assets held by older households, the growth in the proportion of the population that is minority decreases asset growth while the aging of the population promotes asset growth over the coming decades. However, the effects of age are stronger than those for ethnicity, suggesting overall growth in future assets and savings.

8. Housing will be affected by demographic change. Rates of ownership will increase for all racial/ethnic groups as a result of the facts that older persons are more likely to be owners than younger persons and that populations in all racial/ethnic groups are aging. However, faster rates of growth in minority populations, who have lower rates of ownership, will cause overall levels of ownership to grow less rapidly. The counterbalancing of the aging and ethnic effects leads to relative stability in the overall rate of ownership but to substantial changes in the composition of owner and renter households. From 1990 to 2050, the proportion of all owner households who are Anglo declines from 86 percent to 67 percent and the proportion of Anglo renter households declines from 69 to 44 percent. The proportion of older households increases among both owners and renters. Whereas 26 percent of owners and 17 percent of renters were 65 years of age or older in 1990, 39 percent of owners and 32 percent of renters would be 65 years of age or older in 2050.

9. Housing expenditures would show similar patterns to those noted for tenure but would grow extensively in numerical terms. Expenditures for owner-related housing would increase from $174 billion in 1990 to $259 billion in 2050; expenditures for renter housing would increase from $52 to $92 billion. Expenditures are especially concentrated among Anglos, who accounted for 92 percent of all owner expenditures and 65 percent of renter expenditures in 1990. By 2050, the Anglo proportion would decline respectively to 78 and 40 percent. Similarly, expenditures will shift to older households, with persons 45 years of age or older accounting for 67 percent of owner-related expenditures in 2050 compared to 54 percent in 1990 and for 31 percent of renter-related expenditures in 2050 compared to 18 percent in 1990. Both the changing ethnic and age compositions of the future would tend to decrease expenditures on housing relative to those that would prevail if the age and ethnic composition of 1990 existed in 2050.

10. Recreational participation will experience marked impacts due to demographic change. In general, growth in involvement in formal recreational activities will not keep pace with growth in population. An examination of 16 different recreational activities indicates that the number of participants in only one activity (birdwatching) would increase faster than population. Slow growth occurs because participation in formal recreational activities is concentrated among the

young and Anglos and population patterns point to faster growth among older and minority population segments. Growth is particularly slow in such activities as backpacking, tennis, and golf. Recreational involvement will show the same patterns as for other factors examined, however, in that involvement by minority and older persons will increase rapidly. By 2050, minority populations would account for a majority of participants in 7 of 16 activities and for more than 40 percent of all participants in 13 of 16 activities. Similarly, for all activities, rates of increase in the number of participants are larger for age groups 50 years of age or older than for younger age groups.

The specific areas discussed in this chapter merely illustrate some of the many effects that future demographics will have on American business. The information here and in previous chapters suggests many of the important implications that demographic change is likely to have for business in the United States in the coming decades. Some of these implications are discussed below.

As noted in the second chapter, a basic demographic reality, one facing all businesses in the United States, is that the United States is a shrinking segment of the entire international market for goods and services. The population of the United States represented only 4.6 percent of the world's population in 1992 and it is projected to be less than 4.0 percent by 2020. As a result, for many businesses in the United States the fastest-growing markets will be those in other nations. For many firms their futures are determined not only by events in the United States but by events in the world. At the same time, firms located and/or operating in the United States will be impacted by the events shaping its population. Direct impacts such as those on markets or indirect impacts such as those on service demands and tax revenues to pay for such services will impact nearly all firms. It is essential to recognize, then, that domestic demographic change will be especially important to businesses operating largely within the United States and that, even for the most internationally oriented firms in the United States, the demographic patterns of the nation will remain of importance.

The general expectation of slower growth in the U.S. population and in households points to slower growing markets for many products and services. Markets for goods and services that expand largely as a function of the number of persons or households may find that future growth is more difficult to obtain. It is likely as well that such growth will be increasingly localized. Although this work largely examines change at the national level, growth will likely occur in only some regions and will not be uniform across the nation. Demographic analyses of such growth differentials will remain essential to business analyses.

The change in the labor force described in Chapter 4 will also bear on American business. These projections suggested that the workforce will grow more slowly than it has in recent history, will be older, and, if historical relationships between opportunities for education and minority status continue, may be less well educated than previously. This suggests that businesses may need to seek means to retain workers more effectively, be prepared to shift labor demands toward older workers, and put additional resources into worker training. It should also be recognized that the needs of an older population for greater health care and retirement benefits will likely also impact the workforces of American businesses.

Several aspects of the changing labor force should also provide opportunities for business to obtain skilled workers, however. The growth in women's participation in the workforce will continue to create a new pool of talent for jobs across a spectrum of occupations. Individual businesses should take steps to make maximum use of this growing segment. Another population segment with substantial expertise that is likely to be available for employment, at least during the next 20 years, is that of middle-aged managers and other skilled employees. As pointed out in Chapter 4, the aging of the large baby-boom, which has experienced limited opportunities for advancement due to extensive competition, may create a pool of skilled workers for many positions. The dissatisfaction and frustration resulting from limited opportunities for advancement may, while creating problems for some businesses in retaining employees, create opportunities for other industries to obtain skilled managers at very competitive prices. In sum, then, the demographic impacts on the labor force may have substantial implications for business.

The projected change in households discussed in Chapter 5 may also affect business. For example, the increasing fragmentation of households is likely to create an increasing number of households where a single parent will need to divide his or her time and loyalties between family and work. In fact, it is likely that changes in household composition will create increased demands for services and employee benefits to help supplement services traditionally provided by families. This includes both services related to children as well as services related to the middle-aged and the elderly. The present patterns continued into the future will result in fewer elderly persons having children to assist them as they age and fewer family members to provide social and financial support. Businesses aimed at providing alternatives to family-based services for those without families will grow in the coming decades.

The specific demographic changes examined in this chapter will also markedly affect how businesses operate. Many will need to develop products and services that are more clearly oriented to minority and older customers. Recreational industries, for example, may need to increase minority participation during the early years of life when many recreational preferences and practices are adopted and may need to reduce the physical exertion related to some activities to allow participation by older people. Markets for food products are already being carefully segmented to serve specific ethnic markets but these markets are likely to experience even more segmentation. Entertainment and apparel industries, for which expenditure data suggest expenditures are more discretionary than in many other areas, may need to develop additional low-cost alternatives for both minority and elderly residents. The housing industry will need to develop an array of cost alternatives for both rental and owner markets. In fact, what these trends suggest is what most firms are already experiencing—a rapid segmentation of markets for nearly all goods and services that requires firms to increasingly specialize and compete in niche markets.

In fact, in general, the demographics of the future suggest that markets may be increasingly segmented into two very different groups. One segment may consist of an elite market oriented to relatively affluent middle-aged and older Anglos. This market will be one where specialized upscale goods and services are in demand and one in which the convenience and time-saving characteristics of the product or service being offered are likely to be of particular importance. A very different market segment, composed of an increasing population of minority residents with limited resources, may also form. This market is likely to be one in which economics dictate substantial price sensitivity and one that emphasizes mass production of low-cost items. Most firms may be required to produce goods that appeal to one or the other of these markets. Only mass retailers of very basic items needed by all population segments will be able to market to the total population of the United States.

Ethnic-based markets are likely to be particularly significant because they involve differences based not only on price but also on culture and even linguistics. The African-American, Hispanic, and Asian markets are such markets, but the large proportion of growth projected to be due to immigration is likely to expand ethnic markets into additional diverse segments.

The aging of the population, particularly the highly competitive baby-boom generation, may also create opportunities for life-cycle marketing. This entails providing products and services that provide customers with the range of experiences associated with different periods of life. Events or opportunities that were missed or not experienced for some reason are likely to be sought by many aging persons during a time when their numbers are increasing rapidly. The increasing birth rate among older baby-boomers during the late 1980s represents one manifestation of the desire to experience certain events as a cohort ages. Although most such experiences are not as strongly felt as the desire for posterity, it seems likely that many people, particularly baby-boomers, who have foregone some events due to heavy competition during their careers, may want to make up for lost experiences from various life stages. Industries tied to regaining experiences for aging populations may find expanding markets.

The demographic trends may also create new resources for business development. The data shown here related to asset accumulation suggest that the increased savings likely to occur with an older population will generate funds to finance new business ventures as managers of mutual funds, pension funds, and other financial management concerns seek ways to invest savings and retirement funds. This should be especially true in the coming two decades as the baby-boomers save for their retirement.

In numerous ways, then, American business will be impacted by future demographic trends. Such impacts will include changes in the base of labor and capital that business uses to develop products and services and alterations in the demands of customers resulting from their changing numbers and characteristics. In sum, the changing size and characteristics of the population of the United States suggest that business will have to be increasingly creative and flexible in the coming decades. Careful strategic planning, although long included in the management practices of many firms, will be essential. Conditions of the past will not characterize the future, and remaining competitive will likely increasingly involve the ability to recognize future trends and to respond to them appropriately. These are, of course, characteristics that successful businesses have had in the past as well, but they will be especially critical to businesses as they position themselves to compete in the twenty-first century.

CHAPTER SEVEN

Population Change, Services, Revenues, and Expenditures

The United States faces a severe crisis in service delivery and resources to pay for services (Taylor 1983; Executive Office of the President 1986). With the growing federal deficit, the problem is one of attempting to meet the demand for services while controlling costs. As a result, there are continuing discussions about the extent to which growing service demands are a function of costs, changing expectations, or other factors related to services (Gould 1983; Freeman 1981; Schulz 1992). Of equal concern are the projections related to service demands and costs. What are likely to be the levels of future demands, what will the costs be of meeting such needs, and what are likely to be the revenues available to meet such needs? In this chapter, we examine the implications of future population change for the demand and costs for services and for the revenue base to pay for such services.

Given the numerous service needs of a population, the treatment here is limited to two service areas: health and long-term care and educational services. Although many other services could be examined, these two are among those that have the largest associated costs and are the topics of continuing attention (Morrison 1991; Pol and Thomas 1992; Serow et al. 1990). They are, in addition, services that reflect the needs of different population segments, of both young and old.

To determine the implications of population change for these services, we analyze projections of school enrollment and of the likely incidences of diseases and disorders in the United States. We then examine the implications of these projections for the demand for service personnel and service costs. After examining these two examples, we then examine the implications of the changing demographic structure of America for federal tax revenues and expenditures. Again, it is important to clarify that it is only the demographic determinants of services, revenues, and expenditures that are being examined here and that other factors, which are not demographic in origin, will also influence the course of change in these factors. However, the results presented suggest that the demographic factors will have a pronounced influence on future service needs and associated costs and on the ability to pay such costs.

EDUCATION AND HEALTH SERVICE NEEDS:
PAST AND PRESENT

Education and health care services have been among the fastest-growing service segments in America. Examine the historical patterns of educational services in Table 7.1 and selected aspects of health services in Table 7.2. As the tables indicate, historically demand in both areas has risen rapidly. Thus, from 1870 to 1990, the number of elementary and secondary students increased from 6.9 million to 45.9 million and the number of college students from 52,000 to 13.5 million. Similarly, the number of physician visits increased from 1.1 billion to 1.4 billion during the period from 1980 to 1990. Corresponding with these increases are increases in the number of personnel, facilities, and related costs. The number of teachers increased from 207,000 in 1870 to 3.4 million in 1990 and the total costs associated with educational services increased from $63 million in 1870 to $359 billion in 1990. Similarly, the costs associated with health care increased from 9.2 percent to 12.2 percent of the gross national product between 1980 and 1990.

These service demands and costs have tended to exceed overall population growth. For example, from 1980 to 1990 the number of college students increased by 17 percent and expenditures for higher education by 137 percent, and the number of physician visits increased by 25 percent and health care expenditures by 166 percent. However, the population increased by only 9.8 percent in that period. It is evident, then, that educational and health care services have grown faster than would be expected on the basis of population growth alone.

The aging of the population is evident in both school enrollment and in the demand for health services. On the one hand, elementary and secondary enrollments peaked at 51.1 million in 1970 and then declined in both the 1970s and the 1980s. College enrollment more than doubled between 1960 and 1970, increased by more than 44 percent from 1970 to 1980, and then increased by 17 percent in the 1980s—increases but nonetheless ones of declining magnitude. Medical needs, on the other hand, have increased rapidly in the last several decades with the number of physician visits increasing by more than 25 percent from just 1980 to 1990.

The explanation for such changes lies not only in total population growth, but also in the fact that different population segments have reached ages requiring these services at different times. The baby boom played a major role in the growth of educational services during the 1960s, 1970s, and 1980s. Similarly, the aging of the population has had substantial implications for the recent growth in health care services. The reasons for these effects are obvious from examining the data in the top panels of Table 7.3, which show rates of enrollment in education and rates of physician visits by age. Similarly, there are dramatic differences among racial/ethnic groups in both educational involvement and health care usage. The bottom panels of Table 7.3 show substantial race/ethnicity differences.

Table 7.1: Elementary and Secondary and College Enrollment,
Teachers, and Expenditures in the United States, 1870-1990
(enrollment and teachers in thousands, expenditures in
millions of current dollars)

Year	Elementary and Secondary	College	Total
	Enrollment		
1870	6,872	52	6,924
1880	9,867	116	9,983
1890	14,334	157	14,491
1900	16,855	238	17,093
1910	19,372	355	19,727
1920	23,278	598	23,876
1930	28,329	1,101	29,430
1940	28,045	1,494	29,539
1950	28,492	2,659	31,151
1960	40,857	3,640	44,497
1970	51,050	8,005	59,055
1980	46,651	11,570	58,221
1990	45,897	13,539	59,436
	Teachers		
1870	201	6	207
1880	287	12	299
1890	364	16	380
1900	423	24	447
1910	523	37	560
1920	657	47	704
1930	843	82	925
1940	875	147	1,022
1950	914	247	1,161
1960	1,387	381	1,768
1970	2,131	450	2,581
1980	2,300	675	2,975
1990	2,528	824	3,352
	Expenditures		
1870	63	NA	63
1880	78	NA	78
1890	141	NA	141
1900	215	NA	215
1910	426	NA	426
1920	1,036	NA	1,036
1930	2,317	632	2,949
1940	2,344	758	3,102
1950	5,838	2,662	8,500
1960	15,613	7,147	22,760
1970	40,638	25,276	65,914
1980	95,962	62,465	158,427
1990	$211,731	$147,773	$359,504

Source: *Digest of Education Statistics, 1992,* U.S. Department of
Education, Washington, DC: U.S. Government Printing Office, 1992.

Table 7.2: Selected Health Care Data for the United
States for 1980 and 1990

Health Indicators	1980	1990	Percent Change 1980-1990
Physician Contacts (thousands)	1,090,680	1,363,318	25.0
Hospital Discharges (thousands)	36,157	28,209	-22.0
Total Days of Hospital Care (thousands)	258,275	176,960	-31.5
Total Health Expenditures ($ Billions)	$250.1	$666.2	166.4
Health Expenditures as a Percentage of GNP	9.2%	12.2%	32.6

Source: Health, United States, 1991, National Center for Health Statisitics,
U.S. Department of Health and Human Services, Hyattsville, MD:
Public Health Service, 1992. *Vital and Health Statistics,* Series 10, No.
144, U.S. Department of Health and Human Serivces, 1980.

Obviously, then, the growth of educational and health care services has been
extensive in the past and promises to be affected substantially by the differential
rates of population growth, population aging, and change in the racial/ethnic
composition of the future population of the United States. The impacts of such
population patterns on school enrollment and on the incidence of various diseases and disorders are discussed below.

FUTURE EDUCATION AND HEALTH CARE NEEDS

Future Trends in Enrollment

The projections of school enrollment presented here were made by multiplying
1990 rates of school enrollment by age, sex, and race/ethnicity from the National
Center for Educational Statistics (Gerald and Hussar 1992) and the U.S. Bureau of
the Census (1992) by the number of persons projected to be in each age, sex, and

Table 7.3: School Enrollment Rates and Average Physician Contacts by Age and Race/Ethnicity in the United States in 1990

Enrollment Rates by Age

Age	Percent Enrolled
< 5	44.4
5-17	98.0
18-24	36.9
25-34	7.7

- -

Physician Contacts by Age

Age	Average Number of Contacts
< 5	6.9
5-17	3.2
18-24	4.3
25-44	5.1
45-64	6.4
64-74	8.5
75 +	10.1

- -

College Enrollment Rates of 18- to 24-year-olds by Race/Ethnicity

Race/Ethnicity	Enrollment Rates
Anglo	35.2
Black	25.3
Hispanic	16.2

- -

Physician Visits by Race/Ethnicity

Race/Ethnicity	Average Number of Visits
White	5.7
Black	4.9

Sources: Digest of Education Statistics, 1992, U.S. Department of Education, Washington, DC: U.S. Government Printing Office, 1992. *Vital and Health Statistics*, Series 10, No. 181, U.S. Department of Health and Human Services, Washington, DC: U.S. Government Printing Office, 1990.

race/ethnicity group under the scenarios of population growth examined in Chapter 3. The projections of the incidence of diseases and disorders were obtained by using data from the National Health Interview Surveys for 1985, 1986, and 1987 (National Center for Health Statistics 1985; 1986; and 1987). Incidences of various diseases were computed from this sample after grouping all diseases and disorders into the Diagnostic Related Groups (DRGs) used for medicare funding analyses (using classification techniques developed by Averill 1983). Age-, sex-, and race/ethnicity-specific rates of occurrence for diseases and disorders were thus determined for each of 23 DRGs and applied to the population projections examined in Chapter 3. Because a person may be ill with more than one disease or disorder in a given year, the number of incidences will not equal population values.

Tables 7.4 and 7.5 and Figures 7.1 through 7.5 present projections of total school enrollment, with separate projections for elementary and secondary and higher-education enrollment for 1990 through 2050. The tables indicate that the aging of the population will have marked effects on the rates of future growth in enrollment. Whereas total enrollment increased by only 2 percent in the decade from 1980 to 1990, under the middle scenario, projected enrollment would increase by an average of 6.0 percent per decade over the projection period. This is more rapid growth than that from 1980 to 1990 but far less than the booming rates of growth of the 1950s or 1960s, when growth rates of nearly 43 percent and 33 percent respectively were experienced. They are also substantially less than the overall rate of projected population growth. Although population is projected to increase by 10.8, 53.9, 103.7, and 21.0 percent in the low, middle, high, and zero immigration scenarios from 1990 to 2050, enrollment declines by 9.9 percent under the low scenario and increases by 35.7, 99.1, and 3.0 under the middle, high, and zero immigration scenarios.

At the same time, if slow growth were to occur, there could be a net *decrease* in enrollment under several scenarios. Under both the low-growth and the zero immigration scenarios, decline occurs during numerous decades. The lack of growth is particularly evident among Anglos. Under all but the high-growth scenario, the number of Anglos enrolled declines in nearly every decade. Under the low-growth scenario, the number of Anglos would decline by 33.1 percent from 1990 to 2050. Anglo enrollment would decline by 11.9 percent under the middle scenario, and by 19.7 percent under the zero immigration scenario.

Immigration will be essential to growth in future enrollment. In the zero immigration scenario, enrollment peaks in 2000 and declines by nearly 2.0 million by 2050. When compared to the middle scenario, the results suggest that, of the 22.4 million-increase in enrollment projected under the middle scenario, 92 percent would be due to immigrants and their descendants. More so than for any other topic examined to this point, growth in enrollment would be a product of immigration.

Table 7.4: Projections of Total, Elementary and Secondary, and College Enrollment in the United States from 1990-2050 by Race/Ethnicity Under Alternative Scenarios

Year	Anglo	Black	Hispanic	Other	Total
Low Scenario					
			Total		
1990	44,998,396	8,635,613	6,603,047	2,716,061	62,953,117
2000	45,993,491	9,797,259	8,316,190	3,655,395	67,762,335
2010	41,791,198	9,746,040	8,909,312	4,293,971	64,740,521
2020	37,843,028	9,433,609	9,283,595	4,734,163	61,294,395
2030	35,901,926	9,425,121	10,079,501	5,356,246	60,762,794
2040	32,679,220	9,225,365	10,596,371	5,908,586	58,409,542
2050	30,083,573	9,077,959	11,178,258	6,369,048	56,708,838
			Elementary and Secondary		
1990	33,968,895	7,245,924	5,764,963	2,101,835	49,081,617
2000	35,705,276	8,330,687	7,364,542	2,896,674	54,297,179
2010	31,354,616	8,097,197	7,759,116	3,321,719	50,532,648
2020	28,585,931	7,849,963	8,067,570	3,620,552	48,124,016
2030	27,350,921	7,856,734	8,781,280	4,133,423	48,122,358
2040	24,555,307	7,651,268	9,195,192	4,536,135	45,937,902
2050	22,758,751	7,548,987	9,709,551	4,876,827	44,894,116
			College		
1990	11,029,501	1,389,689	838,084	614,226	13,871,500
2000	10,288,215	1,466,572	951,648	758,721	13,465,156
2010	10,436,582	1,648,843	1,150,196	972,252	14,207,873
2020	9,257,097	1,583,646	1,216,025	1,113,611	13,170,379
2030	8,551,005	1,568,387	1,298,221	1,222,823	12,640,436
2040	8,123,913	1,574,097	1,401,179	1,372,451	12,471,640
2050	7,324,822	1,528,972	1,468,707	1,492,221	11,814,722
Middle Scenario					
			Total		
1990	44,998,396	8,635,613	6,603,047	2,716,061	62,953,117
2000	46,544,986	9,992,343	8,822,217	3,981,682	69,341,228
2010	44,162,291	10,818,531	10,799,425	5,349,193	71,129,440
2020	42,473,321	11,782,417	12,873,766	6,707,261	73,836,765
2030	42,204,796	12,953,683	15,160,021	8,094,644	78,413,144
2040	40,584,994	14,098,061	17,324,873	9,476,191	81,484,119
2050	39,622,468	15,429,077	19,546,156	10,800,750	85,398,451

Table 7.4 (Continued)

Year	Anglo	Black	Hispanic	Other	Total

Middle Scenario

Elementary and Secondary

Year	Anglo	Black	Hispanic	Other	Total
1990	33,968,895	7,245,924	5,764,963	2,101,835	49,081,617
2000	36,149,349	8,507,323	7,797,921	3,139,087	55,593,680
2010	33,489,275	9,126,868	9,496,823	4,206,358	56,319,324
2020	32,548,866	10,015,950	11,331,222	5,256,750	59,152,788
2030	32,490,226	11,013,267	13,331,177	6,335,024	63,169,694
2040	30,924,441	11,975,831	15,194,885	7,400,387	65,495,544
2050	30,375,170	13,135,241	17,123,635	8,410,595	69,044,641

College

Year	Anglo	Black	Hispanic	Other	Total
1990	11,029,501	1,389,689	838,084	614,226	13,871,500
2000	10,395,637	1,485,020	1,024,296	842,595	13,747,548
2010	10,673,016	1,691,663	1,302,602	1,142,835	14,810,116
2020	9,924,455	1,766,467	1,542,544	1,450,511	14,683,977
2030	9,714,570	1,940,416	1,828,844	1,759,620	15,243,450
2040	9,660,553	2,122,230	2,129,988	2,075,804	15,988,575
2050	9,247,298	2,293,836	2,422,521	2,390,155	16,353,810

High Scenario

Total

Year	Anglo	Black	Hispanic	Other	Total
1990	44,998,396	8,635,613	6,603,047	2,716,061	62,953,117
2000	47,204,062	10,139,341	9,274,186	4,288,523	70,906,112
2010	47,695,580	11,485,305	12,369,664	6,291,552	77,842,101
2020	50,069,839	13,251,234	16,166,368	8,576,993	88,064,434
2030	53,019,054	15,260,893	20,437,567	10,930,594	99,648,108
2040	54,909,477	17,463,645	25,295,001	13,538,343	111,206,466
2050	57,900,188	20,049,388	30,968,384	16,405,549	125,323,509

Elementary and Secondary

Year	Anglo	Black	Hispanic	Other	Total
1990	33,968,895	7,245,924	5,764,963	2,101,835	49,081,617
2000	36,712,603	8,628,587	8,178,607	3,363,776	56,883,573
2010	36,816,562	9,732,150	10,918,334	4,980,301	62,447,347
2020	39,289,534	11,329,727	14,337,817	6,816,706	71,773,784
2030	41,568,854	13,029,227	18,120,569	8,658,904	81,377,554
2040	42,841,228	14,907,472	22,437,979	10,746,087	90,932,766
2050	45,423,987	17,130,717	27,485,851	13,026,578	103,067,133

Table 7.4 (Continued)

Year	Anglo	Black	Hispanic	Other	Total

High Scenario

College

Year	Anglo	Black	Hispanic	Other	Total
1990	11,029,501	1,389,689	838,084	614,226	13,871,500
2000	10,491,459	1,510,754	1,095,579	924,747	14,022,539
2010	10,879,018	1,753,155	1,451,330	1,311,251	15,394,754
2020	10,780,305	1,921,507	1,828,551	1,760,287	16,290,650
2030	11,450,200	2,231,666	2,316,998	2,271,690	18,270,554
2040	12,068,249	2,556,173	2,857,022	2,792,256	20,273,700
2050	12,476,201	2,918,671	3,482,533	3,378,971	22,256,376

Zero Immigration Scenario

Total

Year	Anglo	Black	Hispanic	Other	Total
1990	44,998,396	8,635,613	6,603,047	2,716,061	62,953,117
2000	45,995,356	9,788,521	7,897,940	3,113,919	66,795,736
2010	42,957,763	10,361,293	8,486,659	3,232,354	65,038,069
2020	40,657,978	11,032,570	9,109,492	3,280,512	64,080,552
2030	39,822,850	11,913,730	9,959,578	3,547,812	65,243,970
2040	37,633,193	12,733,327	10,527,730	3,683,870	64,578,120
2050	36,133,912	13,721,754	11,173,209	3,789,008	64,817,883

Elementary and Secondary

Year	Anglo	Black	Hispanic	Other	Total
1990	33,968,895	7,245,924	5,764,963	2,101,835	49,081,617
2000	35,729,751	8,341,859	7,016,021	2,508,938	53,596,569
2010	32,556,692	8,745,048	7,466,558	2,539,669	51,307,967
2020	31,154,889	9,384,424	8,031,783	2,574,961	51,146,057
2030	30,663,792	10,137,809	8,776,577	2,821,431	52,399,609
2040	28,657,378	10,821,192	9,235,889	2,894,009	51,608,468
2050	27,701,377	11,689,716	9,800,230	2,975,560	52,166,883

College

Year	Anglo	Black	Hispanic	Other	Total
1990	11,029,501	1,389,689	838,084	614,226	13,871,500
2000	10,265,605	1,446,662	881,919	604,981	13,199,167
2010	10,401,071	1,616,245	1,020,101	692,685	13,730,102
2020	9,503,089	1,648,146	1,077,709	705,551	12,934,495
2030	9,159,058	1,775,921	1,183,001	726,381	12,844,361
2040	8,975,815	1,912,135	1,291,841	789,861	12,969,652
2050	8,432,535	2,032,038	1,372,979	813,448	12,651,000

Table 7.5: Percent Change for Selected Time Periods for Projected Total, Elementary and Secondary, and College Enrollment in the United States by Race/Ethnicity Under the Middle Scenario

Time Period	Anglo	Black	Hispanic	Other	Total
Total					
1990-2000	3.4	15.7	33.6	46.6	10.1
2000-2010	-5.1	8.3	22.4	34.3	2.6
2010-2020	-3.8	8.9	19.2	25.4	3.8
2020-2030	-0.6	9.9	17.8	20.7	6.2
2030-2040	-3.8	8.8	14.3	17.1	3.9
2040-2050	-2.4	9.4	12.8	14.0	4.8
1990-2050	-11.9	78.7	196.0	297.7	35.7
Elementary and Secondary					
1990-2000	6.4	17.4	35.3	49.3	13.3
2000-2010	-7.4	7.3	21.8	34.0	1.3
2010-2020	-2.8	9.7	19.3	25.0	5.0
2020-2030	-0.2	10.0	17.6	20.5	6.8
2030-2040	-4.8	8.7	14.0	16.8	3.7
2040-2050	-1.8	9.7	12.7	13.7	5.4
1990-2050	-10.6	81.3	197.0	300.2	40.7
College					
1990-2000	-5.7	6.9	22.2	37.2	-0.9
2000-2010	2.7	13.9	27.2	35.6	7.7
2010-2020	-7.0	4.4	18.4	26.9	-0.9
2020-2030	-2.1	9.8	18.6	21.3	3.8
2030-2040	-0.6	9.4	16.5	18.0	4.9
2040-2050	-4.3	8.1	13.7	15.1	2.3
1990-2050	-16.2	65.1	189.1	289.1	17.9

What is equally apparent, however, is that the patterns are quite diverse for elementary and secondary education relative to higher education. Under the middle scenario, elementary and secondary enrollment would increase by 40.7 percent but college enrollment by only 17.9 percent (see Table 7.5 and Figures 7.1 and 7.2). In addition, total college enrollment declines in both the 1990s and from 2010 to 2020 under the middle scenario (see Figure 7.2), with Anglo enrollment declining

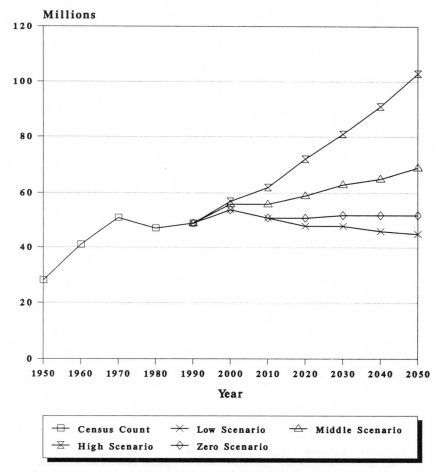

FIGURE 7.1　Elementary and secondary enrollment growth, 1950–2050.

in every decade and by 16.2 percent for the total period from 1990 to 2050. Although Anglo enrollment declines in elementary and secondary schools as well, the substantial growth among minority groups leads to overall growth and to small increases during the projection period in elementary and secondary enrollment.

A comparison of the data for the middle and zero immigration scenarios in Table 7.4 also demonstrates the role of immigration in both elementary and secondary and college enrollment. Rather than increase by nearly 20 million from 1990 to 2050 (as suggested by the middle scenario), elementary and secondary enrollment would increase by only 3.1 million if no immigration were to occur. Simi-

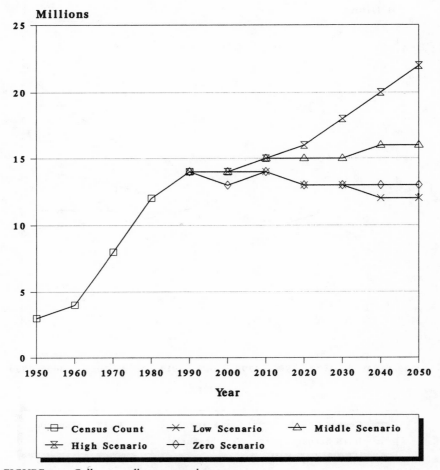

FIGURE 7.2　College enrollment growth, 1950–2050

larly, college enrollment, rather than increase from 13.9 million in 1990 to 16.4 million in 2050, would decline to 12.7 million in 2050 if no immigration were to occur. The importance of immigration as a source of growth in enrollment in education is apparent and could be a major force preventing decline in future higher-education enrollment.

It is the growth in minority populations—both indigenous and immigrant—that will support overall growth in enrollments, with elementary and secondary enrollments being the first to reflect the increasing minority proportion. For both elementary and secondary and for college enrollment, nearly all of the net growth from 1990 to 2050 (see Figure 7.3) will be due to minority population growth. By

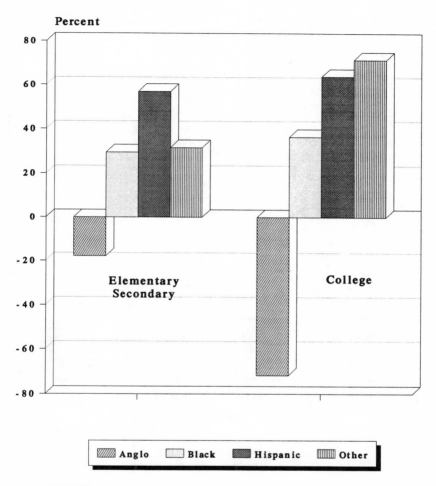

Percent

*Middle Projection Scenario

FIGURE 7.3   Net change in enrollment due to each ethnic group, 1990–2050 (middle projection scenario).

2050, 56 percent of all those enrolled in elementary and secondary education will be non-Anglo; for college enrollment the proportion of non-Anglo students will be more than 43 percent, an increase of 23 percent in the minority proportion of higher-education enrollment from the 20 percent in 1990 (see Figures 7.4 and 7.5). Education will increasingly involve minority students.

Trends in Health Care Needs

The data on the incidence of diseases and disorders show quite different patterns than those for education. These data indicate increases in the number of inci-

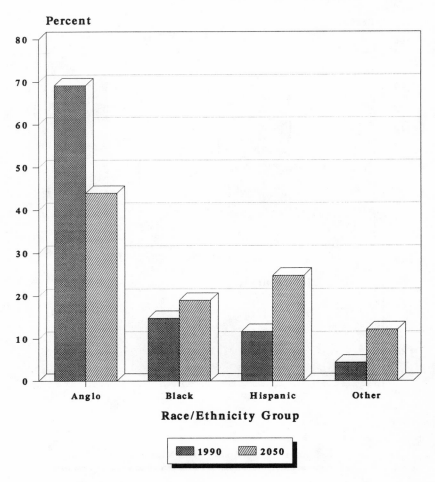

Percent

*Middle Projection Scenario

FIGURE 7.4   Percent enrolled elementary-secondary by ethnicity, 1990 and 2050 (middle projection scenario).

dences for all groups for the total projection period except in the low-growth scenario, and only the number of incidences for Anglos declines even in that scenario. The growth in incidences for every race/ethnicity group is higher than the overall rate of population growth for every scenario. A comparison of Tables 7.6 and 7.7 and Figure 7.6 to Tables 3.2 and 3.3 and Figure 3.1 shows that, although population growth from 1990 to 2050 would be 10.8 percent, 53.9 percent, 103.7 percent, and 21.0 percent in the low, middle, high, and zero immigration scenarios respectively, the incidences of diseases and disorders would increase by 21.8

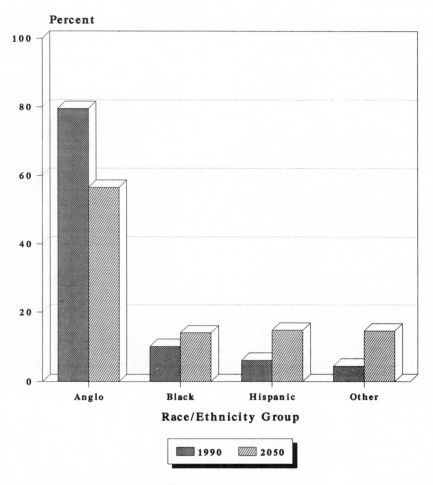

Percent

*Middle Projection Scenario

FIGURE 7.5   Percent of college enrollment by ethnicity, 1990 and 2050 (middle projection scenario).

percent, 67.4 percent, 116.9 percent, and 35.2 percent. Slower-growing populations are generally ones with more rapid aging and higher proportions of age-related health care needs. The aging of the population is sufficiently pervasive, however, that even under the high-growth scenario the incidences of diseases and disorders would exceed overall population change.

The extent to which incidences reflect age is shown in Figure 7.7 (see also Reference Table 7.1). Incidences will be increasingly concentrated in the older ages. In 1990, more than 45 percent of all incidences involved persons 45 years of age or

Table 7.6: Projections of the Incidences of Diseases/Disorders in the United States, by Race/Ethnicty from 1990-2050 Under Alternative Scenarios

Year	Anglo	Black	Hispanic	Other	Total
			Low Scenario		
1990	651,760,177	83,918,053	59,163,781	27,500,015	822,342,026
2000	683,317,804	96,629,120	78,669,778	40,099,897	898,716,599
2010	695,028,025	107,430,847	97,358,828	51,836,965	951,654,665
2020	703,025,748	117,324,434	116,921,025	64,236,179	1,001,507,386
2030	697,096,966	124,585,664	136,021,234	76,653,902	1,034,357,766
2040	660,484,358	128,283,695	153,010,513	88,178,095	1,029,956,661
2050	608,655,955	128,754,770	165,371,915	98,594,227	1,001,376,867
			Middle Scenario		
1990	651,760,177	83,918,053	59,163,781	27,500,015	822,342,026
2000	694,052,322	98,824,620	83,583,207	43,988,342	920,448,491
2010	727,979,527	114,836,156	111,465,938	62,264,604	1,016,546,225
2020	765,731,227	132,472,484	143,499,310	82,630,767	1,124,333,788
2030	797,398,740	150,468,408	179,192,943	104,706,048	1,231,766,139
2040	802,062,803	167,550,328	217,013,366	127,678,839	1,314,305,336
2050	787,170,309	184,243,762	254,087,541	151,029,549	1,376,531,161
			High Scenario		
1990	651,760,177	83,918,053	59,163,781	27,500,015	822,342,026
2000	704,500,700	100,647,614	88,011,931	47,645,319	940,805,564
2010	760,989,700	120,873,022	124,402,605	72,157,660	1,078,422,987
2020	828,086,099	144,670,678	168,483,987	100,437,003	1,241,677,767
2030	898,708,296	171,494,310	221,126,305	132,580,796	1,423,909,707
2040	954,585,916	199,560,056	282,323,662	168,443,769	1,604,913,403
2050	996,880,666	228,605,537	350,676,670	207,739,056	1,783,901,929
			Zero Migration Scenario		
1990	651,760,177	83,918,053	59,163,781	27,500,015	822,342,026
2000	689,181,941	97,361,138	75,359,103	33,997,757	895,899,939
2010	716,214,056	111,187,079	91,671,668	38,734,729	957,807,532
2020	745,634,103	126,137,054	109,149,880	43,675,570	1,024,596,607
2030	767,738,093	140,838,919	126,928,138	48,183,560	1,083,688,710
2040	761,529,158	154,114,880	143,357,527	51,682,122	1,110,683,687
2050	735,181,624	166,527,729	155,640,795	54,307,920	1,111,658,068

Table 7.7: Percent Change for Selected Time Periods in the Incidences of
Diseases/Disorders in the United States by Race/Ethnicity
Under Alternative Scenarios

Time Period	Anglo	Black	Hispanic	Other	Total
		Low Scenario			
1990-2000	4.8	15.1	33.0	45.8	9.3
2000-2010	1.7	11.2	23.8	29.3	5.9
2010-2020	1.2	9.2	20.1	23.9	5.2
2020-2030	-0.8	6.2	16.3	19.3	3.3
2030-2040	-5.3	3.0	12.5	15.0	-0.4
2040-2050	-7.8	0.4	8.1	11.8	-2.8
1990-2050	-6.6	53.4	179.5	258.5	21.8
		Middle Scenario			
1990-2000	6.5	17.8	41.3	60.0	11.9
2000-2010	4.9	16.2	33.4	41.5	10.4
2010-2020	5.2	15.4	28.7	32.7	10.6
2020-2030	4.1	13.6	24.9	26.7	9.6
2030-2040	0.6	11.4	21.1	21.9	6.7
2040-2050	-1.9	10.0	17.1	18.3	4.7
1990-2050	20.8	119.6	329.5	449.2	67.4
		High Scenario			
1990-2000	8.1	19.9	48.8	73.3	14.4
2000-2010	8.0	20.1	41.3	51.4	14.6
2010-2020	8.8	19.7	35.4	39.2	15.1
2020-2030	8.5	18.5	31.2	32.0	14.7
2030-2040	6.2	16.4	27.7	27.0	12.7
2040-2050	4.4	14.6	24.2	23.3	11.2
1990-2050	53.0	172.4	492.7	655.4	116.9
		Zero Migration Scenario			
1990-2000	5.7	16.0	27.4	23.6	8.9
2000-2010	3.9	14.2	21.6	13.9	6.9
2010-2020	4.1	13.4	19.1	12.8	7.0
2020-2030	3.0	11.7	16.3	10.3	5.8
2030-2040	-0.8	9.4	12.9	7.3	2.5
2040-2050	-3.5	8.1	8.6	5.1	0.1
1990-2050	12.8	98.4	163.1	97.5	35.2

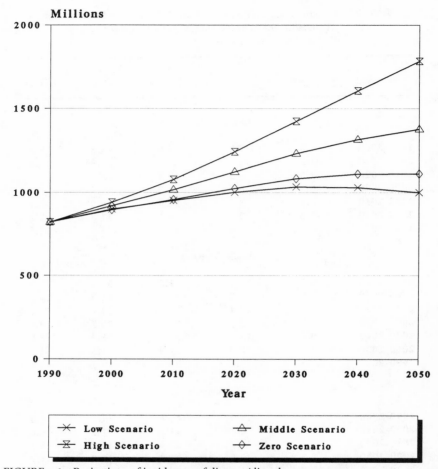

FIGURE 7.6   Projections of incidences of diseases/disorders, 1990–2050.

older. By 2050, 59.9 percent of all incidences will involve persons 45 years of age or older.

The importance of minority population change is also apparent. Of the total increase in incidences of diseases and disorders from 1990 to 2050, non-Anglo populations would account for a majority of incidences for every scenario (see Table 7.1). Under the middle scenario, the proportion of all incidences that involve Anglos would decline from 79.3 percent in 1990 to 57.1 percent by 2050 (see Table 7.6 and Figure 7.8). The rate of minority involvement is less than that for education because minority populations have younger age structures and therefore are projected to have smaller impacts on health and related areas than on education.

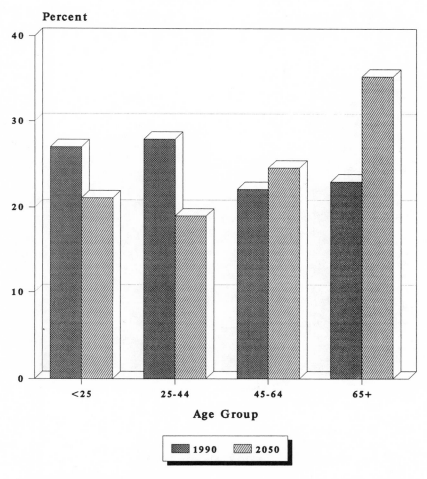

Percent

Age Group

*Middle Projection Scenario

FIGURE 7.7   Percent of incidences by age group, 1990 and 2050 (middle projection scenario).

Nevertheless, these data point to minority populations as a major component in the growth of future health care needs.

The changing age and race/ethnicity composition of the population will differentially affect different types of diseases and disorders. Tables 7.8 and 7.9 provide data on the incidences of diseases and disorders by DRG category. Numbers of incidences by DRG and race/ethnicity category are shown for 1990 and for 2050. These tables show that different diseases and disorders are impacted by growth in different racial and ethnic groups. Diseases more common among the elderly,

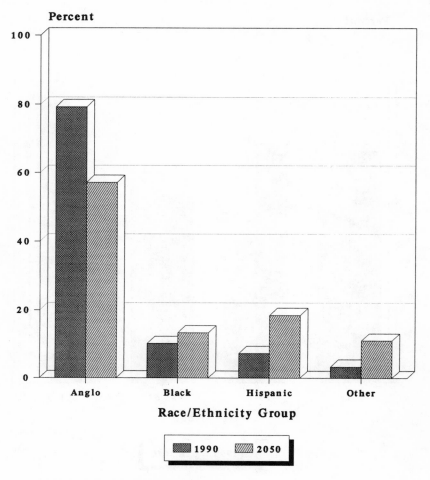

Percent

*Middle Projection Scenario

FIGURE 7.8   Percent of incidences by race/ethnicity, 1990 and 2050 (middle projection scenario).

such as diseases of the circulatory system, increase most rapidly among Anglos, and incidences related to younger ages, such as pregnancy, childbirth, and substance abuse, increase most rapidly among minority groups. These differentials reflect the age structures of the population bases involved. As a result, the proportion of total incidences that would involve Anglo patients by 2050 ranges from 34.3 percent for disorders related to newborns and other infants to nearly 61 percent for diseases of the eye (see Table 7.9). Moreover, the proportion of the net increase in diseases and disorders from 1990 to 2050 accounted for by Anglos ranges from

Table 7.8: Projections of the Incidences of Diseases/Disorders in the United States by Race/Ethnicity and Type of Disease/Disorder, 1990 and 2050 Under the Middle Scenario

Disease/Disorder	Anglo	Black	Hispanic	Other	Total
		1990 Incidences			
Nervous system	17,590,253	2,545,250	1,323,286	770,658	22,229,447
Eye	21,255,991	2,467,378	1,769,659	753,587	26,246,615
Ear, nose, throat	107,303,955	14,251,799	11,467,038	5,235,843	138,258,635
Respiratory system	91,474,982	11,635,187	9,118,901	4,257,235	116,486,305
Circulatory system	79,426,786	9,492,192	5,546,146	2,626,511	97,091,635
Digestive system	57,969,231	7,282,436	4,784,704	2,314,922	72,351,293
Hepatobiliary system	7,946,425	878,417	691,202	330,275	9,846,319
Musculoskeletal system	82,152,035	9,426,467	6,326,249	3,033,370	100,938,121
Subcutaneous tissue and breast	55,059,529	7,141,154	4,794,154	2,440,178	69,435,015
Endocrine, nutritional, and metabolic	14,883,827	2,584,934	1,634,500	517,224	19,620,485
Kidney and urinary	13,150,065	1,897,692	1,084,996	534,966	16,667,719
Male reproductive system	1,830,222	206,150	193,839	57,811	2,288,022
Female reproductive system	8,310,433	1,400,650	928,786	418,043	11,057,912
Pregnancy and childbirth	3,105,492	571,342	501,862	168,636	4,347,332
Newborns and other neonates	374,340	130,138	115,628	22,892	642,998
Blood and immunological	4,030,322	766,327	499,593	168,824	5,465,066
Myeloproliferative	2,256,184	399,598	255,274	84,924	2,995,980
Infectious and parasitic	46,689,007	4,902,541	4,116,451	2,118,465	57,826,464
Mental	7,006,227	1,255,132	720,664	342,954	9,324,977
Substance abuse	1,616,737	413,585	244,523	74,026	2,348,871
Drug poisoning	13,322,353	1,450,357	1,171,297	560,646	16,504,653
Burns	1,064,351	335,560	353,365	50,592	1,803,868
Other	13,941,430	2,483,767	1,521,664	617,433	18,564,294
Total	651,760,177	83,918,053	59,163,781	27,500,015	822,342,026

Table 7.8 (Continued)

2050 Incidences

Disease/Disorder	Anglo	Black	Hispanic	Other	Total
Nervous system	20,609,900	5,314,169	5,567,752	4,068,129	35,559,950
Eye	31,087,130	6,166,033	8,907,131	5,139,081	51,299,375
Ear, nose, throat	110,487,601	27,735,559	39,659,595	24,376,285	202,259,040
Respiratory system	98,889,092	23,285,958	33,327,120	20,870,365	176,372,535
Circulatory system	116,974,194	25,366,682	34,154,148	19,052,790	195,547,814
Digestive system	74,565,652	16,524,750	21,617,913	13,589,147	126,297,462
Hepatobiliary system	9,474,949	1,759,135	2,952,498	1,820,063	16,006,645
Musculoskeletal system	109,146,481	23,195,484	32,414,127	19,223,118	183,979,210
Subcutaneous tissue and breast	63,914,403	14,936,065	19,119,941	12,736,339	110,706,748
Endocrine, nutritional, and metabolic	20,733,184	6,692,384	8,957,923	3,513,775	39,897,266
Kidney and urinary	16,370,750	4,196,434	5,081,745	3,057,559	28,706,488
Male reproductive system	3,163,535	564,582	1,161,352	464,419	5,353,888
Female reproductive system	7,607,235	2,413,754	3,186,301	1,803,835	15,011,125
Pregnancy and childbirth	2,488,832	928,108	1,528,840	655,965	5,601,745
Newborns and other neonates	295,563	210,871	276,557	79,738	862,729
Blood and immunological	4,924,833	1,551,274	2,041,006	933,264	9,450,377
Myeloproliferative	2,981,957	890,624	1,286,878	26,182	5,685,641
Infectious and parasitic	51,712,354	10,484,484	16,469,978	10,643,657	89,310,473
Mental	7,101,627	2,388,269	2,797,033	1,604,772	13,891,701
Substance abuse	1,697,396	839,694	1,252,671	363,387	4,153,148
Drug poisoning	15,908,065	3,133,168	4,9 35,208	3,070,635	27,047,076
Burns	1,082,848	609,909	1,097,009	237,611	3,027,377
Other	15,952,728	5,056,372	6,294,815	3,199,433	30,503,348
Total	787,170,309	184,243,762	254,087,541	151,029,549	1,376,531,161

nearly 44 percent for diseases of the male reproductive system to absolute de-creases in proportions for diseases of the female reproductive system, those related to pregnancy and childbirth, and those involving newborns and other infants (computed from data in Table 7.8). The impacts of the changing population base will be substantial for nearly all types of health care needs in the coming years.

IMPLICATIONS OF POPULATION CHANGE
FOR EDUCATION AND HEALTH CARE

Only some of the many implications of population change for education and health care suggested by the projections presented above can be examined here. Tables 7.10 and 7.11 show the number of elementary and secondary and college teachers required for selected future periods assuming 1990 student-to-teacher ratios and 1990 expenditures per student. They show data by race/ethnicity to show how growth in different ethnic groups will affect the need for teachers, but obviously teachers of any racial/ethnic origin can teach students of any racial/eth-nic origin.

Table 7.10 suggests that the demand for elementary and secondary teachers is likely to increase steadily over the projection period but, when compared to the historical data in Table 7.1, it is obvious that the rate of increase will be slower than in the past. Demand will be robust during the decade of the 1990s as children of the baby-boomers and following generations enter school, with an increase of nearly 400,000 teachers projected to be required between 1990 and 2000. Then the rate slows, however, with the demand being only 400,000 more over the next three decades through 2030 and 400,000 again for the 20-year period from 2030 to 2050. For college teachers, the demand increases by less than 90,000 from 1990 to 2030 compared to an increase of 150,000 in the 1980s alone. From 2030 to 2050, the demand for college teachers increases by another 70,000. For the total 60-year projection period, the growth in demand for college teachers would be roughly 160,000 compared to an increase of 375,000 during the 20-year period from 1970 to 1990. The demand for personnel in higher education will grow much less rap-idly in the future than in the past.

The growth in expenditures for education shown in Table 7.11 suggests a similar picture to that for teachers. During the period from 1990 to 2050, total expendi-tures for education may increase by 40.7 percent for elementary and secondary schools and by 17.9 percent for colleges. By comparison, Table 7.1 shows that ex-penditures increased by 131.1 percent for elementary and secondary education and by 136.6 percent for higher education during the 1980s. Although the increase shown for the 1980-to-1990 period is in current dollars while that for 1990 to 2050 is in constant dollars, even when discounted for the inflation of the 1980s, it is ob-vious that the relative expenditures for education will likely be substantially less in the future than in the past if per-student costs remain as they were in 1990. To the extent that growth in demand and expenditures to meet demand are important indicators, education is likely to experience reduced significance in the future.

Table 7.9: Proportions of the Incidences of Diseases/Disorders in the
United States by Race/Ethnicity and Type of Disease/
Disorder, 1990 and 2050 Under the Middle Scenario

	1990			
Disease/Disorder	Anglo	Black	Hispanic	Other
Nervous system	79.1	11.4	6.0	3.5
Eye	81.0	9.4	6.7	2.9
Ear, nose, and throat	77.6	10.3	8.3	3.8
Respiratory system	78.5	10.0	7.8	3.7
Circulatory system	81.8	9.8	5.7	2.7
Digestive system	80.1	10.1	6.6	3.2
Hepatobiliary system	80.7	8.9	7.0	3.4
Musculoskeletal system	81.4	9.3	6.3	3.0
Subcutaneous tissue and breast	79.3	10.3	6.9	3.5
Endocrine, nutritional, and metabolic	75.9	13.2	8.3	2.6
Kidney and urinary	78.9	11.4	6.5	3.2
Male reproductive system	80.0	9.0	8.5	2.5
Female reproductive system	75.1	12.7	8.4	3.8
Pregnancy and childbirth	71.5	13.1	11.5	3.9
Newborns and other neonates	58.2	20.2	18.0	3.6
Blood and immunological	73.8	14.0	9.1	3.1
Myeloproliferative	75.4	13.3	8.5	2.8
Infectious and parasitic	80.7	8.5	7.1	3.7
Mental	75.1	13.5	7.7	3.7
Substance abuse	68.8	17.6	10.4	3.2
Drug poisoning	80.7	8.8	7.1	3.4
Burns	59.0	18.6	19.6	2.8
Other	75.1	13.4	8.2	3.3

Tables 7.12 through 7.14 suggest that the future will hold quite different implications for health care. Table 7.12 shows health care personnel needs by the race/
ethnicity of the patient. The data are presented in this manner simply to show
how growth in different race/ethnicity groups will effect the likely growth in demand for health care services (because health professionals of any race/ethnicity
origin can treat patients of any race/ethnicity origin). In total, the number of
medical professionals required will increase from 2.6 million in 1990 to 4.1 million
in 2050, an increase of 53.9 percent, reflecting overall population growth.

Tables 7.13 and 7.14 show physician visits and days of hospitalization with associated costs for patients in different age categories. These tables indicate that phy-

Table 7.9 (Continued)

Disease/Disorder	2050			
	Anglo	Black	Hispanic	Other
Nervous system	58.0	14.9	15.7	11.4
Eye	60.6	12.0	17.4	10.0
Ear, nose, and throat	54.6	13.7	19.6	12.1
Respiratory system	56.1	13.2	18.9	11.8
Circulatory system	59.8	13.0	17.5	9.7
Digestive system	59.0	13.1	17.1	10.8
Hepatobiliary system	59.2	11.0	18.4	11.4
Musculoskeletal system	59.4	12.6	17.6	10.4
Subcutaneous tissue and breast	57.7	13.5	17.3	11.5
Endocrine, nutritional, and metabolic	51.9	16.8	22.5	8.8
Kidney and urinary	57.0	14.6	17.7	10.7
Male reproductive system	59.1	10.5	21.7	8.7
Female reproductive system	50.7	16.1	21.2	12.0
Pregnancy and childbirth	44.4	16.6	27.3	11.7
Newborns and other neonates	34.3	24.4	32.1	9.2
Blood and immunological	52.1	16.4	21.6	9.9
Myeloproliferative	52.4	15.7	22.6	9.3
Infectious and parasitic	58.0	11.7	18.4	11.9
Mental	51.1	17.2	20.1	11.6
Substance abuse	40.9	20.2	30.2	8.7
Drug poisoning	58.8	11.6	18.2	11.4
Burns	35.9	20.1	36.2	7.8
Other	52.3	16.6	20.6	10.5

sician contacts and associated costs would increase by 66.7 percent from 1990 through 2050 but that such growth would vary substantially among patients of different ages. Because of the aging of the population, growth would be most extensive among the oldest patients. Whereas the total expenditures for physician visits would increase by 39.3 percent from 1990 to 2050 for persons less than 18 years of age and by only 20.1 percent for those 18 to 44 years of age, the costs of physician services provided to those 65 to 74 years of age would increase by 94.5 percent and costs for persons 75 years of age or older would increase by 232.4 percent. Days of patient care and the costs of hospitalization show similar patterns— both overall and by the age of the patient.

Table 7.10: Projected Numbers of Teachers[a] Required for Elementary and Secondary and Higher Education by Race/Ethnicity of Student and Year Under the Middle Scenario

Year	Anglo	Black	Hispanic	Other	Total
			Elementary and Secondary Teachers		
1990	2,021,958	431,305	343,153	125,109	2,921,525
2000	2,151,747	506,388	464,162	186,850	3,309,147
2030	1,933,942	655,552	793,522	377,085	3,760,100
2050	1,808,046	781,859	1,019,264	500,631	4,109,800
			College Teachers		
1990	702,516	88,515	53,381	39,123	883,535
2000	662,142	94,587	65,242	53,668	875,640
2030	618,762	123,593	116,487	92,389	970,920
2050	589,000	146,104	154,301	152,239	1,041,644

[a] Based on 1990 ratios of 16.8 students per teacher at the Elementary and Secondary level and 15.7 students per teacher at the College level.

Nursing home care and costs show extremely large increases (see Table 7.15). The number of persons in nursing homes would increase from 1.5 million in 1990 to more than 5.8 million in 2050, an increase of 292.5 percent. Costs would increase by 296.1 percent. The effect of the baby-boom generation is particularly apparent when the increases from 2000 to 2030 are examined. During this period the number of residents would increase by nearly 1.8 million and costs would nearly double. Also important, because of the increasing number of physical limitations associated with aging, is the fact that the largest growth in nursing home residents and associated costs is among the oldest of the residents. Whereas the number of residents in the 65-to-74 age group would increase by 94.5 percent from 1990 to 2050, the number of residents 75 to 84 years of age would increase by 158.7 percent and the number of residents 85 years of age or older would increase by 473.1 percent. The aging of the population will have a particularly pronounced

Table 7.11: Projected Expenditures[a] for Elementary and Secondary and Higher Education by Race/Ethnicity of Student and Year Under the Middle Scenario

Year	Anglo	Black	Hispanic	Other	Total
Elementary and Secondary Expenditures					
1990	$174,464,244,720	$37,215,065,664	$29,608,849,968	$10,795,024,560	$252,083,184,912
2000	185,663,056,464	43,693,610,928	40,050,122,256	16,122,350,832	285,529,140,480
2030	166,869,800,736	56,564,139,312	68,468,925,072	32,536,683,264	324,439,548,384
2050	156,006,873,120	67,462,597,776	87,946,989,360	43,196,815,920	354,613,276,176
College Expenditures					
1990	$151,843,140,267	$19,131,848,463	$11,537,902,428	$ 8,456,049,342	$190,968,940,500
2000	143,116,734,579	20,444,270,340	14,101,483,032	11,600,005,365	189,262,493,316
2030	133,740,485,190	26,713,707,072	25,177,695,348	24,224,688,540	209,856,576,150
2050	127,307,551,566	31,579,240,212	33,350,846,607	32,905,263,885	225,142,902,270

[a] Based on 1990 Expenditures or $5,136 per student for Elementary and Secondary Schools and $13,767 per student for Colleges.

Table 7.12: Projected Health Personnel Requirements in the United States by Type and Year Under the Middle Scenario

Health Personnel	Race/Ethnicity of Person Served				
	Anglo	Black	Hispanic	Other	Total
1990					
Physicians	433,824	67,373	51,548	20,780	573,525
Dentists	109,303	16,975	12,988	5,236	144,502
Optometrists	19,189	2,980	2,280	919	25,368
Pharmacists	120,590	18,728	14,329	5,776	159,423
Registered Nurses	1,262,341	196,041	149,996	60,465	1,668,843
Veterinarians	34,249	5,785	4,426	1,784	49,244
Podiatrists	2,406	1,461	1,118	451	12,436
Total	1,991,902	309,343	236,685	95,411	2,633,341
2000					
Physicians	453,592	78,022	70,569	31,541	633,724
Dentists	114,283	19,658	17,779	7,947	159,667
Optometrists	20,064	3,451	3,121	1,395	28,031
Pharmacists	126,085	21,688	19,616	8,768	176,157
Registered Nurses	1,319,863	227,029	205,340	91,779	1,844,011
Veterinarians	38,947	6,699	6,059	2,708	54,413
Podiatrists	9,835	1,692	1,530	684	13,741
Total	2,082,669	358,239	324,014	144,822	2,909,744
2030					
Physicians	478,897	109,654	136,509	70,398	795,458
Dentists	120,659	27,627	34,394	17,737	200,417
Optometrists	21,183	4,850	6,038	3,114	35,185
Pharmacists	133,119	30,481	37,945	19,569	221,114
Registered Nurses	1,393,494	319,071	319,213	204,845	2,314,623
Veterinarians	41,120	9,415	11,721	6,045	68,301
Podiatrists	10,384	2,378	2,960	1,526	17,248
Total	2,198,856	503,476	626,780	323,234	3,652,346
2050					
Physicians	465,444	132,170	186,037	98,796	882,447
Dentists	117,269	27,627	46,872	24,892	222,333
Optometrists	20,588	4,850	8,229	4,370	39,033
Pharmacists	129,380	30,481	51,713	27,462	245,294
Registered Nurses	1,354,350	319,071	541,329	287,476	2,567,743
Veterinarians	39,964	11,349	15,974	8,483	75,770
Podiatrists	10,092	2,866	4,034	2,142	19,134
Total	2,137,087	606,858	854,188	453,621	4,051,754

Table 7.13: Projected Number of Physician Contacts and
Associated Costs (in thousands of 1990
dollars) in the United States by Age of
Patient and Year Under the Middle Scenario

Year/Age of Patient	Number of Contracts	Total Costs
1990		
< 18	286,219,944	$26,226,333
18-44	515,964,485	47,277,825
45-64	296,774,458	27,193,444
65-74	153,905,743	14,102,383
75+	132,666,257	12,156,209
Total	1,385,530,887	126,956,195
2000		
< 18	318,116,412	$29,149,007
18-44	519,337,099	47,586,858
45-64	390,667,072	35,796,824
65-74	155,189,133	14,219,980
75+	167,947,093	15,388,992
Total	1,551,256,808	142,141,661
2030		
< 18	363,496,667	$33,307,200
18-44	567,682,886	52,016,783
45-64	486,835,949	44,608,778
65-74	321,856,385	29,491,700
75+	322,932,350	29,590,291
Total	2,062,804,236	189,014,753
2050		
< 18	398,837,241	$36,545,456
18-44	619,815,178	56,793,665
45-64	550,651,930	50,456,236
65-74	299,339,885	27,428,513
75+	440,961,950	40,405,343
Total	2,309,606,183	211,629,214

Table 7.14: Projected Days of Hospital Care and
Associated Costs (in thousands of 1990
dollars) in the United States by Age of
Patient and Year Under the Middle Scenario

Year/Age of Patient	Days of Care	Total Costs
1990		
< 18	14,902,518	$ 9,403,489
18-44	51,714,690	32,631,970
45-64	41,905,481	26,442,360
65-74	382,329,025	241,249,600
75+	53,689,115	33,877,830
Total	544,540,830	343,605,249
2000		
< 18	16,563,261	$10,451,420
18-44	52,052,725	32,845,270
45-64	55,163,411	34,808,110
65-74	385,517,191	243,261,300
75+	67,967,024	42,887,190
Total	577,263,613	364,253,290
2030		
< 18	18,926,060	$11,942,340
18-44	56,898,383	35,902,880
45-64	68,742,757	43,376,680
65-74	799,548,057	504,514,800
75+	130,688,484	82,464,430
Total	1,074,803,741	678,201,130
2050		
< 18	20,766,126	$13,103,430
18-44	62,123,559	39,199,970
45-64	77,753,773	49,062,630
65-74	743,613,098	469,219,900
75+	178,454,245	112,604,600
Total	1,082,710,800	683,190,530

Table 7.15: Projected Number of Nursing Home
Residents and Total Costs (in 1990 dollars)
in the United States by Age of Resident and
Year for the Middle Scenario

Year/Age of Resident	Residents	Total Costs
1990		
65-74	226,332	$ 310,527,477
75-84	580,180	851,703,844
85+	678,560	1,015,804,843
Total	1,485,072	2,178,036,163
2000		
65-74	228,219	$ 313,116,893
75-84	712,013	1,045,234,878
85+	944,760	1,414,305,166
Total	1,884,992	2,772,656,937
2030		
65-74	473,318	$ 649,392,584
75-84	1,361,303	1,998,393,405
85+	1,846,273	2,763,870,112
Total	3,680,894	5,411,656,101
2050		
65-74	440,206	$ 603,962,234
75-84	1,500,657	2,202,964,784
85+	3,888,664	5,821,330,008
Total	5,829,527	8,628,257,026

impact on the demands for, and costs of, health care and long-term care in the
United States in the coming decades.

IMPLICATIONS FOR PUBLIC COSTS AND REVENUES

Health and education are only two of many services that are required for a nation's population to survive. Defense, transportation, social services, and many
other services are required for a society to exist and each has associated costs.
Populations also generate additional revenue as a result of their generation of in-

come. How will future population change affect both federal government costs and revenues? In this final section, we examine the implications of population change for federal tax revenues and expenditures.

Table 7.16 shows the income tax revenues likely to be paid by households in different income categories assuming that the distribution of households by income is as projected in Chapter 5 and per-household taxes remain at 1990 levels. The data in Chapter 5 indicated that the number of households would increase in lower-income categories more rapidly than in higher-income categories due to the historical patterns of lower income being associated with minority households. The data in this table suggest that tax revenues from individuals in the nation would increase substantially by 2050 but not as rapidly as they would if the composition of the population in 2050 were to reflect the race/ethnicity composition of the population in 1990. Again, it is essential to note that this relationship is a result of the lack of access that minority populations have had to the acquisition of skills and education necessary to earn higher incomes. Nevertheless, unless the incomes of minority populations are increased, tax revenues in 2050 would be $834.3 billion rather than $890.9 billion–$56 billion less than they would be if the composition of 1990 prevails through 2050. Equally important to recognize is that revenues would be substantially higher due to the impact of immigrants and their descendants. A comparison of the zero immigration scenario to the middle scenario shows that immigrants and their descendants would generate an additional $150 billion in revenues each year.

The overall effect of population growth on the federal government's revenues and expenditures is shown in Table 7.17. Because the data in this table were generated by multiplying per capita revenue and expenditure values for 1990 by the total number of persons, they simply reflect the same relative proportional increases as the population, but the results are nevertheless significant. For example, under the projected (middle scenario) patterns, the deficit would increase by more than $100 billion per year by 2050 simply as a result of the increased number of persons in the population. The growth of the population will only accentuate the nation's budgetary problems, if the nation continues to spend more per person than it generates in revenues.

In sum, the projected population patterns of the future would generate substantial new revenues but would also increase costs. The growth of the population will further erode the financial base of the nation, unless the costs and revenues associated with each person are altered.

SUMMARY AND IMPLICATIONS OF POPULATION CHANGE FOR SERVICES, TAXES, AND REVENUES

The analysis of the impacts of future population change on selected services and federal revenues and expenditures presented in this chapter point to the effects of population change. The results suggest that:

Table 7.16: Projected Tax Revenues in the United States Assuming Average Tax by Income Category in 1990[a] and Projected Race/Ethnicity Composition in 2050 Under the Middle and Zero Immigration Scenarios and Assuming the 1990 Race/Ethnicity Distribution in 2050

Household Income	Tax Revenues (in $000)				Percent Change 1990 - 2050		
	1990	Middle Scenario 2050	Zero Immigration Scenario 2050	Assuming 1990 Composition in 2050	Middle Scenario	Zero Immigration Scenario	1990 Distribution
< $5,000	$ 615,302	$ 1,380,112	$ 1,096,586	$ 1,163,218	124.3	78.2	89.1
$5,000-$9,999	3,419,986	5,613,135	4,627,002	5,360,110	64.1	35.3	56.7
$10,000-$14,999	8,450,091	12,032,880	9,766,811	11,487,510	42.4	15.6	35.9
$15,000-$24,999	32,766,619	43,939,890	35,844,490	42,999,730	34.1	9.4	31.2
$25,000-$34,999	43,209,186	75,039,740	61,570,710	75,848,160	73.7	42.5	75.5
$35,000-$49,999	67,503,432	121,134,400	99,786,230	126,022,000	79.5	47.8	86.7
$50,000-$74,999	87,241,466	173,272,100	142,213,900	183,475,800	98.6	63.0	110.3
$75,000-$99,999	44,375,252	98,248,910	80,092,950	105,276,900	121.4	80.5	137.2
$100,000+	159,545,371	303,614,300	248,972,300	339,231,500	90.3	56.1	112.6
Total	447,126,705	834,275,467	683,970,979	890,864,928	86.6	53.0	99.2

[a] From Social Security Information Bulletin 12: (1) 54 Washington, D.C.: Department of the Treasury, Internal Revenue Service, 1992.

Table 7.17: Annual Federal Revenues by Source and Expenditures by Type in 1990 and Projected in 2050 Under the Middle and Zero Immigration Scenarios

Source	1990 Values	2050 Values, Middle Scenario	2050 Values, Zero Immigration Scenario
Revenues			
Individual income tax	$ 373,197,501,139	$ 579,222,685,531	$ 479,915,074,106
Social Security	289,116,327,603	448,724,161,321	371,790,495,284
All other	260,623,704,014	404,502,070,060	335,150,272,560
Total revenues	922,937,532,756	1,432,448,916,912	1,186,855,841,950
Expenditures			
Defense	$ 271,902,034,186	$ 422,006,647,851	$ 349,653,694,055
Postal service	31,216,183,198	48,449,202,925	40,142,596,955
Space	9,637,210,920	14,957,472,044	12,393,016,509
Education	32,543,045,571	50,508,565,018	41,848,881,837
Social service	114,668,842,977	177,972,239,827	147,458,935,570
Transportation	18,680,825,516	28,993,650,521	24,022,695,046
Public safety	5,935,963,248	9,212,935,679	7,633,379,735
Environment and housing	81,392,531,358	126,325,606,286	104,667,106,824
Government administration	11,871,926,496	18,425,871,359	15,266,759,468
Interest on debt	150,249,705,035	233,195,660,165	193,214,311,740
Social Security/Medicaid	280,142,547,869	434,796,370,324	360,250,621,215
All other insurance/ trust/expenditures	32,333,540,986	50,183,402,583	41,579,468,434
All other expenditures	69,974,531,464	108,604,253,537	89,984,076,395
Total expenditures	1,110,548,888,824	1,723,631,878,119	1,428,115,543,783
Net deficit surplus	-187,611,356,068	-291,182,961,207	-241,259,701,833

Source: U.S. Bureau of the Census. Government Finances: 1989-90, Series GF/90-5, Washington, DC: U.S. Government Printing Office, 1991.

1. Historically, both school enrollment and health care demands have risen more rapidly than the growth of the population of the United States.

2. As a result of such changes, there were 45.8 million elementary and secondary students and 13.5 million college students in 1990. These students were being taught by more than 2.5 million elementary and secondary teachers and 824,000 college teachers at a total cost approaching $360 billion per year.

3. Similarly, there were more than 2.6 million health professionals with physician contacts exceeding 1.3 billion and total days of hospital care nearly 544 million in 1990. Total health expenditures were in excess of $666 billion in 1990 (12.2 percent of GNP).

4. Projections of future enrollment suggest an increase of 35.7 percent from 1990 to 2050 under the middle scenario. This is faster growth than the 2-percent growth experienced during the 1980s but less than the 43-percent growth experienced during the 1950s. Growth is projected to be much more rapid among elementary and secondary than among college students. Elementary and secondary enrollment is projected to increase by 40.7 percent from 1990 to 2050 under the middle scenario, but college enrollment is projected to increase only by 17.9 percent. In fact, if slower population growth occurs, the number of persons enrolled in higher education could decline below 1990 levels by 2030. As a result of these patterns, the number of teachers and expenditures in education are likely to show relatively modest growth in the coming decades.

5. Enrollment growth will display the effects of the changing race/ethnicity composition of the population. By 2050, 56 percent of all students enrolled in elementary and secondary schools will be minority and 43 percent of college students will be minority (under the middle scenario) compared to 31 percent of elementary and secondary students and 20 percent of college students in 1990. Of the total net increase in enrollments projected under the middle scenario, nearly all will be due to growth in minority enrollment because Anglo enrollment will decline.

6. Future health care needs show very different patterns than those for education. Whereas educational needs will grow more slowly than the future population, health care needs will increase more rapidly than the population. The incidence of diseases and disorders is projected to increase by 67.4 percent from 1990 to 2050 compared to the increase of 53.9 percent for population.

7. The aging of the population is, in large part, responsible for these increases in incidences but the aging of the population also leads to an aging of the patient population—such that by 2050 (under the middle scenario) 59.9 percent of all incidences of diseases and disorders will be among persons 45 years of age or older (compared to 45.1 percent in 1990).

8. The racial and ethnic changes projected for the population have a somewhat smaller impact on health than on education because health care needs are greater among the elderly, which is composed of a higher proportion of Anglos. However, more than 75 percent of the total net increase in the number of incidences of dis-

eases and disorders would be due to increases in the size of minority populations (under the middle scenario) and, by 2050, the proportion of incidences involving minority group members could increase to 43 percent of all cases.

9. Data on incidences of specific types of diseases and disorders suggest that minority populations will have the largest impacts on diseases and disorders related to younger ages and that Anglos will have larger impacts on diseases of the elderly. For example, by 2050, minority populations would account for more than 55 percent of all incidences of diseases and disorders related to pregnancy, births, and neonates although they would account for only about 40 percent of those related to eye and circulatory diseases and disorders.

10. The implications of the changes in enrollment and in health care are evident when data on projected changes are examined relative to students and patients, personnel, and costs. The required increase in elementary and secondary teachers for the 60-year projection period would be about 1.2 million, similar to that for the 30-year period from 1960 to 1990. The number of college teachers would increase by 160,000 from 1990 to 2050, only 10,000 more for a 60-year period than during the decade of the 1980s, when 150,000 new college teachers were added to colleges and universities in the United States. Because future growth in enrollments is more modest, total expenditures on education should also grow more modestly than in the past.

11. The implications for health care are substantially different than those for education. The number of health care professionals needed would increase as rapidly as the total population and health care costs would be substantially increased because of the aging of the population. For example, from 1990 to 2050, the costs of physician services for persons 65 to 74 years of age would increase by 94.5 percent and the costs among persons 75 years of age or older would increase by 232.4 percent. Nursing home patients would also increase rapidly, from 1.5 to 5.8 million between 1990 and 2050, with the growth being fastest among the oldest. The number of nursing home residents 65 to 74 years of age would increase by 94.5 percent from 1990 to 2050, the number 75 to 84 years of age would increase by 158.7 percent, and the number 85 years of age or older would increase by 473.1 percent (under the middle scenario).

12. Increased service needs have implications for federal government expenditures; thus population growth affects federal revenues as well. Tax revenues would increase substantially but, because of the lower incomes of minority populations, the projected growth produces $56 billion less in taxes in 2050 than would have been the case if the 1990 composition of the population prevailed in 2050. Unless either the amount of revenues per person is increased or expenditures decreased, the growth of the population under current patterns would increase the deficit by more than $100 billion a year by 2050.

The results presented in this chapter for education and health care show that the changing demographics of America are likely to affect different services in very different manners, depending on whether they are services used primarily by the old or the young or by majority-or minority-group members. For those service areas linked to younger populations, such as education, the future may bring slower growth but for those such as health care the projected patterns may bring very rapid growth. Clearly, it is essential to know how a service is affected by demographics to know how it is likely to fare in the coming years.

All services, however, are projected to be markedly impacted by the increased importance of minority populations. Although these impacts are greatest among those services involving younger populations, because minority populations are younger than majority populations, the impacts are pervasive in nearly all service areas. For nearly all services the client population is likely to become more diverse.

These findings show the importance of careful planning of public services, because, as is evident above, it is not always obvious how services will be impacted by future patterns. Unless the implications of demographic change are examined and taken into account, services may either fail to be developed requiring costly accelerated facility expansion, or may be overbuilt in anticipation of levels of need that never materialize. There is little doubt that public-service planning is likely to be of increased importance in the coming decades.

The results also present some sobering findings related to the growth in need and the likely resources to meet such need. On the one hand, the aging population base will increase some needs substantially at the very time that this large population segment declines in productivity and resources. On the other hand, the population in the productive ages is likely to be increasingly composed of minority residents who, as noted in Chapter 5, have experienced more limited access to resources and are thus likely to also have fewer resources to pay for services. The findings related to revenues and expenditures suggest that, since population members are costing more for service provision than they are paying in revenues, population growth will lead to larger deficits. In addition, the other trends presented in this and earlier chapters suggest that the gap may further widen unless service costs are reduced or the income- and revenue-generating capability of the population is increased. In fact, there is little in the analysis presented here to suggest that the fiscal crisis in America is a short-term phenomenon. Rather, demographic factors suggest that it will continue for the foreseeable future and could worsen without cost containment and revenue maintenance or enhancement.

What is suggested by the findings in this chapter, then, is that governing America and providing the American population with public services is likely to be increasingly difficult in the future. Competing needs among groups with diverse levels of resources, increasing needs coupled with stagnant or declining revenues and other resources, and growing diversity that is likely to lead to increasingly diverse views about the appropriate course for the future are all suggested by the demographic future of the nation. For those who would govern, and for those who would serve the public in the provision of services, it is likely that the future will be an especially challenging one.

CHAPTER EIGHT

Summary, Conclusions, and Implications

In this work, we have examined the implications of future demographic change in the United States for selected areas of American society. We have examined the implications of three major demographic changes—the rate of population growth and of immigration in producing that growth; the growth of minority populations; and the aging of the population. The implications of these three de-mographic events have been examined in regard to their impact on the labor force; household structure, income, and poverty; business; and services, public revenues, and public expenditures in America. In this final chapter, we summa-rize the key findings of the work, delineate the general trends that are evident in the findings, and suggest some of the overall implications of the findings for the future of the United States.

SUMMARY OF MAJOR FINDINGS

The findings from the analyses in individual chapters have been previously pre-sented in the summaries for those chapters and will not be repeated here. Rather, in this section, general findings that have emerged from the demographic analysis and from examinations of topical areas are presented. Among the most important of these findings are the following:

1. Rates of future growth will be slower than those of the past. For example, in the 1980s the population of the United States increased by 9.8 percent, but pro-jected patterns (under the middle scenario) show rates of growth as large as those of the 1980s only for the decade of the 1990s and an average rate of growth of about 8.9 percent per decade for the total projection period from 1990 to 2050. Similarly, the civilian labor force of the United States increased by 16.7 percent during the 1980s but is projected to increase by an average of 7.4 percent per de-cade in the future. The number of households, which increased by 13.8 percent during the 1980s, would increase by 10.6 percent per decade from 1990 to 2050.

2. The projected growth in the population, households, and the labor force will be heavily dependent on immigration. Of the net growth from 1990 to 2050 under the middle scenario, 61 percent of the 134-million increase in population is projected to be due to immigrants and their descendants; for the labor force, 72.2 percent of the 54.9-million increase would be due to immigrants and their descendants; and for households, 47.1 percent of the 58.6-million increase is projected to be due to immigrants and their descendants.

3. Increasing ethnic diversity will be a pervasive pattern. For example, the minority population of the nation will increase from 24.3 percent in 1990 to 47.3 percent in 2050 (under the middle scenario), with 89.8 percent of the net growth in the population from 1990 to 2050 being due to growth in minority populations. Among households, the increase will be from 19.9 percent being minority households in 1990 to 41.2 percent in 2050; 74.7 percent of the net growth in households from 1990 to 2050 would be due to increases in the number of minority households. For the labor force, the minority proportion increases from 21.7 percent in 1990 to 45.0 percent in 2050, with 98 percent of the net change being due to growth in the minority labor force.

4. Aging will also be pervasive. In 1990, 12.6 percent of the population was 65 years of age or older but, by 2050, 20.6 percent of the population would be 65 years of age or older. Similarly, 21.7 percent of all households had a householder who was 65 years of age or older in 1990 but, by 2050, 32.6 percent of all households would have a householder who was 65 years of age or older. For the labor force, the percentage that is 55 years of age or older would increase overall from 12.3 percent in 1990 to 18.9 percent in 2050.

5. Relative to the labor force, the demographic trends noted above will lead to a slower-growing, more ethnically diverse, and older labor force. Unless the existing relationships between levels of education and occupational patterns and minority status and age change, these patterns will also lead to an extensive increase in the number of retirees from the workforce with related implications for retirement costs for the public and private sectors, a decline in the overall occupational and educational status of the workforce, higher rates of unemployment, and reduced earning power. Retirement costs would nearly double from those of the 1980s by 2050, the percentage of persons in managerial and professional specialties would decline relative to that in 1990, the number of unemployed would increase by more than 87 percent, and the number of workers with less than a high school education would increase by more than 5 percent compared to the levels of 1990. Given trends that suggest that future labor needs will be for persons with more technical skills and higher levels of education, the implications of such trends are that America's labor force could become less competitive in the future, unless the historical relationships between minority status and educational and occupational attainment are altered.

6. Patterns of change in populations and households are related to income and poverty. Trends in American households, the major income earning and consum-

ing unit, suggest that the number of households with children will increase and the number of family households will grow faster than the number of nonfamily and childless households, reversing historical trends in household change. However, the number of married-couple households does not increase as rapidly as one-parent households, which generally have more limited socioeconomic resources. Because minority households tend to have lower incomes and are expected to grow more rapidly than majority households, future patterns would lead to a larger proportion of households with low incomes and to lower levels of aggregate income growth than if the ethnic distribution of 1990 prevailed in the future. Average income per household would decline from 1990 to 2050 and the percentage of families in poverty would increase by 2050 relative to 1990 levels. For example, aggregate income would increase by nearly $2.0 trillion from 1990 to 2050 but would be $325 billion less in 2050 under the middle scenario projection than if the 1990 ethnic distribution prevailed in 2050. The proportion of families in poverty would increase from 10.0 percent in 1990 to 13.1 percent in 2050. A higher proportion of aggregate income would also be in minority households, with the percentage of aggregate income in minority households increasing from 15 percent in 1990 to 35 percent in 2050.

7. Demographic trends would differentially impact business in America. Consumer income, discretionary income, owner housing, and participation in many forms of organized recreational activities are higher among majority households. In the future, each of these factors will shift toward greater involvement of minority households. However, consumer income, discretionary income, net worth, and owner-related housing expenditures are projected to continue to be disproportionately concentrated among majority households. Whereas 80.1 percent of all households in 1990 were Anglo households, 84.0 percent of consumer expenditures, 88.3 percent of discretionary income, 91.2 percent of net worth, and 92 percent of homeowner-related expenditures in 1990 were in Anglo households. In 2050, 58.8 percent of all households would be Anglo as would 63.0 percent of consumer expenditures, 71.6 percent of discretionary income, 75.2 percent of net worth, and 77.5 percent of owner-related expenditures. Although growth in the number of persons from 1990 to 2050 increases the total level of expenditures, discretionary income, net worth, housing-related expenditures, and the number of persons involved in recreation, the increase in the minority population (if historical relationships between minority status and income and recreational involvement do not change) will decrease the overall levels of each of these factors relative to what would occur if the 1990 ethnic composition of the population were to prevail. The aging of the population has less uniform effects, increasing total expenditures, net worth, levels of housing ownership, and owner-related expenditures—but decreasing involvement in recreation.

8. Demographic change will impact different types of services in very different ways, but will likely increase both the level of public revenues and expenditures and increase the budget deficit, unless relationships between demographic factors

and service needs, costs, and revenues are changed. Educational services are disproportionately impacted by young age groups and show higher rates of enrollment, beyond mandatory ages of attendance, for majority- rather than minority-group members. The slower rates of population growth, the changing ethnic distribution of the population, and the aging of the population will bring about slower overall levels of growth in enrollment than occurred in the 1960s and 1970s but more rapid growth than during the 1980s. The growth will be primarily among elementary and secondary students with college enrollments increasing only modestly during the projection period. Overall, growth in educational enrollments and in teachers and expenditures related to such enrollments will be modest. The ethnic composition of those enrolled will, however, change dramatically toward larger enrollments among minority students, with 56 percent of all elementary and secondary students and 43.4 percent of college students being minority by 2050. Health and long-term care show very different patterns. The aging of the population increases needs for health and long-term care services substantially. The incidences of diseases and disorders would increase by 67.4 percent from 1990 to 2050 compared to a 53.9-percent increase in the population. Overall, by 2050, 59.9 percent of all incidences would be among those 45 years of age or older compared to 45.1 percent in 1990, and the proportion of such incidences involving minorities would increase from 20.7 percent in 1990 to 42.9 percent in 2050. In general, the largest increases in incidence among minorities would occur for diseases/disorders associated with younger ages (such as health care related to pregnancy); Anglo proportions remain highest for diseases/disorders more common among older persons (for example, diseases of the circulatory system).

As a result of the growth in health care requirements, the demand for health care professionals would increase by more than 50 percent from 1990 to 2050, the number of physician contacts and associated costs would increase by more than 66 percent, and the number of nursing home residents would increase by more than 296 percent. Both public revenues and expenditures would increase as well but, because current patterns are such that expenditures per person exceed revenues per person, the projected population growth would add an additional $100 billion to the budget deficit each year by 2050.

Clearly, the changes suggested by the analysis of the implications of slower population growth, increasing ethnic diversity, and the aging of the population are extensive. These changes would impact not only the number of Americans, but the characteristics of the American workforce and households, the wealth of American households and families, the level and forms of business opportunities in the American economy, the types of services required, and the level of financial resources available to the nation to pay for services. Although all of the implications described above were arrived at by assuming that the 1990 relationships between demographic and other factors will continue in the future, which is unlikely to be the case, they show, nevertheless, that the demographic future of America is likely to have implications for many aspects of American society.

Table 8.1: Indices of Dissimilarity (based on race/ethnicity categories) Between Populations, Households, or Labor Forces and Selected Socioeconomic Factors, 1990 and 2050

Socioeconomic Factor	Index of Dissimilarity, 1990	Index of Dissimilarity, 2050
Household income	4.9	7.0
Household expenditures	5.8	9.4
Household discretionary income	8.2	14.1
Household net worth	11.5	19.0
Percent of labor force in managerial/professional occupations	7.3	12.6
Percent of population enrolled in elementary and secondary school	4.2	6.5
Percent of population enrolled in college	4.7	7.2

GENERAL IMPLICATIONS FOR AMERICAN SOCIETY

Having summarized the findings from the analysis, it is important to ascertain whether there are general themes that emerge from the findings: What will the demography of tomorrow mean for the United States? The trends suggest several emergent themes, which are summarized below.

A Nation of Diversity, Maturity, and Inequality

Much of the analysis of demographic trends described here suggests that, coupled with the diversity created by slower growth and changing ethnic and aging patterns, the United States is likely to experience increasing diversity in socioeconomic resources and increasing differences between the wealthiest and poorest Americans. This growing inequity can be seen by examining the index of dissimilarity values for selected items shown in Table 8.1. The index of dissimilarity as used here indicates the differences between the percentage of households, the population, and the labor force in certain categories and the percentage of the factor of interest in the same categories. For example, the index of dissimilarity for household income shows the difference in the distribution of households by race/ethnicity and the distribution of aggregate household income by race/ethnicity. If the two distributions were identical, that is, each race/ethnicity group had the same percentage of aggregate income as it did of all households, then the index of dissimilarity value would be zero; if all income was obtained by a single group it would have a value of 100 percent. Since the size of the index value varies widely

**Table 8.2: Indices of Dissimilarity (based on age categories) Between
Populations, Households, or Labor Forces and Selected
Socioeconomic Factors, 1990 and 2050**

Socioeconomic Factor	Index of Dissimilarity, 1990	Index of Dissimilarity, 2050
Annual expenditures	10.2	12.2
Annual discretionary income	12.1	14.3
Homeowners	10.4	9.9
Size of civilian labor force	17.6	21.7
Incidence of diseases/disorders	13.9	16.8
Annual costs of physician contacts	11.1	12.8

with the item being examined, the findings of greatest interest in Table 8.1 are how
the size of these indices change over the projection period from 1990 to 2050.

An examination of the indices in Table 8.1 suggests that the effects of projected
demographic change on each of these factors is to increase the differences between racial/ethnic groups. For example, although the data presented earlier indicate that a larger share of total aggregate household income would be controlled
by minority households in 2050 than in 1990, minority populations would actually experience a decline in their **relative** share of income compared to their proportion of the population. Similarly, minorities would experience a relative decline in their share of consumer spending, discretionary income, net worth,
employment in managerial and professional occupations, and enrollment in education. The picture is clear: The projected demographic trends are likely to lead to
greater inequality in America if the relationships between socioeconomic factors
and race/ethnicity are not altered from their present patterns.

Similar patterns emerge relative to the indices of dissimilarity by age shown in
Table 8.2. Although data were not available to examine all of the same factors that
were examined for race/ethnicity, it is obvious that the aging of the population
will generally increase inequality between the young and the old. The old will gain
a disproportionate share of resources relative to the young.

These patterns could be particularly important because America historically
has been a nation focused on youth and the perpetuation of youth and a nation
controlled by majority ethnic groups—yet America's population will be increasing elderly and minority. The aging of the population and the increased proportion of minorities in the population, coupled with the fact than an increasing
amount of resources will be controlled by the elderly and minorities, could substantially alter the treatment of the elderly and minorities in America. Addition-

ally, it is likely to enhance the already substantial political influence of the elderly and substantially enhance the political clout of minority populations.

A Nation in Need

The data presented here also suggest that the projected demographic trends will likely produce a population that is not only (as suggested above) a nation with increasing inequality but also one with increasing levels of need as well. Both the aging of the population, which means more health problems and higher rates of dependency, and the increase in minority populations, which involves increases in the number and proportion of persons with low incomes and high rates of poverty, suggest that the relative level of need in the population of the United States will increase. The increasing rates of poverty, the reduced levels of average household income, the increasing number of physician visits and increasing physician costs, and the increasing number of nursing home residents expected to result from the projected changes in the population suggest that the demographics of the future are likely to increase the overall level of need in American society. This need, in turn, is likely, as suggested by the values shown for public costs, to lead to a nation with a substantial increase in costs for social and human services.

A Nation of Dissension

Although the United States has been among the most successful nations in the world in integrating diverse interests and concerns, it is nevertheless evident that the themes noted above may also have the potential to increase conflict between rich and poor, young and old, families with children and those without, immigrants and natives, and among minority- and majority-group members. It might be argued that the political fabric of the nation will become more complex, its people more difficult to unite around common issues and concerns, and that special interests will become even more diverse in composition and divergent in their social, economic, and political ends. Political and social climates change rapidly, such that any such projected theme must be seen as highly speculative, but nevertheless, the potential for diversity and divergence and increasing levels of need to lead to dissension must be acknowledged.

A Nation of Potential Opportunity

The growth of the minority population, with its relative youth, can also be seen as a potential source of opportunity for the United States. If the inequalities noted throughout this work are addressed, the growth of the minority population could bring with it substantial changes in the social and economic structure of the United States. Similarly, as noted in Chapter 6 on business impacts, the diversity is likely to represent opportunities for new businesses to serve new market segments. Such diversity may also provide conduits for innovative ideas for public- and private-sector social and economic development.

It is clear, however, that addressing relative socioeconomic inequalities among groups is likely to be necessary to allow the nation to capitalize on the virtues of diversity. Table 8.3 presents data showing projections of selected factors examined in this work. The projected values under the middle scenario for 2050 are compared to a set of projections in which the total population and the number of households is projected to be of the same size as those projected under the middle scenario for 2050; but Anglo levels for 1990 for the factors examined (for example, average household income values for Anglos) are assumed to apply to all race/ethnicity groups. Thus, values for 2050 are as if the entire population in 2050 had the socioeconomic characteristics of Anglos.

Table 8.3 shows that the closure of differences between minority and majority populations would have substantial socioeconomic impacts on the nation. Aggregate income and consumer expenditures would increase by between 12 and 10 percent; the poverty rate would decline by more than 35 percent; discretionary income would increase by more than 80 percent; net worth would increase by 28 percent; the number of unemployed would decline by nearly 50 percent; the number of persons employed in services would decline by more than 18 percent; the number employed in managerial and professional occupations would increase by 10 percent; and college enrollment would increase by nearly 19 percent. Housing and recreational patterns show alternative patterns of growth and decline, depending on which component one examines, but both still show substantial effects from altering race/ethnicity differentials. The effects of closing the differentials between minority and majority residents represent not only opportunities for minority residents but opportunities for improving the socioeconomic welfare of the entire nation.

It would, of course, be naive to suggest that such differences can be eliminated immediately or easily. A substantial investment of resources would be required to eliminate them and a substantial long-term effort would likely be necessary. Data such as those in Table 8.3 suggest, however, that reducing these differences is of national significance as well as important to the groups involved.

A Nation Challenged

Whether viewed as a vehicle creating opportunities or one creating difficulties and dissension, there is little doubt that the projected demographic future is one that will challenge the nation's resources and leadership. Never before in the history of the United States has its population grown as slowly over such an extended period, never has it been so ethnically diverse, and never has it been as old. Nor has it often attempted to integrate as large a number of immigrants in as short a period.

These future populations are ones likely to require extensive resources both to assist those with limited means, due to age or impoverishment, and to provide the education, training, technology, and other factors needed to create an economi-

Table 8.3: Comparison of Projections of Selected Items for 2050 Under the Middle Scenario and Projections Completed for 2050 Assuming 1990 Anglo Rates Apply to All Racial/Ethnic Groups

Item	Middle Scenario Projections for 2050	Projection for 2050 Assuming 1990 Anglo Rates	Percent Difference
Annual aggregate income	$5,419,373,929,000	$6,069,515,316,132	12.0
Annual consumer expenditures	$3,735,982,547,633	$4,106,799,774,865	9.9
Percent of families in poverty	13.1%	8.4%	-35.9
Annual expenditures for:			
Owner housing	$258,910,528,142	$298,966,103,100	15.5
Renter housing	$92,405,589,451	$82,890,478,395	-10.3
Annual discretionary income	$638,154,178,448	$1,152,099,199,452	80.5
Net worth	$13,174,581,948,614	$16,860,047,603,516	28.0
Labor force (selected characteristics)			
Managerial and professional occupations	43,921,593	48,385,721	10.2
Service occupations	26,271,426	21,370,082	-18.7
Unemployed	1,873,924	937,969	-49.9
Persons enrolled in college	16,353,810	19,451,684	18.9
Annual recreational participants:			
Baseball	30,658,901	24,593,771	-19.8
Tennis	37,375,224	42,337,782	13.3
Golf	33,154,952	42,621,869	28.6

cally competitive labor force. Meeting needs and creating opportunities for the nation will be challenging.

Similarly, the challenge to leadership is likely to be extensive. Integrating the diverse groups in the population sufficiently to provide bases for developing and obtaining passage of legislation, and creating and allocating the resources needed to address needs and opportunities, will be difficult. Leadership has always been complex but it is likely to be especially difficult for future leaders as they attempt to obtain the level of consensus necessary to govern and lead the nation.

CONCLUSION: KNOWING THE FUTURE IS IMPOSSIBLE, BUT ASSESSING IT IS ESSENTIAL

In this work, I have attempted to examine the implications of projected population change in the United States for a number of socioeconomic dimensions of American society. The major conclusions and implications from this work are based on projections of the population for an extended period of time in the future and on projections of the likely relationships between demographic and other factors assuming, in large part, that these relationships will continue over a 60-year period. The projections are made without regard to the many other dimensions, such as changes in the world economy, that will alter the future. Given that the projected patterns may be altered by future events, it is certain that nearly all of these projections will be incorrect in the exact numerical values they project for the future, especially the distant future. Some will likely be incorrect even in the direction of the effects projected. Caution in the use of these and all other projections must thus be reiterated.

It is also important to recognize that there will be substantial regional and local variation from more general patterns described for the nation. In general, the populations of the Northeast and Midwest regions of the nation are growing slower, are older, and have lower proportions of minority-group members than those of the South or West. Thus, as noted above, nine of the ten fastest-growing states from 1980 to 1990 were in the South and West. Of the ten states with the highest median age in 1990, seven were in the Northeast and Midwest. Of the ten states with the highest proportion of Black residents, nine were in the South, and of the ten states with the highest proportion of Hispanic residents, seven were in the West and Southwest. Similarly, there will be variations from rural to urban, suburban to city, and in many other areas. For those who want to know the applicability of the patterns described in this book for their area, analyses of local and regional patterns will be essential.

Despite such cautions, it is nevertheless evident that it is necessary to know the future if we wish to alter it. Examining the course of events that will unfold if current patterns continue into the future is essential if we are to capitalize on the opportunities and mitigate the problems they may create. Thus, studies such as that represented by this work must be completed. Clearly, additional studies examining implications in other areas, using more sophisticated analytical methods and examining the roles of other factors in conjunction with demographic dimensions, should be completed. This analysis has been simply an initial attempt to examine the long-term implications of population change in America. There will and must be many more.

Despite the limitations of projections and the need for additional analyses, the examples provided here should make clear that demographic factors will play a critical role in the future of the United States. Although demography is not destiny, it does provide the skeletal base on which much of the social, economic, and political structure of the nation is built.

It has often been noted that to ignore the past is to destine oneself to repeat its mistakes. It can be asserted, as well, that to ignore the future is to eliminate the opportunity to alter it. I am hopeful that this effort has enhanced that opportunity and that future analyses will provide additional indications of what the future may be and of how it can be altered.

Notes

1. It is also essential to realize that population projections, such as those utilized here, are usually made using explicit assumptions about future patterns in the three demographic processes of births (fertility), deaths (mortality), and the movement of persons (migration) into (immigration), and out of (emigration), the country (Day 1992). These three demographic processes are, in turn, impacted by a multitude of economic, social, and other factors. Fertility, for example, has been seen as being determined both by economic patterns, which reflect conditions at a given point in time, or cyclical patterns, which are generational rather than a product of prevailing economic conditions (Ahlburg 1982). It is evident that projections of future fertility have often been inaccurate (Carter and Lee 1986). Mortality, too, is often difficult to predict because it is not clear whether past improvements in longevity will continue, reverse, or accelerate as a result of breakthroughs likely to result from biotechnology and other medical advancements (Stoto and Durch 1993). As a result, widely different projections have often existed for such groups as the elderly (Alho and Spencer 1990).

Immigration is also complex and is often seen as the most difficult demographic process to project (Spencer 1986). The projection of immigration is particularly difficult because its level in the United States is often a product of legislation; immigration laws such as the Immigration Reform and Control Act of 1986 or the Immigration Act of 1990 can vastly alter projections of future growth. In addition, such world events as the dissolution of the Soviet Union, the opening of relations with China, and various trade agreements may also impact immigration patterns to the United States (Acevado and Espenshade 1992).

2. There is no totally satisfactory means of either identifying racial/ethnic groups or for referring to racial/ethnic groups (McLemore 1991). I define race/ethnicity in this work by using the categories of Anglo, Black, Other, and Hispanic, with the first three groups being persons of the White, Black, and all Other racial groups (combining Asian and Pacific Islander; American Indian, Aleut, and Eskimo; and other racial groups) who are not of Hispanic origin. By so doing, I reduce the number of persons in groups such as Black, Asian, American Indian, and other groups. This is done so that sums across groups including the Hispanic ethnic group will be equal to the total population and because the numbers of persons who are Black and Hispanic; Asian, Indian, Aleut, or Eskimo and Hispanic; and Asian and Pacific Islander and Hispanic is small (roughly 2.6 percent of Blacks, 8.5 percent of American Indians, Aleuts, and Eskimos, and 4.2 percent of Asians and Pacific Islanders). This also substantially reduces the size of the "Other" racial category because that category consisted largely of Hispanics who did not define themselves as in the White, Black, Asian and Pacific Islander, or American Indian, Aleut, or Eskimo categories (thus, only 2.5 percent of the persons in the Other race category were not Hispanics). I have chosen to define race/ethnicity in this manner because I believe values for individual race/ethnic groups

that sum to the total population provide a clearer understanding of trends and patterns and that including Hispanics among such groups is essential because of the major role this group plays in future population growth in the United States. Obviously, alternative categories could be employed and might be preferable for other uses.

I have also chosen to aggregate all non-Hispanic, Asian, and Pacific Islanders; American Indians, Aleuts, and Eskimo; and the Other racial group into a category I refer to as "Other." This reduces the number of categories in the presentation of information. Space limitations required eliminating more detailed information for numerous items. This aggregation admittedly ignores substantial differences among individual groups within the Other category and, again, other modes of presentation might have been used. Those used delineate the largest ethnic groups in the United States and provide substantial detail in the results presented for these groups.

I refer to non-Hispanic Whites as Anglos. Some may object to this term because of the name's roots in largely western European Anglo-Saxon traditions. Obviously many non-Hispanic Whites are not of western European heritage. Similarly, I use the terms Black and Hispanic even though some may prefer the terms African-American and Latino (or other terms). I have selected reference names that I believe are commonly understood and hope that in so doing I have not failed to adequately or appropriately refer to any group.

3. This is because an unanticipated change is likely to have altered conditions less in a shorter period of time. Most projections are based on assumptions that use patterns from the past as a means of anticipating the future. Larger numerical errors are necessary to produce larger rates of error in large population areas thus making it more likely to have larger percentage and other "rates" of error in smaller areas.

4. Cohort-component methods involve projections made by making specific assumptions about the demographic processes of fertility, mortality, and migration. Understanding such a set of projections requires one to understand the assumptions being made about the demographic processes—assumptions about what will happen to fertility, mortality, and migration in the future. There is substantial uncertainty about the future of all three of these processes in the United States.

Fertility has shown periodic fluctuations from a general pattern of long-term decline. The best known of these peaks is the well- publicized baby-boom period from 1946 to 1964. Fertility increased from a total fertility rate of about 2.5 children per woman in 1946 to nearly 3.6 at the height of the baby boom in 1957 and then gradually declined to pre-boom levels by the mid-1960s. Citing less dramatic but nevertheless significant and repeated changes in fertility, Lee and others (Lee 1974; Carter and Lee 1986) have argued that many of the past projections of the U.S. population have been too conservative because they assume that long- term declines in fertility will continue when in fact much of history suggests periodic fluctuations. Richard Easterlin, an economic demographer, maintains that fertility is inversely related to the size of a cohort so that large cohorts have small numbers of births and small cohorts have larger numbers of births because the economic fortunes of a cohort are tied to its size (Easterlin 1987). Large cohorts that experience substantial competition tend to depress their fertility, perceiving that there are too many competitors, while small cohorts failing to experience such competition opt for larger numbers of births. However the history of fertility is viewed, it is clear that fertility may change over time and is not readily predictable (Ahlburg and Land 1992).

Mortality has declined substantially over time, with life expectancy at birth having increased from less than 50 years in 1900 to more than 75 years in 1992. For more than 25 years, mortality has been declining at a rate of 1 to 2 percent per year (Ahlburg and Vaupel 1990), but there is a continuing debate about both the ultimate life span of humans and about how substantial declines in mortality may be in the future (Stoto and Durch 1993). As a result, there is substantial debate about mortality at older ages and substantial diversity in the existing projections of elderly and retirement populations (Ahlburg 1993).

Similarly, immigration has, as noted in Chapter 2, been highly variable over time but has recently been higher than anticipated. Thus, whereas previous projections of the population of the United States maintained an assumption of net immigration of 500,000 per year (Spencer 1989) and more recent projections assume nearly 900,000 per year (Day 1992), the number of immigrants has exceeded both of these levels for several years and levels of 1 to 2 million per year for an extended period are thought to be reasonable by some researchers (Ahlburg and Vaupel 1990).

5. Any time that an analyst chooses to emphasize only a few of several scenarios and selects any specific period of time for examination, questions can be legitimately posed about the analyst's rationale. Clearly space and other limitations did not allow all 10 scenarios that are available from the Census projections to be utilized and it was thus necessary to select only some scenarios for the analysis. I have chosen to utilize four scenarios, a zero immigration scenario, and the lowest, middle, and highest projection scenarios from the U.S. Bureau of the Census (1992). The middle scenario, which is used in all parts of the analysis, is employed because it is the scenario that the Census Bureau indicates is among the most likely to occur and is the scenario that is traditionally used in projection analyses. As such, it was deemed appropriate to utilize it extensively, since it should display those patterns that are projected to be among those most likely to occur in the future. The high scenario was used because, as noted by Ahlburg (1993), there are several projections available for the United States that suggest that the Census Bureau's projections are too low. To address this concern and to demonstrate what may happen if higher growth rates prevail, the high scenario was employed for several basic parts of the analysis. The low scenario is used because it clearly displays how Anglo, compared to minority, populations are impacted by slower population growth. It also provides useful comparative data against which to evaluate the other scenarios. The zero immigration scenario is used because it allows one to compare the total population change occurring under each of the other scenarios relative to that which would occur without immigration. Given the attention presently being paid to immigration concerns, this scenario was deemed to be useful for demonstrating the role that immigration may play in future growth in the nation. In sum, the use of these four scenarios allows the implications of alternative patterns of change in rates of population growth and in population characteristics to be identified and allows one to clearly demonstrate the uncertainty inherent in population projections by showing alternatives that produce a wide range of values. The presentation of these alternative values hopefully serves to remind the reader that projections are indeed subject to uncertainty.

The use of the entire projection period from 1990 through 2050 might also be questioned, since it is emphasized in this work and throughout the projection literature (Keyfitz 1981) that projections for periods of the length encompassed by the chosen time period are unlikely to be accurate. As noted in this text, however, the intent of the work is to examine the implications of certain patterns of change in the population (slower population growth, population aging, and the increase in the minority population) rather than to present values appropriate for detailed planning. The use of a longer period of time more clearly demonstrates the long-term implications of the patterns analyzed. In addition, the use of certain periods of time relatively distant in the future was necessary to demonstrate key points about the trends analyzed in this work. For example, the growth of the elderly population begins to occur most rapidly after 2011, when the baby-boomers begin to enter the elderly ages (65 years of age or older), and does not fully manifest itself until 2030, when all of the baby-boomers are 65 years of age or older. In addition, it is evident that these aging patterns begin to stabilize after 2030 so that the aging of the population proceeds relatively slowly after 2030. By including the total projection period available through 2050, both the effect of the baby-boom generation and the stabilization of the aging of the population could be demonstrated. Had the analysis not been extended through 2050, it could have been maintained that I failed to account for the full aging of the baby-boom phenomenon and was not using the full range of data available that would have made this phenomenon apparent. Similarly, it is evident that differential rates of growth in minority, compared to majority, populations show more marked effects on total population patterns when the total projection period is examined and that the implications of differentials in rates of growth become more apparent over longer time periods. It was thus deemed appropriate to take a more inclusive approach in showing various periods of time in order to more fully demonstrate the effects of the trends that are the focus of the work.

6. The population projections from the U.S. Bureau of the Census shown in Chapter 3 are of the resident population and the projected labor-force participation rates are rates for the civilian noninstitutional population. In order to obtain the projected civilian noninstitutional population from the resident population for use in these projections, ratios were computed of the civilian noninstitutional population to the resident population for the census date in 1990 and assumed to prevail throughout the projection period. The projections of labor-force participation rates from the U.S. Bureau of Labor Statistics are for the years 1990 through 2005. We have used the Bureau of Labor Statistics (1991) labor-force participation rates projected for 1990 to 2005 to project patterns for these years and held rates for each age, sex, and race/ethnicity group constant at the level of 2005 for the projections from 2006 through 2050. Because the labor-force participation rates used in this analysis are from data from the Bureau of Labor Statistics and based on annual averages, and the population used is the civilian noninstitutional population adjusted from the resident population from the U.S. Bureau of the Census, values shown here for 1990 and 2000 differ slightly from those published by the Bureau of Labor Statistics and the Bureau of the Census.

Reference Tables

Reference Table 2.1: Total Fertility Rates and Number of Children Ever Born (per Woman) by Selected Characteristics of Women in the United States, 1990

Characteristic	Total Fertility Rate
Total, all women	2.1
Race/Ethnicity	
White	2.0
Black	2.5
Hispanic	3.0

Characteristic	Number of Children Ever Born
Education	
<High School	2.6
High School	2.1
College	1.7
1-3 years	1.8
4 years	1.7
5+ years	1.5
Labor Force Status	
Employed	1.8
Unemployed	2.3
Not in the Labor Force	2.4
Occupation	
Managerial and Professional	1.6
Technical, Sales, and Administrative Support	1.8
Service Occupations	2.1
Farming, Forestry, and Fishing	2.7
Precision Production, Craftsmen, and Repair	1.9
Operators, Fabricators, and Laborers	2.2

Source: Total fertility rates from "Advance Report of Final Natality Statistics, 1990," *Monthly Vital Statistics Report,* Vol. 41, No. 9, Washington, DC: National Center for Health Statistics. Number of Children ever born from "Fertility of American Women: June 1990," *Current Population Reports,* P-20, No. 454, Washington, DC: U.S. Bureau of the Census. For a definition of the total fertility rate see text Table 2.3.

Reference Table 2.2: Death Rates by Age, Race, and Hispanic Origin: United States, 1989 (rates are deaths per 100,000 population)

Race, Hispanic origin[a], and age	1989
White	
Under 1 year	815.5
1-14 years	29.4
15-24 years	91.5
25-44 years	150.8
45-64 years	761.2
65 years and over	4,957.6
Black	
Under 1 year	2,023.7
1-14 years	48.4
15-24 years	150.8
25-44 years	373.6
45-64 years	1,355.2
65 years and over	5,585.3
Hispanic[a]	
Under 1 year	1,013.5
1-14 years	32.9
15-24 years	121.4
25-44 years	201.4
45-64 years	611.1
65 years and over	3,516.9
Asian or Pacific Islander	
Under 1 year	659.5
1-14 years	25.9
15-24 years	55.6
25-44 years	80.6
45-64 years	386.8
65 years and over	2,379.2
American Indian or Alaskan Native	
Under 1 year	1,316.4
1-14 years	46.8
15-24 years	157.4
25-44 years	286.3
45-64 years	891.5
65 years and over	3,471.0

[a]Data shown only for states with an Hispanic-origin item on their death certificates. The race groups include persons of both Hispanic and non-Hispanic origin. Conversely, persons of Hispanic origin may be of any race.

Source: National Center for Health Statistics: *Vital Statistics of the United States,* Vol. II, Mortality, Part A, Public Health Service, Washington, DC: U.S. Government Printing Office. Death rates for Hispanics, Asian or Pacific Islanders, and American Indian or Alaskan Natives were computed by the Office of Analysis and Epidemiology, National Center for Health Statistics, 1991.

Reference Table 2.3: Population, Percent Population by Age, and Percent Change by Age in the United States 1970, 1980, and 1990

	Population						Percent Change	
Age Group	1970		1980		1990		1970-1980	1980-1990
	Number	%	Number	%	Number	%		
< 18	69,644,081	34.3	63,754,960	28.1	63,604,432	25.6	-8.5	-0.2
18-24	23,697,340	11.7	30,022,207	13.2	26,737,766	10.8	26.7	-10.9
25-44	47,995,234	23.6	62,716,549	27.7	80,754,835	32.5	30.7	28.8
45-54	23,219,957	11.4	22,799,787	10.1	25,223,086	10.1	-1.8	10.6
55-64	18,589,812	9.1	21,702,875	9.6	21,147,923	8.5	16.7	-2.6
65+	20,065,502	9.9	25,549,427	11.3	31,241,831	12.5	27.3	22.3
All Ages	203,211,926	100.0	226,545,805	100.0	248,709,873	100.0	11.5	9.8

Source: Censuses of Population and Housing, 1970, 1980, and 1990, Summary Tape File 1A.

Reference Table 2.4: Households in the United States by Type, 1970-1990

Type of Household	Year			Percent Change	
	1970	1980	1990	1970-1980	1980-1990
Total (thousands)	63,401	80,776	91,947	27.4	13.8
Percent Family	81.2	73.7	70.2	15.7	8.4
Married couple	70.6	60.8	55.2	9.8	3.2
Male only	1.9	2.1	3.4	41.1	84.3
Female only	8.7	10.8	11.6	58.3	22.3
Percent Nonfamily	18.8	26.3	29.8	77.0	29.0

Source: Data for 1970 and 1980 from the United States Department of Commerce, Bureau of the Census. "Household and Family Characteristics: March 1990 and 1989," *Current Population Reports* P-20, No. 447, Washington, DC: U.S. Government Printing Office, 1990. Data for 1990 from the Summary Tape File 1A data file from the 1990 Census.

Reference Table 2.5: Selected Socioeconomic Characteristics of the Population in the United States, 1940-1990

Characteristic	Year					
	1940	1950	1960	1970	1980	1990
Population 25 Years of Age or Older by Level of Educational Attainment						
College (%)						
4 years and over	4.6	6.2	7.7	10.7	16.2	21.3
1-3 years	5.5	7.4	8.8	10.6	15.7	17.9
High School (%)						
4 years	14.3	20.8	24.6	31.1	34.6	38.4
1-3 years	15.2	17.4	19.2	19.4	15.3	11.2
Elementary School (%)						
8 years	28.2	20.8	17.6	12.7	7.9	4.8
5-7 years	18.5	16.4	13.8	10.0	6.7	4.1
0-4 years	13.7	11.1	8.3	5.5	3.6	2.4
Median Years of Education	8.6	9.3	10.6	12.1	12.5	12.7

Reference Table 2.5 (Continued)

Labor Force by Occupation and Industry for the Population of the United States, 1950-1990

Characteristic	1950		1980		1990	
	Number	Percent	Number	Percent	Number	Percent
Occupation:						
White Collar	20,750,383	37.3	51,745,154	56.1	67,251,980	58.1
Blue Collar	34,756,930	62.7	40,352,237	43.9	48,429,222	41.9
Industry:						
Extractive and Construction Industries	11,374,479	20.5	9,681,365	10.0	11,053,550	9.6
Manufacturing	14,575,692	26.3	21,914,754	22.4	20,462,078	17.7
Transportation, Communication, and Utilities	4,368,302	7.9	7,087,455	7.2	8,205,062	7.1
Wholesale and Retail Trade	10,547,569	19.1	19,933,926	20.4	24,556,692	21.2
Services	12,044,705	21.7	33,874,389	34.7	45,865,743	39.6
Government	2,488,778	4.5	5,147,466	5.3	5,538,077	4.8

Reference Table 2.5 (Continued)

Poverty Data

Year	Percent of Families Below Poverty	Percent of Persons Below Poverty
1960	20.7	22.2
1970	10.9	12.6
1980	11.5	13.0
1989	10.0	13.1

^aOccupation and industry data for different years are not directly comparable because of changes in categories over time.

Source: Data on education from "School Enrollment: Social and Economic Characteristics of Students," *Current Population Reports* P-20, No. 433, Washington, DC: U.S. Government Printing Office and *Digest of Education Statistics, 1992,* Washington, DC: U.S. Department of Education, 1992. Employment Data for 1940–1970 from U.S. Bureau of the Census. *Historical Statistics of the United States* (Series D11-25). Washington, DC: U.S. Government Printing Office, 1975. Employment data for 1980 and 1990 from the Summary Tape File 3A for the U.S. from the 1980 and 1990 Censuses. Washington, DC: United States Department of Commerce, Bureau of the Census. Income and poverty data from "Money, Income and Poverty Status in the United States, 1989," *Current Population Reports* P-60, No. 168, Washington, DC: U.S. Government Printing Office, 1990.

Reference Table 2.5 (Continued)

Income Data (in 1989 dollars)

Year	Median Household Income Value (dollars)	Median Household Income Standard Error (dollars)	Mean Household Income Value (dollars)	Mean Household Income Standard Error (dollars)
1970	27,913	102	31,962	102
1975	27,197	111	31,758	99
1980	26,651	137	31,697	116
1981	26,020	136	31,085	113
1982	25,919	117	31,236	116
1983	26,167	118	31,883	118
1984	26,751	122	32,777	121
1985	27,218	148	33,496	133
1986	28,168	146	34,800	141
1987	28,447	134	35,377	144
1988	28,537	138	35,656	158
1989	28,906	161	36,520	161

Reference Table 3.1: U.S. Bureau of the Census' Alternative Projections of the Percent of the Male and Female Population in the United States by Age and Race/Ethnicity from 1990-2050 Under the Middle Scenario

Age Group	Percent of Population by Age and Race/Ethnicity				
	Anglo	Black	Hispanic	Other	Total

1990 Census

Males by Race/Ethnicity

1990
< 18	24.6	34.2	34.9	31.4	26.9
18-24	10.4	12.8	15.2	12.8	11.2
25-34	17.4	17.9	20.4	19.0	17.8
35-44	15.8	13.7	13.1	15.9	15.3
45-54	10.9	8.3	7.3	9.5	10.2
55-64	9.0	6.2	4.9	5.8	8.2
65-74	7.5	4.4	2.7	3.7	6.6
75-84	3.6	2.0	1.2	1.6	3.1
85+	0.8	0.5	0.3	0.3	0.7

Females by Race/Ethnicity

1990
< 18	22.1	29.8	34.5	29.0	24.3
18-24	9.6	11.9	13.2	11.6	10.3
25-34	16.5	18.1	19.0	19.1	17.0
35-44	15.0	14.3	13.3	16.9	14.9
45-54	10.6	8.9	8.0	9.8	10.1
55-64	9.4	7.2	5.8	6.8	8.7
65-74	9.0	5.6	3.7	4.4	8.0
75-84	5.7	3.2	1.9	1.9	5.0
85+	2.1	1.0	0.6	0.5	1.7

2000-2050 Projections

Males by Race/Ethnicity

2000
< 18	24.3	34.5	34.3	31.3	27.0
18-24	9.2	11.5	11.8	10.9	9.8
25-34	13.0	14.2	17.7	16.5	13.9
35-44	16.8	15.4	16.1	16.4	16.5
45-54	14.6	11.1	9.7	11.6	13.5
55-64	9.6	6.3	5.2	6.7	8.6
65-74	7.1	4.4	3.3	4.1	6.1
75-84	4.3	2.0	1.5	2.0	3.7
85+	1.1	0.6	0.4	0.5	0.9

Reference Table 3.1 (Continued)

Age Group	Percent of Population by Age and Race/Ethnicity				
	Anglo	Black	Hispanic	Other	Total
Males by Race/Ethnicity					
2010					
< 18	22.0	33.0	32.6	30.0	25.3
18-24	9.7	12.1	12.1	11.2	10.5
25-34	12.5	13.4	15.0	15.2	13.0
35-44	12.8	12.5	14.5	14.9	13.2
45-54	15.8	12.6	12.4	12.5	14.7
55-64	13.4	8.8	7.3	8.4	11.7
65-74	7.9	4.7	3.7	4.8	6.7
75-84	4.5	2.2	1.8	2.3	3.7
85+	1.4	0.7	0.6	0.7	1.2
2030					
< 18	20.6	32.1	30.5	27.7	24.5
18-24	8.3	11.1	11.1	10.7	9.4
25-34	11.5	12.9	14.5	15.0	12.5
35-44	12.9	12.3	13.0	14.1	12.9
45-54	11.9	9.8	10.2	11.5	11.3
55-64	11.5	8.6	9.1	9.2	10.5
65-74	13.0	8.3	7.2	6.8	10.8
75-84	8.2	3.8	3.4	3.7	6.4
85+	2.1	1.1	1.0	1.3	1.7
2050					
< 18	20.0	32.0	28.8	25.9	24.3
18-24	8.1	10.8	10.8	10.2	9.3
25-34	11.8	12.8	14.1	14.5	12.7
35-44	11.9	11.5	12.5	13.8	12.2
45-54	11.8	9.9	10.7	12.0	11.3
55-64	12.6	9.1	9.1	9.6	11.0
65-74	11.1	7.2	6.8	7.1	9.2
75-84	8.3	4.2	4.9	4.6	6.5
85+	4.4	2.5	2.3	2.3	3.5
Females by Race/Ethnicity					
2000					
< 18	22.0	29.9	33.5	28.1	24.5
18-24	8.4	10.6	11.4	10.4	9.2
25-34	12.5	14.4	16.3	16.7	13.3
35-44	16.1	15.9	15.3	16.7	16.0
45-54	14.3	12.2	10.2	12.3	13.5
55-64	9.7	7.3	6.0	7.4	8.9
65-74	8.0	5.3	4.2	5.1	7.1
75-84	6.4	3.1	2.3	2.5	5.3
85+	2.6	1.3	0.8	0.8	2.2

220

Reference Table 3.1 (Continued)

Age Group	Percent of Population by Age and Race/Ethnicity				
	Anglo	Black	Hispanic	Other	Total

Females by Race/Ethnicity

Age Group	Anglo	Black	Hispanic	Other	Total
2010					
<18	20.1	28.4	31.5	26.9	23.1
18-24	9.0	11.1	11.6	10.4	9.7
25-34	11.9	13.4	14.8	15.5	12.7
35-44	12.5	13.0	13.8	15.2	12.9
45-54	15.4	13.8	12.0	12.8	14.6
55-64	13.5	10.2	8.0	9.3	12.1
65-74	8.5	5.6	4.6	5.6	7.4
75-84	5.8	3.0	2.6	3.0	4.9
85+	3.3	1.5	1.1	1.3	2.6
2030					
<18	18.9	27.4	28.9	25.1	22.4
18-24	7.8	10.2	10.6	9.9	8.7
25-34	11.1	13.0	14.2	14.8	12.3
35-44	12.5	12.8	13.1	14.0	12.8
45-54	11.8	10.8	10.7	11.9	11.4
55-64	11.6	9.9	9.2	9.8	10.8
65-74	13.2	9.1	7.5	7.6	11.2
75-84	9.1	4.9	4.1	4.5	7.3
85+	4.0	1.9	1.7	2.4	3.1
2050					
<18	18.3	27.1	27.0	23.8	22.1
18-24	7.6	10.0	10.1	9.6	8.7
25-34	11.3	13.1	13.8	14.1	12.4
35-44	11.6	12.2	12.6	13.6	12.2
45-54	11.6	10.9	11.0	11.9	11.4
55-64	12.5	10.3	9.7	9.8	11.2
65-74	10.8	7.5	7.3	7.8	9.3
75-84	8.7	5.1	5.2	5.3	7.0
85+	7.6	3.8	3.3	4.1	5.7

Source: See text Table 3.2

Reference Table 3.2: U.S. Bureau of the Census' Alternative Projections of the Population in the United States by Race/Ethnicity and Sex from 1990-2050 Under Alternative Scenarios

Year	Population by Race/Ethnicity				Total Population
	Anglo	Black	Hispanic	Other	

Low Scenario

Males by Race/Ethnicity

Year	Anglo	Black	Hispanic	Other	Total Population
1990	91,656,591	13,779,127	11,388,059	4,415,641	121,239,418
2000	94,728,257	15,638,532	14,523,523	6,052,272	130,942,584
2010	94,316,633	16,754,903	16,983,605	7,583,973	135,639,114
2020	92,553,920	17,581,174	19,353,704	9,126,495	138,615,293
2030	88,368,091	17,972,544	21,456,199	10,638,691	138,435,525
2040	82,217,746	18,038,452	23,191,082	12,031,869	135,479,149
2050	76,042,787	17,952,652	24,689,600	13,335,485	132,020,524

Females by Race/Ethnicity

Year	Anglo	Black	Hispanic	Other	Total Population
1990	96,471,705	15,437,166	10,966,000	4,595,584	127,470,455
2000	99,149,086	17,455,866	14,169,058	6,391,181	137,165,191
2010	98,699,007	18,841,467	16,844,377	8,054,537	142,439,388
2020	97,377,126	19,978,934	19,512,789	9,715,529	146,584,378
2030	94,235,617	20,694,057	22,008,640	11,336,481	148,274,795
2040	88,769,170	21,008,811	24,199,861	12,828,769	146,806,611
2050	82,297,640	21,028,199	26,100,517	14,199,664	143,626,020

Middle Scenario

Males by Race/Ethnicity

Year	Anglo	Black	Hispanic	Other	Total Population
1990	91,656,591	13,779,127	11,388,059	4,415,641	121,239,418
2000	96,212,893	16,001,663	15,491,929	6,631,658	134,338,143
2010	99,001,637	18,066,122	19,792,343	9,151,674	146,011,776
2020	101,555,738	20,306,324	24,557,480	11,888,431	158,307,973
2030	102,368,505	22,483,711	29,612,656	14,793,988	169,258,860
2040	101,148,138	24,661,590	34,835,245	17,798,529	178,443,502
2050	99,266,162	26,998,361	40,150,633	20,855,565	187,270,721

Females by Race/Ethnicity

Year	Anglo	Black	Hispanic	Other	Total Population
1990	96,471,705	15,437,166	10,966,000	4,595,584	127,470,455
2000	100,488,042	17,832,800	15,110,213	7,046,267	140,477,322
2010	102,666,812	20,134,567	19,519,219	9,776,699	152,097,297
2020	104,606,032	22,604,464	24,394,288	12,688,946	164,293,730
2030	105,305,752	25,067,867	29,584,532	15,734,368	175,692,519
2040	104,438,646	27,623,103	34,991,984	18,851,805	185,905,538
2050	102,574,371	30,317,227	40,524,379	21,987,382	195,403,359

Reference Table 3.2 (Continued)

	Population by Race/Ethnicity				Total Population
Year	Anglo	Black	Hispanic	Other	

High Scenario

Males by Race/Ethnicity

1990	91,656,591	13,779,127	11,388,059	4,415,641	121,239,418
2000	97,618,646	16,347,316	16,389,685	7,172,445	137,528,092
2010	103,586,429	19,211,027	22,385,472	10,616,459	155,799,387
2020	110,320,320	22,548,405	29,443,924	14,522,017	176,834,666
2030	116,231,071	26,186,470	37,559,387	18,881,106	198,858,034
2040	121,499,189	30,254,168	46,869,936	23,737,605	222,360,898
2050	127,022,520	34,838,063	57,498,246	29,075,531	248,434,360

Females by Race/Ethnicity

1990	96,471,705	15,437,166	10,966,000	4,595,584	127,470,455
2000	102,020,073	18,138,150	15,953,059	7,666,665	143,777,947
2010	107,598,732	21,135,020	21,942,899	11,418,749	162,095,400
2020	114,050,344	24,638,874	29,001,199	15,597,455	183,287,872
2030	120,422,984	28,495,919	37,157,868	20,194,988	206,271,759
2040	126,711,937	32,759,664	46,595,672	25,258,599	231,325,872
2050	132,698,306	37,439,406	57,405,710	30,762,383	258,305,805

Zero Immigration Scenario

Males by Race/Ethnicity

1990	91,656,591	13,779,127	11,388,059	4,415,641	121,239,418
2000	95,298,035	15,702,641	13,822,389	5,141,544	129,964,609
2010	96,906,098	17,360,266	15,853,913	5,682,304	135,802,581
2020	98,165,822	19,137,717	18,003,842	6,233,861	141,541,242
2030	97,581,736	20,790,296	20,035,802	6,740,616	145,148,450
2040	94,901,979	22,389,724	21,877,291	7,149,018	146,318,012
2050	91,564,231	24,106,433	23,536,873	7,528,366	146,735,903

Females by Race/Ethnicity

1990	96,471,705	15,437,166	10,966,000	4,595,584	127,470,455
2000	99,667,299	17,528,516	13,487,498	5,335,605	136,018,918
2010	100,757,351	19,410,616	15,670,362	5,856,203	141,694,532
2020	101,482,925	21,395,883	17,962,994	6,368,473	147,210,275
2030	100,863,836	23,303,877	20,163,213	6,833,716	151,164,642
2040	98,612,167	25,239,436	22,219,494	7,216,534	153,287,631
2050	95,341,968	27,254,464	24,107,413	7,570,108	154,273,953

Source: See text Table 3.2

Reference Table 3.3: U.S. Bureau of the Census' Projections of the Net Numerical Change in the Population in the United States from 1990-2050 by Race/Ethnicity Under Alternative Scenarios and Proportion of Net Change Due to Each Race/Ethnicity Group

Race/ Ethnicity	Net Numerical Change	Proportion of Net Change
Low Scenario		
Anglo	-29,787,869	-110.7
Black	9,764,558	36.3
Hispanic	28,436,058	105.6
Other	18,523,924	68.8
Total	26,936,671	100.0
Middle Scenario		
Anglo	13,712,237	10.2
Black	28,099,295	21.0
Hispanic	58,320,953	43.5
Other	33,831,722	25.3
Total	133,964,207	100.0
High Scenario		
Anglo	71,592,530	27.7
Black	43,061,176	16.7
Hispanic	92,549,897	35.9
Other	50,826,689	19.7
Total	258,030,292	100.0
Zero Immigration Scenario		
Anglo	-1,222,097	-2.3
Black	22,144,604	42.3
Hispanic	25,290,227	48.4
Other	6,087,249	11.6
Total	52,299,983	100.0

Source: See text Table 3.2

Reference Table 5.1: Median Household Income in the United States
by Age of Householder and Race/Ethnicity,
1989

Age of Householder	Total	White	Black	Hispanic[a]
<25	$17,376	$18,547	$10,975	$17,032
25-34	30,672	32,574	19,815	24,335
35-44	38,779	40,982	26,539	28,350
45-54	42,607	44,853	28,680	31,012
55-64	32,922	34,434	21,186	25,744
65-74	20,553	21,403	12,000	15,047
75+	$13,150	$13,663	$ 8,398	$ 9,636

[a] Hispanics can be of any race.

Source: Data derived from the Summary Tape File 3C from the 1990 Census.

Reference Table 5.2: Median Household Income in the
United States by Race/Ethnicity,
1979 and 1989 and Percent Change
1979-1989

Race/ Ethnicity of Householder	Median Household Income		Percent Change 1979-1989
	1979	1989	
Total	$16,841	$30,056	78.5
White	17,680	31,687	79.2
Black	10,943	20,082	83.5
American Indian	12,256	20,317	65.8
Asian	19,966	37,169	86.2
Hispanic[a]	$13,502	$24,284	79.9

[a] Hispanics can be of any race.

Source: Data derived from Summary Tape File 3C from the
1980 and 1990 Censuses.

Reference Table 5.3: Average (Mean) Household Income in
the United States by Type of
Household, 1990

Household Type	Mean Income
Family household	
Married couple with children	$48,880
Married couple without children	48,538
Male householder with own children	27,592
Male householder without own children	37,908
Female householder with own children	16,568
Female householder without own children	29,876
Nonfamily household	$24,100

Source: Data derived from the Summary Tape File 3C from
the 1990 Census.

Reference Table 5.4: Number and Percent of Persons in Poverty in the United States by Race/Ethnicity, 1980 and 1990, Percent Change 1980-1990 and Proportion of 1980-1990 Net Change Due to Each Group

| | Persons in Poverty | | | | Percent Change | Proportion of Net Change in Persons in Poverty[b] |
| Race/ Ethnicity | 1980 | | 1990 | | | |
	Number	%	Number	%	1980-1990	
Total	27,392,580	12.4	31,742,864	12.8	15.9	100.0
White	17,331,671	9.4	19,025,245	9.5	9.8	38.9
Black	7,648,604	29.9	8,441,429	28.2	10.4	18.2
American Indian, Aleut, and Eskimo	408,067	27.5	603,188	30.8	47.8	4.5
Asian and Pacific Islander	475,677	13.1	997,196	13.7	109.6	12.0
Other	1,528,561	13.5	2,675,816	27.6	75.1	26.4
Hispanic[a]	3,371,134	23.5	5,403,492	24.2	60.3	46.7

[a] Hispanics can be of any race.

[b] Because data are shown by both race and Hispanic-origin categories, the sum of values for the categories excluding Hispanics sums to 100 percent. Hispanics may be of any race and are thus included in the values for racial groups as well as being shown as a separate ethnic group.

Source: Data derived from the Summary Tape File 3C from the 1980 and 1990 Censuses.

Reference Table 5.5: Income Distribution of Households in the United States by Age of Householder for 1990 and Projected for 2050 Under the Middle Scenario

Income Category	< 25 Years of Age					25-34 Years of Age				
	1990		2050		Pct. Chg. 1990-2050	1990		2050		Pct. Chg. 1990-2050
	Number	%	Number	%		Number	%	Number	%	
$< 5,000	730,609	14.5	1,065,729	16.5	45.9	1,100,710	5.5	1,466,624	6.9	33.2
$5,000-$9,999	730,955	14.5	970,007	15.0	32.7	1,225,222	6.2	1,530,982	7.2	25.0
$10,000-$14,999	769,056	15.2	970,273	15.1	26.2	1,552,336	7.8	1,846,080	8.7	18.9
$15,000-$24,999	1,277,735	25.3	1,568,380	24.3	22.8	3,920,679	19.8	4,288,216	20.3	9.4
$25,000-$34,999	781,553	15.5	940,295	14.6	20.3	3,956,443	19.9	4,049,305	19.2	2.3
$35,000-$49,999	505,409	10.0	613,307	9.5	21.3	4,216,048	21.2	4,165,011	19.7	-1.2
$50,000-$74,999	196,101	3.9	245,138	3.8	25.0	2,784,204	14.0	2,731,566	12.9	-1.9
$75,000-$99,999	37,102	0.7	46,982	0.7	26.6	678,481	3.4	666,479	3.2	-1.8
$100,000+	20,836	0.4	25,804	0.5	23.8	415,531	2.2	395,416	1.9	-4.8
Total for age group	5,049,356	100.0	6,445,915	100.0	27.7	19,849,654	100.0	21,139,679	100.0	6.5

Reference Table 5.5 (Continued)

Income Category	35-44 Years of Age					45-54 Years of Age				
	1990		2050		Pct. Chg. 1990-2050	1990		2050		Pct. Chg. 1990-2050
	Number	%	Number	%		Number	%	Number	%	
$ < 5,000	792,599	3.9	1,218,698	4.9	53.8	588,780	4.1	1,220,305	5.0	107.3
$5,000-$9,999	929,679	4.6	1,370,994	5.5	47.5	639,818	4.5	1,291,495	5.3	101.9
$10,000-$14,999	1,126,932	5.5	1,610,248	6.5	42.9	753,357	5.3	1,473,045	6.0	95.5
$15,000-$24,999	2,920,073	14.3	3,855,646	15.6	32.0	1,788,529	12.5	3,304,414	13.6	84.8
$25,000-$34,999	3,403,654	16.7	4,134,223	16.7	21.5	2,008,071	14.0	3,486,440	14.3	73.6
$35,000-$49,999	4,574,448	22.4	5,236,049	21.1	14.5	2,852,864	19.0	4,702,476	19.3	64.8
$50,000-$74,999	4,184,077	20.5	4,675,093	18.9	11.7	3,154,718	22.1	5,018,462	20.6	59.1
$75,000-$99,999	1,352,045	6.6	1,495,629	6.0	10.6	1,330,180	9.3	2,081,748	8.5	56.5
$100,000+	1,109,606	5.5	1,187,760	4.8	7.0	1,186,896	8.3	1,806,737	7.4	52.2
Total for age group	20,393,073	100.0	24,784,340	100.0	21.5	14,303,213	100.0	24,385,122	100.0	70.5

Reference Table 5.5 (Continued)

Income Category	55-64 Years of Age					65-74 Years of Age				
	1990		2050		Pct. Chg.	1990		2050		Pct. Chg.
	Number	%	Number	%	1990-2050	Number	%	Number	%	1990-2050
$ < 5,000	746,791	6.0	1,759,250	7.1	135.6	843,505	7.3	1,962,112	9.0	132.6
$5,000-$9,999	946,742	7.6	2,095,833	8.5	121.4	1,870,877	16.2	3,866,582	17.7	106.7
$10,000-$14,999	985,533	8.0	2,058,651	8.4	108.9	1,619,271	14.1	3,064,609	14.0	89.3
$15,000-$24,999	2,058,087	16.6	4,140,665	16.8	101.2	2,623,765	22.8	4,754,693	21.7	81.2
$25,000-$34,999	1,885,498	15.2	3,669,024	14.9	94.6	1,682,484	14.6	3,020,312	13.8	79.5
$35,000-$49,999	2,177,757	17.6	4,171,386	16.9	91.6	1,365,249	11.9	2,477,457	11.3	81.5
$50,000-$74,999	2,004,456	16.2	3,807,494	15.5	90.0	900,024	7.8	1,651,885	7.5	83.5
$75,000-$99,999	804,381	6.5	1,531,442	6.2	90.4	300,156	2.6	550,357	2.5	83.4
$100,000+	770,169	6.3	1,398,875	5.7	81.6	311,253	2.7	541,831	2.5	74.1
Total for age group	12,379,414	100.0	24,632,620	100.0	99.0	11,516,584	100.0	21,889,838	100.0	90.1

Reference Table 5.5 (Continued)

Income Category	75 + Years of Age				
	1990		2050		Pct. Chg. 1990-2050
	Number	%	Number	%	
$< 5,000	1,030,826	12.2	3,809,805	14.0	269.6
$5,000-$9,999	2,320,186	27.4	7,64,374	28.1	230.8
$10,000-$14,999	1,430,538	16.9	4,516,677	16.5	215.7
$15,000-$24,999	1,627,072	19.2	5,002,648	18.3	207.5
$25,000-$34,999	825,002	9.8	2,528,682	9.3	206.5
$35,000-$49,999	597,845	7.1	1,848,739	6.8	209.2
$50,000-$74,999	372,069	4.4	1,152,600	4.2	209.8
$75,000-$99,999	120,787	1.4	377,911	1.4	212.9
$100,000+	131,794	1.6	387,419	1.4	195.5
Total for age group	8,456,119	100.0	27,300,905	100.0	222.9

Reference Table 6.1: Consumer Expenditures by Category in the United States in 1990 and Projected to 2050 Under the Zero Immigration Scenario

Year	Total	Food	Alcohol	Housing	Apparel
1990	$2,501,623,506,367	$404,766,038,877	$23,029,673,659	$772,538,459,292	$121,750,975,098
2000	2,782,215,309,786	452,822,564,609	24,544,910,642	853,890,747,165	135,877,584,730
2030	3,028,752,667,542	508,728,270,118	25,259,677,072	937,176,566,927	142,511,123,273
2050	3,007,322,271,216	509,518,611,992	24,638,591,133	936,215,103,279	141,476,464,032

Year	Transportation	Health	Entertainment	Personal	Reading
1990	$469,243,143,552	$131,825,339,365	$124,651,509,578	$22,776,234,120	$14,347,121,878
2000	520,471,781,933	147,814,958,190	137,311,720,264	25,567,081,711	15,849,081,785
2030	553,561,578,448	184,943,990,607	141,474,091,149	29,831,967,563	17,506,072,018
2050	545,651,572,409	184,970,576,290	137,382,821,380	29,908,957,610	17,084,453,274

Year	Education	Tobacco	Miscellaneous	Cash	Insurance
1990	$33,841,482,389	$25,197,642,415	$37,634,450,034	$77,372,781,504	$242,648,654,606
2000	38,852,686,499	27,735,398,073	41,528,656,983	89,563,613,863	270,384,523,339
2030	37,454,112,830	29,644,058,932	45,732,370,490	104,190,701,851	270,738,086,264
2050	37,157,667,760	29,064,230,675	44,784,563,035	104,048,352,423	265,420,305,924

Reference Table 6.2: Consumer Expenditures in the United States by Category and Race/Ethnicity in 1990 and Projected to 2050 Under the Middle Scenario

Anglo

Year	Total	Food	Alcohol	Housing	Apparel
1990	$2,102,479,290,649	$329,720,030,874	$20,206,839,919	$640,394,131,171	$99,892,273,079
2000	2,293,431,701,682	359,854,699,695	21,287,872,917	692,826,046,131	109,235,973,485
2030	2,427,187,227,015	387,009,173,453	21,704,361,984	736,298,381,550	110,815,860,579
2050	2,354,161,680,667	374,890,286,462	20,891,555,841	715,980,949,748	106,609,401,705

Year	Transportation	Health	Entertainment	Personal	Reading
1990	$397,076,824,935	$116,024,639,873	$110,189,957,607	$18,212,927,283	$12,791,615,896
2000	432,873,850,592	128,033,169,308	119,903,970,003	19,921,741,596	13,944,216,049
2030	449,464,505,499	156,340,991,674	122,625,634,529	22,486,586,586	15,327,879,813
2050	434,512,146,854	154,625,589,752	117,801,392,430	21,902,472,690	14,854,899,386

Year	Education	Tobacco	Miscellaneous	Cash	Insurance
1990	$28,393,948,610	$21,631,563,395	$32,683,388,139	$68,028,113,999	$207,233,035,869
2000	31,972,164,260	23,492,517,622	35,401,054,618	77,598,950,636	227,085,474,770
2030	30,343,484,256	24,542,287,756	38,451,419,090	90,161,395,816	221,615,264,430
2050	29,451,798,268	23,591,485,747	37,069,780,050	89,477,928,203	212,501,993,531

Reference Table 6.2 (Continued)

Black

Year	Total	Food	Alcohol	Housing	Apparel
1990	$178,656,971,312	$33,050,102,420	$1,149,242,742	$57,969,238,733	$10,635,002,117
2000	219,586,755,603	40,320,301,950	1,389,544,701	70,733,993,752	13,018,359,177
2030	311,753,886,780	58,565,468,986	1,889,248,722	100,103,495,909	17,894,317,410
2050	373,162,309,733	70,463,121,109	2,266,226,932	120,008,058,807	21,336,572,812

Year	Transportation	Health	Entertainment	Personal	Reading
1990	$31,188,611,179	$7,258,984,461	$5,840,122,641	$2,654,247,157	$709,026,305
2000	38,358,261,056	8,893,681,512	7,210,337,746	3,285,385,882	894,505,649
2030	54,032,340,729	14,276,335,417	9,911,211,097	4,644,132,384	1,278,639,170
2050	64,175,836,798	17,374,034,007	11,831,525,292	5,492,826,647	1,536,447,081

Year	Education	Tobacco	Miscellaneous	Cash	Insurance
1990	$1,892,607,589	$2,086,838,492	$2,033,553,708	$5,349,965,856	$16,839,427,912
2000	2,457,766,946	2,522,985,138	2,511,897,944	7,019,012,748	20,970,721,402
2030	3,130,978,442	3,666,670,658	3,785,044,742	9,800,145,085	28,775,858,029
2050	3,729,573,647	4,434,576,227	4,576,630,594	11,654,779,263	34,282,100,517

Reference Table 6.2 (Continued)

Hispanic

Year	Total	Food	Alcohol	Housing	Apparel
1990	$140,770,105,176	$28,614,940,417	$1,223,114,388	$47,426,741,792	$7,742,937,125
2000	206,622,608,302	42,443,930,072	1,718,728,538	69,297,379,516	11,386,160,310
2030	417,889,230,116	88,247,193,996	3,243,574,721	141,076,968,998	22,022,818,279
2050	576,963,308,267	122,387,193,449	4,440,227,607	195,615,929,675	30,216,291,446

Year	Transportation	Health	Entertainment	Personal	Reading
1990	$25,445,185,006	$5,366,623,276	$5,561,342,355	$1,310,265,610	$493,787,167
2000	37,135,781,575	8,104,476,423	8,134,919,815	1,938,283,138	734,734,074
2030	73,321,796,974	18,391,022,966	15,314,975,140	4,132,502,252	1,440,729,848
2050	99,760,037,676	26,107,739,092	20,925,068,412	5,725,589,123	1,990,182,634

Year	Education	Tobacco	Miscellaneous	Cash	Insurance
1990	$1,572,767,944	$1,009,697,110	$1,801,730,624	$2,156,101,839	$11,044,870,523
2000	2,308,903,705	1,485,780,470	2,683,675,529	3,131,125,180	16,118,729,957
2030	4,083,022,353	2,982,053,218	5,351,145,249	6,966,660,505	31,314,765,617
2050	5,493,498,406	4,082,835,406	7,348,214,144	10,136,196,330	42,734,304,867

Reference Table 6.2 (Continued)

Other

Year	Total	Food	Alcohol	Housing	Apparel
1990	$79,717,139,230	$13,380,965,166	$450,476,610	$26,748,347,596	$3,480,762,777
2000	129,389,589,646	21,756,793,094	704,319,155	43,119,908,710	5,568,539,380
2030	301,875,569,167	51,294,340,279	1,564,113,639	98,702,942,459	12,911,505,000
2050	431,695,248,966	73,510,571,496	2,219,478,618	140,920,577,848	18,278,107,505

Year	Transportation	Health	Entertainment	Personal	Reading
1990	$15,532,522,43	$3,175,091,755	$3,060,086,975	$598,794,070	$352,692,510
2000	24,956,926,171	5,275,309,427	4,948,300,929	973,554,960	571,069,238
2030	57,335,416,067	14,525,900,509	11,710,576,022	2,316,634,848	1,392,308,663
2050	81,361,051,806	21,934,466,760	16,787,122,081	3,355,647,545	2,032,735,510

Year	Education	Tobacco	Miscellaneous	Cash	Insurance
1990	$1,982,158,246	$469,543,418	$1,115,777,563	$1,838,599,810	$7,531,320,302
2000	3,295,853,305	749,510,937	1,832,197,225	3,163,296,429	12,474,010,686
2030	7,565,802,599	1,745,652,599	4,068,822,111	7,249,892,206	29,491,662,166
2050	10,697,291,503	2,495,079,390	5,762,033,556	10,367,810,811	41,973,274,537

Reference Table 6.3: Consumer Expenditures in the United States in 1990 and 2050 by Category and Age of Householder Under the Middle Scenario

1990

Age of Householder	Total	Food	Alcohol	Housing	Apparel
15-24	$78,953,895,852	$13,348,477,784	$1,619,341,770	$23,395,358,741	$4,977,635,560
25-34	528,430,948,903	80,993,543,252	6,470,245,562	175,770,305,259	26,068,986,688
35-44	683,755,109,985	108,548,556,037	6,022,860,322	215,353,308,138	37,057,595,220
45-54	503,142,615,771	79,418,630,559	3,854,421,305	143,298,410,853	25,323,246,873
55-64	348,053,376,478	57,472,247,748	2,807,531,726	100,568,210,276	16,005,301,758
65-74	231,904,003,515	42,820,948,989	1,627,315,175	70,367,535,964	8,641,134,162
75+	127,383,555,863	22,163,634,508	627,957,799	43,785,330,061	3,677,074,837

Age of Householder	Transportation	Health	Entertainment	Personal	Reading
15-24	$17,148,009,342	$1,822,679,867	$4,019,484,239	$669,294,325	$370,497,182
25-34	105,711,463,683	17,946,258,730	27,509,286,767	4,054,142,041	2,664,125,636
35-44	124,145,888,226	26,929,143,003	36,066,876,484	5,614,423,166	3,871,510,439
45-54	100,394,383,636	21,804,287,542	25,831,177,906	4,315,564,298	2,674,220,904
55-64	64,388,120,428	21,191,314,336	17,908,156,812	3,551,509,798	2,035,799,572
65-74	39,489,734,787	24,090,560,395	9,964,214,327	2,983,084,242	1,774,730,536
75+	17,965,543,450	18,041,095,492	3,352,313,043	1,588,216,250	956,237,609

Reference Table 6.3 (Continued)

1990 (Continued)

Age of Householder	Education	Tobacco	Miscellaneous	Cash	Insurance
15-24	$3,894,946,347	$1,064,630,427	$958,178,618	$778,845,356	$4,886,516,294
25-34	5,892,151,211	5,423,665,018	7,039,242,830	8,137,438,725	54,750,093,501
35-44	8,701,073,124	6,430,181,682	11,117,174,963	17,931,527,123	75,964,992,058
45-54	10,015,607,882	5,126,555,282	6,532,330,290	18,898,961,614	55,654,816,827
55-64	4,439,879,557	4,034,580,718	5,478,577,993	11,267,276,911	36,904,868,845
65-74	413,809,884	2,362,937,485	4,425,754,840	10,682,244,791	12,259,997,938
75+	484,014,384	755,091,803	2,083,190,500	9,676,486,984	2,227,369,143

2050

Age of Householder	Total	Food	Alcohol	Housing	Apparel
15-24	$96,942,335,517	$17,939,515,151	$1,769,419,624	$29,903,740,659	$6,326,219,747
25-34	542,157,065,244	86,868,761,948	6,137,132,539	182,288,795,728	27,553,539,198
35-44	781,922,405,471	128,337,042,987	6,723,251,284	252,879,591,622	42,539,852,401
45-54	824,518,109,194	138,491,664,177	5,647,613,756	243,394,665,376	41,041,209,111
55-64	682,548,855,517	116,481,618,495	4,927,268,951	199,920,753,683	32,721,051,348
65-74	418,064,835,054	82,131,153,887	2,642,690,429	128,417,470,658	14,971,324,396
75+	389,828,941,636	71,001,415,871	1,970,112,415	135,720,498,352	11,287,177,267

Reference Table 6.3 (Continued)

2050 (Continued)

Age of Householder	Transportation	Health	Entertainment	Personal	Reading
15-24	$19,279,194,272	$2,225,111,064	$4,742,598,583	$916,096,564	$441,795,911
25-34	109,100,886,998	17,958,831,753	26,187,675,500	4,341,220,007	2,512,061,534
35-44	142,584,300,038	29,323,578,254	39,090,281,542	6,644,928,814	4,101,668,600
45-54	159,720,468,881	32,706,480,623	38,006,247,668	7,470,322,140	4,014,951,226
55-64	126,727,900,726	40,173,377,827	32,260,710,921	6,921,604,462	3,586,906,504
65-74	70,323,604,257	42,801,201,572	16,435,831,326	5,436,147,123	2,900,124,177
75+	52,072,717,962	54,853,248,518	10,621,762,675	4,746,216,895	2,856,756,659

Age of Householder	Education	Tobacco	Miscellaneous	Cash	Insurance
15-24	$4,243,760,848	$1,182,988,082	$1,036,879,277	$1,117,336,842	$5,817,678,893
25-34	6,229,536,667	5,109,177,992	6,636,439,444	7,984,041,923	53,248,964,013
35-44	10,406,189,858	7,147,086,661	12,602,288,511	18,996,455,719	80,545,889,180
45-54	17,182,951,127	7,403,071,624	11,037,233,638	29,228,996,631	89,172,233,216
55-64	9,166,379,050	7,345,358,761	10,476,167,167	20,011,518,847	71,828,238,775
65-74	807,283,879	4,000,358,294	7,086,738,708	17,252,973,964	22,857,932,384
75+	1,336,060,395	2,415,935,356	5,880,911,599	27,045,390,681	8,020,736,991

Reference Table 7.1: Percent of Incidences of Diseases/Disorders in the United States by Age and Race/Ethnicity from 1990-2050 Under the Middle Scenario

Age Group	Anglo	Black	Hispanic	Other	Total
1990					
<1	0.1	0.2	0.2	0.1	0.1
1-4	5.7	8.7	11.6	8.3	6.6
5-17	11.6	14.1	17.3	16.3	12.3
18-24	7.4	8.7	11.2	9.9	8.0
25-44	27.4	29.0	29.4	33.6	27.9
45-64	22.7	21.6	18.7	20.2	22.1
65-74	13.2	9.8	6.7	7.2	12.3
75+	11.9	7.9	4.9	4.4	10.7
2000					
<1	0.0	0.1	0.2	0.1	0.1
1-4	5.0	8.0	10.1	7.6	5.9
5-17	11.7	14.3	16.8	15.9	12.6
18-24	6.4	7.5	8.8	8.5	6.8
25-44	24.2	26.8	28.5	30.4	25.2
45-64	26.9	25.7	21.9	23.5	26.2
65-74	12.0	9.3	7.5	8.0	11.0
75+	13.8	8.3	6.2	6.0	12.2
2030					
<1	0.0	0.1	0.1	0.1	0.1
1-4	4.0	6.9	7.9	6.0	5.1
5-17	9.2	12.1	13.4	13.6	10.4
18-24	5.3	6.7	7.4	7.6	6.0
25-44	18.3	21.0	21.7	24.9	19.7
45-64	24.0	25.2	24.8	24.4	24.4
65-74	18.9	15.5	13.5	11.7	17.0
75+	20.3	12.5	11.2	11.7	17.3
2050					
<1	0.0	0.1	0.1	0.1	0.1
1-4	4.0	6.8	7.0	5.4	5.0
5-17	8.6	11.8	12.1	12.5	10.1
18-24	5.1	6.4	6.9	7.2	5.9
25-44	17.5	20.2	20.3	23.3	19.0
45-64	24.5	25.4	24.6	24.2	24.6
65-74	15.5	13.0	12.4	11.8	14.2
75+	24.8	16.3	16.6	15.5	21.1

References

Acevado, D., and T.J. Espenshade

1992 "Implications of a North American Free Trade Agreement for Mexican migration into the United States." *Population and Development Review* 18:729–744.

Ahlburg, D.A.

1982 "How accurate are the U.S. Bureau of the Census' projections of total live births?" *Journal of Forecasting* 1:365–374.

1993 "The Census Bureau's new projections of the U.S. population." *Population and Development Review* 19:159–174.

Ahlburg, D.A., and C.J. De Vita

1992 "New realities of the American family." *Population Bulletin* 47 (2):2–37.

Ahlburg, D.A., and K.C. Land

1992 "Population forecasting: Guest editors' introduction." *International Journal of Forecasting* 8:289–299.

Ahlburg, D.A., and J.W. Vaupel

1990 "Alternative projections of the U.S. population." *Demography* 27:639–652.

Alho, J., and B.D. Spencer,

1990 "Error models for official mortality forecasts." *Journal of the American Statistical Association* 85:609–616.

Armstrong, J.S.

1985 *Long-Range Forecasting.* New York, NY: Wiley.

Ascher, W.

1978 *Forecasting: An Appraisal for Policy Makers and Planners.* Baltimore, MD: John Hopkins.

Averill, R.F.

1983 *The Revised ICD-9-CM Diagnosis Related Groups.* Yale University. New Haven, CT: DRG Support Group.

Bluestone, B., and B. Harrison

1986 "The great American job machine: The proliferation of low wage employment in the U.S. economy." Study prepared for the Joint Economic Committee. Washington, DC.

Bradbury, K.L.

1986 "The shrinking middle class." *New England Economic Review* (September/October):41–55.

Brody, H.

1993 "Great expectations: Why predictions go awry." *Journal of Consumer Marketing* 10 (1):23–27.

Bumpass, L.L.

1990 "What's happening to the family? Interactions between demographic and institutional change." *Demography* 27 (4):483–498.

Bumpass, L.L. and J.A. Sweet.

1989 "National Estimates of Cohabitation." *Demography* 26:615–625.

Burtless, G.

1993 "The fiscal challenge of an aging population." In O.S. Mitchell (ed.), *As the Workforce Ages*. Ithaca, NY: ILR Press.

Camerer, C.F., and E.J. Johnson

1990 "The process-performance paradox in expert judgment: How can experts know so much and predict so badly?" Unpublished manuscript, Wharton School, University of Pennsylvania.

Carter, L., and R.D. Lee

1986 "Joint forecasts of U.S. marital fertility, nuptiality, births, and marriage using time series models." *Journal of the American Statistical Association* 81:902–911.

Chatterjee, A.

1991 "How to profit from demographic trends." *Business Quarterly* (Summer):20–24.

Clark, A.M.

1991 "'Trends' that will impact new products." *The Journal of Consumer Marketing* 8 (1):35–40.

Clark, B., and P. Lempert

1993 "Riding the age wave." *Retail Business Review* (June):18–20.

Clawson, M.

1985 "Outdoor recreation: Twenty-five years of history, twenty-five years of projection." *Leisure Sciences* 7:73–99.

Coffey, W.

1983 *303 of the World's Worst Predictions*. New York, NY: Tribeca Communications.

Crone, T.M.

1990 "The aging of America: Impacts on the marketplace and workplace." *Federal Reserve Bank of Philadelphia Business Review* (May–June):3–13.

Day, J.F.

1992 "Population projections of the United States by age, sex, race, and Spanish origin, 1992–2050." *Current Population Reports*, Series P-25, No. 1092. U.S. Bureau of the Census. Washington, DC: U.S. Government Printing Office.

Dunn, W.

1991 "Survival by the numbers." *Nation's Business* (August):14–21.

Eargle, J.

1990 "Household wealth and asset ownership: 1988." *Current Population Reports*. Series P-70, No. 22. U.S. Bureau of the Census. Washington, DC: U.S. Government Printing Office.

Easterlin, R.A.

1987 *Birth and Fortune: The Impact of Numbers on Personal Welfare*. Chicago: University of Chicago.

Eggebeen, D.J., and D.T. Lichter

1991 "Race, family structure, and changing poverty among American children." *American Sociological Review* 56:801–17.

Executive Office of the President
1986   *Up from Dependency.* Washington, DC: U.S. Government Printing Office.
Exter, T.G.
1993   "Discretionary income: Who, where, how much?" Paper presented at the Southern Demographic Association meetings. New Orleans, LA (October 21–23).
Foot, D.K.
1992   "Let us now appraise famous trends." *Canadian Business* 65 (November):63–67.
Fosler, R., W. Alonso, J. Meyer, and R. Kern
1990   *Demographic Change and the American Future.* Pittsburgh, PA: University of Pittsburgh Press.
Freeman, R.A.
1981   *The Wayward Welfare State.* Stanford, CA: Hoover Institution Press.
Fullerton, H.N.
1989   "New labor force projections spanning 1988 to 2000." *Monthly Labor Review* 112 (11):3–12.
1991   "Labor force projections: The baby boom moves on." *Monthly Labor Review* 114 (11):31–44.
Galston, W.A.
1993   "Causes of declining well-being among U.S. children." *Aspen Institute Quarterly* 5 (Winter):52–77.
Gerald, D.E., and W.J. Hussar
1992   *Projections of Education Statistics to* 2003. National Center for Education Statistics. Washington, DC: U.S. Government Printing Office.
Gill, R.T., N. Glazer, and S.A. Trernstrom
1992   *Our Changing Population.* Englewood Cliffs, NJ: Prentice-Hall, Inc.
Gould, F.
1983   "The growth of public expenditures." In C.L. Taylor (ed.), *Why Governments Grow.* Beverly Hills, CA: Sage Publications.
Gruen, N.J.
1992   "America, circa 2001." *Journal of Property Management* (January/February):41–43.
Heller, P.S.
1989   "Aging, saving, and pensions in the group of seven countries: 1980–2025." *International Monetary Fund: Working Paper* 89 (13).
Heller, P.S., and R. Hemming
1986   "Aging and social expenditure in major industrial countries." *Finance and Development* (December):18–21.
Jamison, E.
1991   *World Population Profile:* 1991. Washington, DC: U.S. Bureau of the Census.
Jasper, C.R., and P.R. Lan
1992   "Apparel catalog patronage: Demographic, lifestyle and motivational factors." *Psychology and Marketing* 9 (4):275–296.
Johnston, W.B., and A.H. Packer
1987   *Workforce* 2000. Indianapolis, IN: Hudson Institute.
Karoly, L.A.
1992   *The Trend in Inequality Among Families, Individuals, and Workers in the United States.* Santa Monica, CA: Rand.

Kelly, J.R.

1987 *Recreation Trends Towards the Year 2000*. Champaign, IL: Management Learning Laboratories.

Keyfitz, N.

1981 "The limits of population forecasting." *Population and Development Review* 7:579–593.

Kotlikoff, L.J. (ed.)

1989 *What Determines Savings?* Cambridge, MA: MIT Press.

Lee, R.D.

1974 "Forecasting births in a post transition population: Stochastic renewal with serially correlated errors." *Journal of the American Statistical Association* 69:607–617.

Leventhal, R.C.

1991 "The aging consumer: What's all the fuss about anyway?" *The Journal of Consumer Marketing* 8 (1):29–34.

Loomis, D.K., and R.B. Ditton

1988 "Technique for projecting the future growth and distribution of marine recreational fishing demand." *North American Journal of Fisheries Management* 8:259–263.

Manton, K.G., E. Stallard, and B. Singer

1992 "Projecting the future size and health status of the U.S. elderly population." *International Journal of Forecasting* 8:433–458.

Market Opinion Research

1986 "Participation in outdoor recreation among American adults and the motivations which drive participation." Working Papers. Washington, DC: President's Commission on Americans Outdoors.

Masson, P.R., and R.W. Tryon

1990 "Macroeconomic effects of projected population aging in industrial countries." *International Monetary Fund: Staff Papers* 37 (3):453–485.

McLemore, S.D.

1991 *Racial and Ethnic Relations in America*. Boston, MA: Allyn and Bacon.

Meyer, S.A.

1992 "Saving and demographics: Some international comparisons." *Business Review* (March/April):13–23.

Mills, L.

1991 "Understanding national and regional housing trends." *Business Review* (September/October):15–23.

Mitchell, O.S.

1993 *As the Workforce Ages*. Ithaca, NY: ILR Press.

Morrison, P.A.

1987 "Changing demographics: What to watch for." *Business Economics* (July):5–8.

1991 *The Changing Demographic Context of Postsecondary Education*. Santa Monica, CA: Rand.

Murdock, S.H., and D.R. Ellis

1991 *Applied Demography: An Introduction to Basic Concepts, Methods and Data*. Boulder, CO: Westview Press.

Murdock, S.H., F.L. Leistritz, R.R. Hamm, S. Hwang, and B. Parpia
1984 "An assessment of the accuracy of a regional economic-demographic projection model." *Demography* 21 (3):383–404.

Murdock, S.H., K. Backman, E. Colberg, Md. N. Hoque, and R.R. Hamm
1990 "Modeling demographic change and characteristics in the analysis of future demand for leisure sciences." *Leisure Sciences* 12:79–102.

Murdock, S.H., R.R. Hamm, P.R. Voss, D. Fannin, and B. Pecotte
1991a "Evaluating small-area population projections." *Journal of the American Planning Association* 57 (Fall):432–443.

Murdock, S.H., K. Backman, Md. N. Hoque, and D. Ellis
1991b "The implications of change in population size and composition on future participation in outdoor recreational activities." *Journal of Leisure Research* 23:238–259.

Murdock, S.H., K. Backman, R.B. Ditton, Md. N. Hoque, and D. Ellis
1992 "Implications of future demographic change for participation in fishing in Texas." *North American Journal of Fisheries Management* 12:548–558.

Murdock, S.H., D. Loomis, R.B. Ditton, and Md. N. Hoque
1993 "The implications of demographic change for recreational fisheries management in the twenty-first century." Paper presented at the annual meetings of the American Fisheries Society. Portland, OR (August 28–September 2).

National Center for Education Statistics
1992 *Projections of Education Statistics to 2003.* U.S. Department of Education. Washington, DC: U.S. Government Printing Office.

National Center for Health Statistics
1985, 1986, 1987 National Health Interview Survey. (Public-use data tape and documentation). Springfield, VA: National Technical Information Service.
1993 *Vital Statistics of the United States,* Vol. II, Mortality, Part A. Public Health Service. Washington, DC: U.S. Government Printing Office.

Pant, P.N., and W.H. Starbuck
1990 "Innocents in the forest: forecasting and research methods." *Journal of Management* 16 (2):433–460.

Pflaumer, P.
1992 "Forecasting U.S. population totals with the Box-Jenkins approach." *International Journal of Forecasting* 8:329–338.

Pol, L.G.
1987 *Business Demography: A Guide and Reference for Business Planners and Marketers.* New York: Quorum Books.

Pol, L.G., and R.K. Thomas
1992 *The Demography of Health and Health Care.* New York, NY: Plenum Press.

Robey, B.
1985 *The American People: A Timely Exploration of a Changing America and the Impact of New Demographic Trends Around Us.* New York, NY: Truman, Tally Books.

Schulz, J.H.
1992 *The Economics of Aging.* New York, NY: Auburn House.

Serow, W.J., D.F. Sly, and J.M. Wrigley
1990 *Population Aging in the United States.* Westport, CT: Greenwood Press.

Shryock, H., and J. Siegel

1976   *The Methods and Materials of Demography.* Washington, DC: U.S. Government Printing Office.

Silvestri, G., and J. Lukasiewicz

1991   "Occupational employment projections." *Monthly Labor Review* 114 (11):64–94.

Social Security Administration

1993   "Current Operating Statistics: List of Tables." *Social Security Bulletin* 56 (1)(Spring):102–148. Washington, DC: U.S. Government Printing Office.

Spencer, G.

1986   "Projections of the Hispanic population: 1983 to 2080." *Current Population Reports.* Series P-25, No. 796. U.S. Bureau of the Census. Washington, DC: U.S. Government Printing Office.

1989   "Projections of the population of the United States, by age, sex, and race: 1983 to 2080." *Current Population Reports.* Series P-25, No. 1018. U.S. Bureau of the Census. Washington, DC: U.S. Government Printing Office.

Sternlieb, G., and J.W. Hughes

1986   "Demographics and housing in America." *Population Bulletin* 41:2–34. Washington, DC: Population Reference Bureau, Inc.

Stoto, M.A., and J.S. Durch (eds.)

1993   *Forecasting Survival, Health, and Disability Workshop Summary.* (March 1992) Washington, DC: National Academy Press.

Taylor, C.L.

1983   *Why Governments Grow: Measuring Public Sector Size.* Beverly Hills, CA: Sage Publications, Inc.

Texas Parks and Wildlife

1986   1985 Texas Outdoor Recreation Plan. Austin, TX: Texas Parks and Wildlife Department.

United Nations

1992   "The revision of world population prospects." *Population Newsletter* (54)(December).

U.S. Bureau of the Census

1992   "School enrollment and social and economic characteristics of students: October 1990." *Current Population Reports,* Series P-20, No. 460. U.S. Bureau of the Census. Washington, DC: U.S. Government Printing Office.

U.S. Bureau of Labor Statistics

1991   "Outlook to 2005 for the economy, the labor force and employment." *Monthly Labor Review* 114 (11)(November).

U.S. Department of Education

1992   *Digest of Education Statistics,* 1992. Washington, DC: U.S. Department of Education.

U.S. Immigration and Naturalization Service

1991 and 1992   *Statistical Yearbook of the Immigration and Naturalization Service.* Washington, DC: U.S. Immigration and Naturalization Service.

Wacker, W.

1992   "The demography of tomorrow." *Retail Business Review* (August):12–19.

Wilkin, J.C., M.P. Glanz, R.V. Gresch, and S.H. An

1984   *Economic Projections for OASDI Cost Estimates,* 1983. Washington, DC: Social Security Administration.

Wolfe, K.E.

1989   "Financial and demographic conditions associated with local and regional railroad service failures." *Transportation Quarterly* 43 (1):3–28.

About the Book and Author

Demographic change is increasing the demand for living space, jobs, social services, and health care. Aging baby-boomers will join the already swelling ranks of senior citizens. Minority groups constitute the majority in some regions. Family structure is more diverse. Immigrants are expanding the workforce.

Steve Murdock lays out the implications of these and other population trends for business, government, and the public in this concise and accessible book. Using data from the most recent census and projections of future populations. Murdock provides a brief historical overview of recent demographic change in the United States and explains the effects of future population patterns on the labor force; household and family composition; business markets and services; income, wealth, and poverty; and health, education, and other human services.

What will an older population mean for growth in business markets? How will projected population change affect the quality of the available workforce? What are the implications of larger immigrant populations for competition in the workforce? Businesspeople, policymakers, and general readers will find in this book the answers to these and other questions that are relevant now and as we move into the twenty-first century.

Steve H. Murdock is professor and head of the Department of Rural Sociology, and a professor of sociology, at Texas A&M University. Professor Murdock is also Chief Demographer for the Texas State Data Center. He has worked in the area of population analysis for more than two decades and has published widely in the area of applied population analysis.

Index